FOAL

CONFRONTING
UNDERGROUND JUSTICE

CONFRONTING UNDERGROUND JUSTICE

Reinventing Plea Bargaining for Effective Criminal Justice Reform

William R. Kelly
with Robert Pitman

ROWMAN & LITTLEFIELD
Lanham • Boulder • New York • London

Published by Rowman & Littlefield
An imprint of The Rowman & Littlefield Publishing Group, Inc.
4501 Forbes Boulevard, Suite 200, Lanham, Maryland 20706
www.rowman.com

Unit A, Whitacre Mews, 26-34 Stannary Street, London SE11 4AB

British Library Cataloguing in Publication Information Available

Library of Congress Cataloging-in-Publication Data

Names: Kelly, W. R. (William Robert), 1950–, author. | Pitman, Robert, 1942– , author.
Title: Confronting underground justice : reinventing plea bargaining for effective criminal justice reform / William R. Kelly with Robert Pitman.
Description: Lanham, Maryland : Rowman & Littlefield, 2018. | Includes bibliographical references and index.
Identifiers: LCCN 2018012131 (print) | LCCN 2018013018 (ebook) | ISBN 9781538106495 (Electronic) | ISBN 9781538106488 (cloth : alk. paper)
Subjects: LCSH: Plea bargaining—United States. | Law reform—United States. | Criminal justice, Administration of—United States.
Classification: LCC KF9654 (ebook) | LCC KF9654 .K45 2018 (print) | DDC 345.73/072—dc23
LC record available at https://lccn.loc.gov/2018012131

Printed in the United States of America

CONTENTS

ACKNOWLEDGMENTS

First, I would like to express my profound gratitude to my wife and partner Emily, who has supported and encouraged this reform journey, has made this work possible, and has made life absolutely marvelous.

I am most grateful for my collaborator Robert Pitman. Judge Pitman's contributions to this work included discussion of broad themes, the identification and recruitment of interviewees, content regarding mediation of criminal cases, and references from our previous book. To present readers with diverse and independent viewpoints, we each individually contributed select passages. Specific criticisms and recommendations of a political nature are mine alone.

Obtaining the interviews that we conducted for this book was greatly facilitated by the assistance of Jim Bethke, executive director of the Texas Indigent Defense Commission, and Robert Kepple, executive director of the Texas District and County Attorneys Association. Their efforts in securing willing interviewees is greatly appreciated.

I would like to express my appreciation to the Charles Koch Foundation for financial support to me for this research. I would also like to thank David Snyder, the program coordinator for academic grants at the Charles Koch Foundation, for his enthusiasm and encouragement. The foundation's commitment to meaningful criminal justice reform makes this kind of research and policy development possible. I also want to thank the University of Texas and the Department of Sociology for institutional support. The ideas expressed in this book do not necessarily reflect those of any of those who supported this work.

This research benefited tremendously from the very able research assistance provided by several undergraduate students of mine. I am very grateful to Jose Pena, Anh-Linh Kearney, and Ana Prado, who were instrumental in conducting interviews, reviewing research, and assisting in preparation of the manuscript.

I am also grateful to the district attorneys who gave us access to their prosecutors and the chief public defenders who gave us access to their defense lawyers. We very much appreciate the dozens of public defenders, prosecutors, and judges who took the time to candidly share their experiences, perceptions, and opinions about their roles and responsibilities, plea bargaining, recidivism, improving the criminal justice system, and a variety of other topics.

I also must thank our publisher, Rowman & Littlefield, and our terrific editor, Kathryn Knigge. Thank you, Kathryn, for supporting this work and once again making the process seamless and enjoyable.

I also want to acknowledge Elizabeth Henneke and Alycia Welch at the Lone Star Justice Alliance for implementing some of the ideas developed here and in our previous book *From Retribution to Public Safety: Disruptive Innovation of American Criminal Justice* (Rowman & Littlefield, 2017). Their efforts provide the road maps for serious criminal justice reform.

Many of the ideas in this book have been test-driven in my upper-division criminal justice classes at the University of Texas. I thank the hundreds of students who have listened and provided feedback as these ideas evolved.

INTRODUCTION

We find ourselves in the midst of perhaps the greatest public policy failure in U.S. history. For five decades, we have been trying to punish bad behavior out of criminal offenders. Our tough-on-crime approach has required a fundamental transformation in how we think about crime and punishment as well as how we administer criminal justice, including a variety of exceptional statutory, procedural, policy, and funding changes. The results include the massive expansion of incarceration and correctional control, the expenditure of at least $2 trillion in direct criminal justice costs, recidivism rates well north of 65 percent, and a failed war on drugs, to name a few. In the process, we have created an extraordinarily expensive, nearly perfect recidivism machine.

It is hard to comprehend why we tolerate such poor performance, especially with such devastating consequences in terms of victims, families, offenders, communities, tax dollars, and public resources. The failures of the criminal justice system expose all of us unnecessarily to the risk of criminal victimization. Moreover, every time an offender is rearrested and reenters the justice system, the cash register starts ringing again. If what is being described above were a publicly traded corporation, it wouldn't last five minutes on the New York Stock Exchange. Even with such poor return on investment, it nevertheless has persisted for decades as public policy in federal, state, and local criminal justice systems throughout the nation.

There are many factors that come into play in understanding how we got here. These include the usual suspects—mass incarceration and the expansion of prison and jail capacity, mandatory sentencing, and the war on drugs, among others. We suggest that one of the most important elements that doesn't often make the list is plea negotiation. The vast majority—more than 95 percent—of all criminal convictions are based on a guilty plea pursuant to a plea negotiation. Not only does plea negotiation dramatically expedite criminal convictions, but we argue that it also perpetuates the nearly exclusive reliance on punishment.

The key decisions that prosecutors ordinarily make once they decide that a defendant is guilty are based on answering two questions—how much harm has been perpetrated by the offender and thus how much punishment is due. Punishment is what is negotiated, and time is the typical currency of that negotiation. Time is the severity of punishment, years in prison or on probation, and months in jail.

We make the case in the following chapters for why plea negotiation is a primary facilitator of tough-on-crime policies. We also argue that there are characteristics of plea negotiation, such as procedural short-cuts and due process concerns, that enhance its role in facilitating the tough-on-crime agenda.

Having established the primacy of plea bargaining in the tough-on-crime playbook, we then turn to the primary purpose of this book, which is broader criminal justice reform with a particular focus on reducing recidivism. In our analysis, it is not possible to achieve meaningful justice reform absent fundamental changes to plea negotiation. That includes addressing the key procedural and due process issues associated with the current practice of plea bargaining.

Also in our analysis, it is impossible to achieve essential justice reform without reconsideration of the roles and responsibilities of the prosecutor. Current policies, practices, and law place prosecutors in the position of being the most influential decision makers in the justice system. They decide whom to prosecute, what charges to bring against individuals, what charges to indict individuals for, what to plea negotiate, and, in many instances, what that sentence shall be. In effect, prosecutors are judge, jury, and sentencer. Thus, serious discussions about reform must focus a good deal of effort on prosecutors and prosecutorial decision making.

Plea negotiation was developed not as a better way of doing justice but rather as the only way the court system can function due to a variety of constraints and demands. Underfunding and extraordinary caseloads and court dockets have made plea bargaining a necessity. We do not expect that to change; thus, we assume that plea negotiation is here to stay. We also assume that prosecutors' relative power and discretion will persist. Therefore, our recommendations for reform focus on modifying the plea process and the role of the prosecutor to shift the primary outcomes of justice decision making from the principal question of how much punishment to the question of how do we effectively reduce the likelihood of this individual reoffending—from tough on crime to recidivism reduction.

Because the plea process focuses on speed and because the primary end game in U.S. criminal justice policy is punishment, we generally have had neither the time nor the inclination to ask questions about why offenders commit crime. Very little time and effort is spent with serious inquiries about things like mental illness, substance use disorders, neurocognitive impairment, and a variety of other criminogenic or crime-related conditions, circumstances, and situations. One of our key recommendations involves the use of independent, neutral panels of professional clinical experts (such as psychiatrists, psychiatric nurse practitioners, psychologists, and clinical social workers) who are charged with screening and assessing defendants as they enter the justice system. The goal is to identify the often complicated situations of many individuals in the justice system—essentially half have a mental illness, the vast majority have a substance use disorder, large percentages have neurodevelopmental or neurocognitive impairments, about one in six have significant intellectual deficiencies, and many have complex comorbidities. Moreover, there are the very common educational, employment, family, and medical problems that often plague offenders, most of whom are products of poverty and disadvantage. These expert panels are also responsible for developing recommendations to prosecutors regarding diversion, treatment, and rehabilitation. The point is to provide prosecutors with the information necessary to engage in problem solving and make better decisions regarding recidivism reduction.

We also introduce the concept of the plea mediator, much like the mediator in civil litigation. It is our contention that the plea mediator can help level the playing field that is necessarily due to the profound imbalance in power and resources between the prosecutor and the defendant. The presence and involvement of the plea mediator can also serve to mitigate several of the due process and procedural complaints about plea negotiation.

The vast majority of criminal defendants are indigent and thus do not have the resources to retain their own counsel. They rely on either public defenders or appointed/assigned counsel. In most jurisdictions today, public counsel are seriously underfunded. As a result, they have extraordinary caseloads that prohibit spending sufficient time with clients. The obvious remedy is increased funding for public defense. While we make that recommendation, we also believe there is a bigger picture regarding criminal defense. Again, the goal is to reduce the likelihood of reoffending, and there is a primary role for defense counsel in achieving this goal. The concept is holistic defense, which places defense counsel in the position of problem solving a variety of clients' problems and issues in addition to the immediate criminal matter. As is the case with prosecutors, we envision a significant shift in the roles and responsibilities of defense counsel as well as significant reallocation of resources.

Finally, our analysis of plea negotiation highlights a number of important decisions and actions that occur prior to plea negotiation in the pretrial system, actions such as pretrial detention and supervision. These decisions have substantial consequences downstream for defendants, everything from the likelihood of a criminal conviction and length of sentence to short-term and longer-term recidivism. As a result, we make recommendations about significantly reforming the pretrial system to better facilitate the system goal of recidivism reduction.

We will be the first to admit that our recommendations are bold and very difficult to achieve. It is quite challenging to institute the statutory changes, procedural changes, policy changes, and reallocation of funding that are necessary in what we recommend. It is even more difficult to shift thinking about crime and punishment—to change the culture of criminal justice. Moreover, the venue for most of these changes is local jurisdictions, the more than 3,100 counties and county equivalents that are in effect the criminal justice systems in the United States. We do spend some time discussing these challenges as well as identifying solutions, incentives, and funding strategies.

Chapter 1 describes current criminal justice policy and how we got to this point. Chapter 2 is a brief overview of plea bargaining. Part of our research and analysis involves interviews with dozens of prosecutors, public defenders, and judges. Chapter 3 discusses the methodology and presents a brief overview of the interview results. Plea negotiation has been subject to a good deal of criticism, and we summarize the key points of contention in chapter 4. Many of plea bargaining's critics have offered solutions, and we discuss those and offer our take on them within the context of broader criminal justice reform and recidivism reduction. Chapter 6 presents our recommendations for consequential reform of plea negotiation, and chapter 7 focuses on changing the pretrial system and public defense. We wrap up with a discussion of challenges, incentives, and funding strategies in chapter 8.

THE RELENTLESS PURSUIT OF PUNISHMENT

Cynthia Powell[1] dropped out of high school at age seventeen and soon after gave birth to a daughter. The father left one month later. Cynthia raised her daughter Jackie by herself, and when Jackie had a premature daughter, Cynthia devoted much of her life to caring for her granddaughter.

Among other challenges, Cynthia suffered from uncontrollable diabetes. When it worsened, resulting in acute pain in her legs, she was prescribed Lorcet, which contains the pain medication hydrocodone. In April 2002, Cynthia decided to sell some of the Lorcet pills to make ends meet. The $300 sale involving thirty-five pills was made to an undercover police officer in Sunrise, Florida.

Cynthia was arrested for sale of a controlled substance weighing 29.3 grams. She had no prior arrests or convictions, and because she had nothing of value to offer the prosecution, she pled guilty to selling between twenty-eight grams and thirty kilos of hydrocodone. That charge carried a mandatory twenty-five-year prison sentence.

Michael Giles was a serviceman in the U.S. Air Force. He served six years on tours in Iraq and Kuwait. On February 6, 2010, Giles was invited by some friends to a nightclub. While he was there, a sizable brawl broke out between two rival fraternities. Michael went in search of his friends in the parking lot. He made his way to the rental car they came in and retrieved his legally owned handgun. Although he had no involvement in the fraternity brawl, Michael was attacked by some of the participants. Fearing for his safety, he fired two shots at the attackers. One was hit in the leg, but it was not a serious injury.

Michael was arrested. All agreed, including the prosecutor, that he had been attacked. Nevertheless, the prosecutor argued that he did not think Michael needed to fire his weapon to defend himself. He was subsequently convicted of aggravated battery, resulting in a twenty-five-year mandatory sentence despite the fact that he had no prior arrests or convictions.

These profiles illustrate what is becoming an all-too-familiar story of an American criminal justice system relentlessly in pursuit of punishment. The headlines are common. The scale and reach of our criminal justice system is unparalleled. The United States incarcerates more people than any other country (1.7 million in prisons and jails). We have the largest correctional population (consisting of individuals in prison and jail plus those on community supervision, such as probation and parole) in the world (nearly 7 million). We have the highest incarceration rates (adjusted for population size) in the world and the highest rates of correctional control. In effect, we have created and expanded a criminal justice system that is designed to deliver the maximum punishment to as many people as possible.

The statistics reflect the hard reality.[2] Between 1975 and today, the number of people in U.S. prisons and jails increased by 400 percent at the state level and 600 percent at the federal level. The population under correctional control increased 375 percent over the past four decades. We incarcerate approximately 700 per 100,000 population, compared to 440 in Russia, 434 in Rwanda, 221 in Kazakhstan, 146 in the United Kingdom, 118 in China, 114 in Canada, and 78 in Germany. Jails are the entry point to the U.S. criminal justice system for many criminal offenders and an important component of the bigger picture of incarceration. Local jails house 730,000 individuals on any given day, and more than 11 million individuals enter and exit U.S. jails annually.

Why and how we went down this path is increasingly well documented,[3] but we will take a few pages to summarize some of the essentials.

UNDERSTANDING WHY

The "why" in part involves a coincidence of circumstances and events that the United States experienced in the 1960s and 1970s: high crime rates, race riots, sometimes violent and typically disruptive Vietnam War protests, and the high-profile assassinations of Martin Luther King Jr. and Robert Kennedy. A palpable lack of law and order led presidential candidate Richard Nixon in 1967 and 1968 to declare war on crime and disorder and, soon after that, to declare war on drugs. The problem Nixon identified was a lack of law and order. His solution—and that of the Republican Party—was punishment.

Other circumstances helped set the stage for this dramatic shift in policy. The U.S. Supreme Court of the 1960s under Chief Justice Earl Warren handed down a number of landmark due process decisions designed to protect the rights of criminal suspects and defendants. This was seen by some, including Nixon, as a threat to the rule of law, giving criminals ways to "get off on technicalities."

Two major pieces of civil rights legislation passed by Congress in 1964 and 1965—the Civil Rights Act and the Voting Rights Act—also served to threaten the status quo, especially in the South. Then there was the expanding use of drugs in inner cities and college campuses. Few poor minorities and college students supported Nixon and the Republican Party, posing little electoral risk to launching the war on drugs.

The coincidence of these circumstances and threats provided much of the motivation for launching a sea change in criminal justice policy, the birth of what has come to be called "tough on crime" or "crime control." Crime control is a set of policies, procedures, laws, and funding decisions that have resulted in the massive expansion of criminal justice at the local, state, and federal levels, an expansion on a scale unrivaled in U.S. history and probably in the history of the world.

The origin of crime control makes sense given the realities the nation was facing in the 1960s and 1970s. We were experiencing real threats as well as perceived threats over things like Supreme Court decisions and civil rights legislation. There was a sense that how we were administering criminal justice was not working; otherwise, we would not be facing such a law-and-order crisis. And one cannot ignore how well crime and punishment resonated with the public and, importantly, with the electorate. One of the primary reasons Nixon won the 1968 presidential election was his tough-on-crime rhetoric. Another outcome of the 1968 election was the politicization of criminal justice policy, something that plays a much longer-term role regarding how we think about and conduct criminal justice in this country.

While the launch of crime control can be rationalized given the circumstances of the time (although, ironically, there was really no scientific evidence that indicated that more punishment for more people would reduce crime or reoffending), it is much harder to justify the forty-five-year run of our punishment experiment. If high crime rates, race riots, and Vietnam War protests were the primary components of the law-and-order problem, one would assume that once they were mitigated, the "solution" would be modified accordingly. Crime rates peaked in 1981, fluctuated during the 1980s, and then began a sustained decline during the 1990s. Today, we have the lowest crime rates since 1966. The race riots ended in 1970, with occasional riots in the aftermath of dramatic events like the acquittal of the police officers in the Rodney King beating trial. The Vietnam War ended in 1974, as did the protests. Drug use in the United States has declined substantially since the late 1970 and 1980s.[4] All indications were that the primary threats to law and order that brought about crime control in the first place had, for the most part, abated. Nevertheless, crime control continued on an unremitting path of expansion.

During the first fifteen years or so of crime control, tough punishment was exclusively owned by the Republican Party, beginning with Nixon and through Ronald Reagan and George H. W. Bush. Reagan was responsible for shepherding changes to federal sentencing laws making sentencing much tougher. He also provided considerable financial support for the expansion of state prison capacity. There is little doubt that politics plays a central role in sustaining our penchant for punishment. Few public officials have lost elections for being tough on crime. We just have to recall the Willie Horton TV ads during the 1988 presidential campaign between George H. W. Bush and Michael Dukakis, where Dukakis was portrayed quite successfully as soft on crime.

The politics of crime control took an unusual turn in the 1992 presidential campaign when the Clinton camp and the national Democratic Party decided it was time for liberals to be tough on crime and to take some of the political leverage for themselves. From that point forward, crime control became bipartisan, giving added momentum to the ever-expanding criminal justice system.

Part of the politics of crime control has been the role of fear. Clearly, fear was front and center early on with high rates of predatory crime, large swaths of cities burning during the race riots, and campus protests, including events like the Kent State killings. The crack epidemic in the mid-1980s further heightened fear as inner-city violence spiked, initially and mistakenly attributed to the pharmacological properties of crack and later to be correctly understood as a result of gang violence in the course of establishing crack markets. Fear seemed ever present, and elected officials could be counted on to come to the rescue with new, often draconian mandatory prison sentences and changes in parole laws requiring inmates to serve longer proportions of their sentences before being eligible for release.

The attacks on the World Trade Center and the Pentagon on September 11, 2001, added a new fear of terrorism. While fear of terrorism is different in important ways from fear of crime, the threat of terrorism subsequent to September 11 was an important element in the bigger picture of crime control. During Super Bowl XXXVI in 2002, President Bush proclaimed in a TV ad that drug traffickers fund terrorism and thus that drug use and drug dealing support terrorism. The dots had been connected between terrorism and at least some forms of traditional street crime.

Today, in the Trump era of American politics, fear is being leveraged in the form of "illegal immigrants" who, we have been told, are rapists and murderers. The "sanctuary city" statutes, building a wall between Mexico and the United States, and a variety of other anti-immigrant initiatives have kept fear alive and well. That, coupled with concerns over the opioid epidemic, has apparently caused Attorney General Jeff Sessions to regress federal charging and sentencing policy back to the 1980s and 1990s by requiring U.S. attorneys, the federal prosecutors responsible for charging and prosecuting federal offenders, to charge the most serious crimes possible in order to trigger mandatory sentences and maximize punishment, a policy that had been relaxed by the Obama administration. Sessions has also repealed the Cole Memorandum, the Obama administration's policy to not enforce federal marijuana laws in states that have legalized recreational use. What is puzzling is that Session's directives have been implemented in an era when criminal justice reform, focusing generally on reducing prison populations, among other things, is either under way or under serious discussion in the vast majority of states and the federal system.

Money is a key player in the sustainability of crime control policies, as the private sector has a strong foothold in the corrections business. Publicly traded corporations, such as CoreCivic (previously known as Corrections Corporation of America) and the GEO Group (previously known as Wackenhut), operate a number of private prisons and detention centers. The higher the population in these facilities, the more money the private sector makes. Thus, they have substantial interests in tough on crime policies and spend considerable sums of money on lobbying efforts to promote those policies.

Financial issues are important for local jurisdictions that are home to various criminal justice offices and institutions. For example, prisons tend to be located in smaller towns and rural areas, localities for which a prison is a significant economic driver because of employment and sales and property tax revenue. What used to be "not in my backyard" became "please build it here."

UNDERSTANDING HOW

The "how" of tough on crime involves a variety of policy, statutory, procedural, and funding decisions at all levels of government. Some are obvious and deliberate and others more subtle and indirect in their effects. All play key roles in expanding and sustaining crime control.

Retribution and Anger-Based Decision Making

There are tens of thousands of state and federal prosecutors in the United States and thousands of state and federal judges involved in criminal law enforcement. While there is variation given so many prosecutors and judges and so many jurisdictions, retribution, "an eye for an eye," has been the primary theme in the decisions they have made. We have created a harm-based system of punishment where the key questions have been how much harm was perpetrated by the offender and thus how much punishment fits the crime. We have tended to be driven by anger and moral outrage, "throwing the book" at those offenders who make us angry.

Retribution is an entirely legitimate motivation for punishing someone. It is simple, it is responsive to the actions of the offender, it is somehow thought to be proportional to the offender's actions, it is grounded in Western religion and culture, and, importantly, it makes sense to us. As such, it is an ideal platform for maximizing punishment by focusing mainly on harm, with little thought given to mitigation.

Expanding Correctional Capacity

The hallmark of U.S. justice policy has been the expansion of the correctional population. That requires a corresponding expansion of correctional capacity. The most significant expansion is of prisons and jails, the institutions of incarceration. The capital investment in prisons has been substantial, leading to a 430 percent increase in prison capacity over the past forty years. We have also seen massive expansion of jails at the local level, essentially on the same scale and at the same rate as prisons.[5]

The expansion of probation and parole has occurred in a much more cost-efficient manner compared to prison and jail. To a large extent, expanding community supervision populations is a matter of expanding caseload sizes for probation and parole officers. In effect, that is what we have seen over the past few decades as officer caseloads have exceeded by a considerable amount professional standards for caseload size.[6]

Sentencing Reform

Sentencing reform is the label applied to the radical rewriting of sentencing laws in the United States. It was driven in part by liberal concerns about sentencing bias as a result of perceived excessive discretion by judges when sentencing offenders. When there is so much discretion, extralegal factors like race or ethnicity can enter the calculus. Sentencing reform was also a result of conservative perceptions that judges tend to be too lenient when they have wide latitude in fixing criminal sentences. There were two different sets of concerns with the common solution of limiting judicial discretion. Sentencing reform limited the latitude that judges have by creating so-called determinate—that is, fixed or predetermined—sentences, including the proliferation of mandatory sentences. When sentences are determinate or prescribed, they are closely tied to the offense(s) of conviction. Thus, judges have little latitude. When judges have little discretion, the argument goes, there is little opportunity for lenience or discrimination.

Whatever the motivation, the end result of sentencing reform was enhanced punishment for those who are convicted in the American criminal justice system. That was accomplished by legislators who determined what the punishment should be on conviction of particular crimes. Across the board, state legislatures and Congress embraced the tough punishment provisions of crime control, and that was reflected in the sentencing laws they created.

Sentencing reform also included provisions for increasing the length of time offenders served. A defining characteristic of sentencing prior to the changes discussed above was early release from prison on parole. In many situations, the laws across the country allowed offenders to be released after serving a relatively small proportion of the sentence. It was not uncommon for inmates to be released after serving one-fifth, one-fourth, or one-third of the sentence that was imposed.

So-called truth-in-sentencing laws require much lengthier time served. A typical truth-in-sentencing law requires violent offenders to serve 85 percent of the sentence imposed. The combination of mandatory sentences and truth-in-sentencing laws dramatically increased the severity of punishment for large numbers of criminal offenders, in turn increasing the size of the prison population and raising incarceration rates.

Prosecutors as Key Decision Makers

Sentencing reform was designed to reduce the amount of discretion used by judges in the sentencing of criminal offenders. That intention was largely successful. However, that discretion did not just evaporate. Rather, it moved upstream to the prosecutor. As sentencing became more directly tied to the conviction offense(s), what someone is charged with and convicted of becomes the primary driver of the sentence. These changes have elevated prosecutors to the status of being the most important decision makers in the criminal justice system. They decide whom to prosecute, what evidence to use, what to charge offenders with, what to indict them for, what to offer in a plea negotiation, and what sentence to recommend. These are the decisions that drive the outcomes.

Recent research[7] has provided compelling statistical evidence that prosecutors have played a primary role in the growth of crime control and incarceration in recent decades through their charging decisions. During the 1990s and 2000s, crime rates for violent and nonviolent crimes dropped consistently. Arrests declined as well. At the same time, the filing of felony cases increased. However, the likelihood that a felony conviction resulted in a prison admission remained essentially stable.

In effect, while the drivers of criminal convictions—crimes and arrests—were declining, prison populations grew significantly. That was not due to significant increases in the probability of a felony conviction resulting in a sentence of incarceration. The only notable change over this period of time was prosecutors' charging decisions. The odds of an arrest leading to a felony charge increased between the early 1990s and the late 2000s from one in three to roughly two in three.

It is important to underscore the profound power that prosecutors have today in the administration of American criminal justice. This will be a consistent theme of this book, as we focus much of our attention on how prosecutors shape and implement criminal justice policy.

Overcriminalization: The Expansion of the Criminal Law

A man is sentenced to forty-five days in jail for selling hot dogs without a proper city permit. A teenager was in distress while swimming in a river, so a boater swam over to rescue her. He was charged with obstructing a government operation since he did not wait for the rescue team to arrive. A woman who routinely helped her neighbor's kids board a school bus in front of her house without being paid to do so was charged for illegally operating a day care facility without a license in violation of state regulations. One can be incarcerated for up to one year in Rhode Island for selling or exchanging pillows and mattresses without the tags required by statute.[8]

These examples illustrate what is called overcriminalization, the use of the criminal law and criminal penalties in a variety of situations that are rightly considered regulatory or civil matters. It is, in effect, the criminalization of behaviors that are outside of the realm of common law crimes like robbery, burglary, and assault. Overcriminalization is exemplified in laws criminalizing social problems, such as homelessness, acting out in school, and truancy, as well as public health problems, such as mental illness and addiction.

Overcriminalization is reflected in enhancements to the criminal code. An example is the law of parties. Jack is an accomplice to a robbery with Mike. In the course of the robbery, Mike pulls out a gun and kills a bystander. Jack can be convicted of murder in Texas under the law of parties even if he had no awareness that Mike had a gun or any intention of harming someone, if the offense was committed in furtherance of the unlawful purpose and was one that should have been anticipated.

The growth of overcriminalization is reflected elsewhere in federal law, which includes nearly 5,000 criminal laws spread across 27,000 pages of the U.S. Code. Moreover, there are more than 300,000 federal regulations for which there are criminal penalties if violated. One result is that tremendous numbers of criminal laws do not appear in the penal or criminal code but, rather, in obscure volumes of regulatory agencies. Moreover, this trend has placed lawmaking and law-enforcing responsibilities in the hands of bureaucrats.

This is not just a federal problem. The Manhattan Institute[9] conducted an analysis of Michigan law and found that of the 1,209 felonies and 1,893 misdemeanor crimes in the state, the majority (48 percent of felonies and 76 percent of misdemeanors) are not contained in the penal code, meaning they are regulatory violations. These regulatory violations created without legislative input span agriculture, the environment, trade and commerce, workplace safety, and public health, among others. Moreover, these regulatory violations do not require that individuals understand that they have broken the law.

There are two primary problems associated with overcriminalization. One is that with the ever-increasing number of laws, it is not realistic for individuals to be aware of all of these potential violations. In effect, overcriminalization has rendered archaic the maxim "Ignorance of the law is no excuse."

The other issue bears directly on the growth of the criminal justice system. Overcriminalization dramatically expands the reach of criminal justice, resulting in increasing numbers of individuals coming in the front door and being prosecuted, convicted, and punished. Where sentencing reform increases the severity of punishment, which is one of the goals of crime control, overcriminalization increases the number of people being punished, which helps accomplish the other goal of more people being punished.

The Role of Plea Negotiation

The vast majority of all criminal convictions (95 percent or more) are obtained from a plea deal, an agreement between the government and the defendant that resolves the case at hand. What is typically bargained is time: time in prison or jail or on probation. Plea negotiation dramatically expedites the processing, conviction, and punishment of criminal defendants. As such, a procedural mechanism that was developed to manage increasing caseloads has become a primary enabler or facilitator of crime control policies. One of the important consequences of this heavy reliance of plea negotiation is that it places tremendous power and discretion in the hands of prosecutors. In effect, prosecutors have become judge and jury as well as prosecutor since they determine who is innocent or guilty and determine more often than not what the punishment will be.

We limit the discussion of plea negotiation here since it is a primary focus of this book. The subsequent chapters discuss plea bargaining in detail.

Lax Enforcement of Criminal Intent

In order to lawfully convict someone of a crime, the government, in theory, is required to prove two things: the criminal act, or actus reus, and criminal intent, or mens rea. Despite that requirement, mens rea has taken a backseat in criminal prosecution during the decades of tough-on-crime policies.

First, Congress and state legislatures have created an increasing number of criminal laws for which there is no intent requirement. These are called strict liability crimes, for which the only necessary element is the criminal act. Not only does prosecution and conviction for such strict liability crimes require no criminal intent, there is also no requirement that someone is even aware that the act is criminal.

A 2010 analysis of laws proposed in the 109th Congress found that the majority (57 percent) had inadequate or absent mens rea requirements.[10] Moreover, the hundreds of thousands of federal regulatory laws with criminal consequences typically do not require criminal intent or any knowledge that the act is illegal.

Analysis of Michigan law[11] reveals that more than one-quarter (26 percent) of felonies and the majority (59 percent) of misdemeanors do not require evidence of criminal intent. A similar lack of criminal intent requirements was found in North Carolina.[12] In 2014, Idaho passed a new law making battery against a health care worker a felony. One problem is that an exemption for mentally ill individuals was removed before the bill became law.[13] The result is that a mentally ill individual potentially could be prosecuted for a felony under the law absent any criminal intent to commit that crime.

In addition to absent or inadequate mens rea requirements, we argue that the extraordinarily high plea negotiation rate has largely rendered mens rea irrelevant.[14] The primary evidence in a negotiated plea is whether the defendant committed the criminal act. The evidence of that is the defendant's confession. Once the defendant confesses to the facts of the criminal act, the deal is done. Intent is largely irrelevant.

The lax treatment of criminal intent has substantially contributed to crime control efforts by facilitating the criminal conviction of large numbers of criminal offenders.[15]

The Failure of Public Substance Abuse Treatment

Wittingly or unwittingly, the war on drugs has played a primary role in the expansion of the American criminal justice system. The war on drugs was launched at the time that crime control took hold and continued in lockstep with the expansion of the criminal justice system. As the number of drug-related criminal statutes has grown and as criminal penalties have increased, largely through mandatory minimum sentences, the number of drug law offenders in the criminal justice system has grown dramatically. In 1980, there were 590,000 people arrested on drug-related charges. In 2015, that had increased to 1.6 million, and nearly one-half of those were for marijuana.[16] Today, 25 percent of prison admissions are for drug offenses. From a purely statistical perspective, the scale of prison expansion could not have been accomplished without the sheer numbers provided by drug offenses. But there is a good bit more to the story.

The most common disorder among individuals involved in the criminal justice system is addiction, dependence or abuse of alcohol, illicit drugs, and prescription medication. We have discussed elsewhere how substance use disorders impact brain functioning and brain structure and in turn how they affect behavior.[17] The link between substance abuse and crime is not new. Large-scale studies confirm what many prosecutors, judges, and probation officers see every day—substance use is widespread, and what we have been doing to deal with it is not working.

There are major challenges to effectively reducing the prevalence of substance abuse among the criminal justice population. One is that very few individuals in the general population in need of treatment for a substance use disorder receive it, and most of those who do don't receive evidence-based treatment. Another major problem is that many of the individuals in the criminal justice system in need of treatment for a substance use disorder do not receive it, and most of those who do don't receive evidence-based treatment. The effect is that we are unable not only to effectively prevent substance-abusing individuals from criminality and thus criminal justice involvement but also to effectively reduce recidivism of those with substance use disorders who are in the criminal justice system.

The National Center on Addiction and Substance Abuse at Columbia University conducted extensive research on substance abuse treatment in the United States and published an extraordinarily comprehensive report in 2012.[18] Among their findings is that 90 percent of individuals who meet the diagnostic criteria for drug and alcohol addiction do not receive treatment. The experts at Columbia conclude,

> There is no other disease that affects so many people, has such far-reaching consequences and for which there is such a broad range of effective interventions and treatments that is as neglected as the disease of addiction.[19]

A primary reason for this situation is that there is a profound disconnect between substance abuse treatment and the medical community. Substance abuse treatment does not typically occur in the context of medical practice or in a medical setting despite the professional recognition decades ago that addiction and substance abuse are medical disorders. Rather, a separate, typically non–medically based substance abuse treatment industry has grown over the years. Therein lies much of the problem. The majority of substance use disorder treatment providers lack the knowledge, skills, and expertise to implement evidence-based practices. They are not required to have medical training, and for most individuals providing services, there are no advanced degree require- ments (many states require only a high school degree or General Equiv- alency Diploma; fourteen states[20] have no license requirements at all).[21] Moreover, the economics of substance abuse treatment favor a less skilled, peer-based approach since including medical professionals in- creases overhead significantly. A result is that treatment providers and substance abuse counselors are significantly unregulated and have few requirements for meeting any medical standards or providing evidence- based practices.

To make matters worse, as many as 70 to 80 percent of the 13,000 treatment providers in the United States use as the primary treatment modality a twelve-step program such as Alcoholics Anonymous (AA) or Narcotics Anonymous (NA).[22] AA and NA are not evidence-based prac- tices. The *Handbook of Alcoholism Treatment Approaches* is a research- based clinical assessment of effective treatment modalities. The hand- book ranks AA thirty-eighth out of forty-eight approaches in terms of effectiveness. The American Society of Addiction Medicine created a joint policy statement in 1997 in conjunction with the American Acade- my of Addiction Psychiatry and the American Psychiatric Association that distinguished between substance abuse treatment and self-help groups like AA or NA. The policy statement includes the following:

> It is important to distinguish between professional treatment and self help. Treatment involves, at a minimum, the following elements:
>
> 1. A qualified professional who is in charge and shares responsibility for the overall care of the patient;
> 2. A thorough evaluation performed, including diagnosis, determina- tion of the state and severity of illness and an assessment of the accompanying medical, psychiatric, interpersonal and social prob- lems;
> 3. A treatment plan, guided by professionally accepted practice guidelines;

4. A professional who is responsible for treatment and refers the patient to additional services that may be required.

Self help groups . . . should not be confused with or substituted for professional treatment.[23]

The National Institute on Drug Abuse has also published the *Principles of Effective Treatment*,[24] which highlights, among other things, that no single treatment approach is appropriate for everyone; that treatment should address the multiple needs of the individual, not only their substance abuse; that behavioral therapies provided by professionals are appropriate interventions; that medications are an important component of treatment for many individuals; and that the common comorbidities with mental illness should be considered and treated. These elements go far beyond the self-help model of AA and NA. Of particular importance is the fact that these self-help groups do nothing to address mental health problems. Moreover, medications like the opioid antagonist naltrexone have been shown to be effective in treating alcohol and drug abuse, and acamprosate has been shown to reduce symptoms of protracted withdrawal from alcohol. However, many AA and NA groups discourage the use of medications.[25]

These problems with substance abuse treatment extend to the criminal justice population as well. While there is considerable variation across states and local jurisdictions in terms of how and how well they address substance abuse disorders among the justice-involved population, it is accurate to conclude that the vast majority of those in need of substance abuse treatment do not receive evidence-based care. Less than 20 percent of prison inmates who need drug and alcohol treatment receive any formal treatment.[26] The most common service provided is drug education. Approximately 20 percent of prison inmates with substance abuse problems participate in twelve-step self-help programs while incarcerated.[27]

There is very limited capacity for diversion-based treatment. For example, drug courts have been found to be reasonably successful in treating substance use disorders; however, they have the capacity to address at best 10 percent of the need.[28] Moreover, most criminal justice treatment efforts utilize community-based treatment providers. Those providers suffer from the same deficiencies we described above. Additionally, a very common go-to remedy in the justice system is AA or

NA. Judges routinely order offenders to go to AA, and attending AA meetings is a common condition of probation. AA meetings are often brought into local jails and prisons for inmates who want to attend. It's not that this is necessarily bad. The problem, as noted above, is that AA and related programs are not treatment.

To further aggravate the situation, most of the 600,000 or so offenders whom judges, prosecutors, and probation officers send to drug treatment are sent to community-based facilities. The relative lack of oversight and regulation we noted above plays out in unfortunate ways in some treatment centers. For example, Phoenix House runs several drug and alcohol treatment centers in New York State. The New York Office of Alcoholism and Substance Abuse Services suspended admissions to five of Phoenix House's facilities for a variety of problems. A report by that office stated that the facilities had "persistent regulatory violations and resident/patient care concerns dating back several years" and detailed the following: sex among the residents; common use of drugs, including cocaine, heroin, and marijuana; sexual violence and assaults; insufficient and inadequately trained staff; and poor security.[29]

Christian Alcoholics and Addicts in Recovery (CAAIR) was started in 2007 by executives of a chicken processing company in Oklahoma. The goal was to provide addiction treatment and a workforce for their chicken processing plants. The Center for Investigative Reporting conducted an extensive investigation of CAAIR and found little drug treatment and much unpaid work. The 280 or so offenders whom Oklahoma courts send to CAAIR each year process chicken for companies like Walmart, Popeye's, KFC, and PetSmart. They were not paid for this work. *Reveal*, the center's radio program, interviewed dozens of former participants and employees as well as judges and reviewed court records and tax filings, among other things. They found that

> drug courts in Oklahoma are required to send defendants for treatment at certified programs with trained counselors and state oversight. CAAIR is uncertified. Only one of its three counselors is licensed, and no state agency regulates it.[30]

Participants stated that there was essentially no treatment. The therapeutic model was based on faith and work. Many described it as slave labor. The Center for Investigative Reporting found similar "treatment" facilities in Oklahoma and Arkansas called DARP (Drug and Alcohol

Recovery Program). Participants work in factories and chicken process- ing plants for no pay. They receive little addiction treatment. Partici- pants also work in businesses in Alabama and North Carolina.[31]

The unfortunate reality summarized by the experts at the National Center at Columbia is that "the vast majority of people in need of addiction treatment do not receive anything that approximates evi- dence-based care."[32] The fact that there is so much variation in over- sight, quality, modalities, and training for staff highlights the caution that simply finding an available bed for an offender referral is not the same as receiving evidence-based treatment and impacting recidivism. If the goal is to reduce recidivism and wisely invest taxpayer money, we have to get much more sophisticated about how we address substance use disorders and criminal behavior.

The Failure of Public Mental Health Treatment

As is the case with substance abuse, the expanding scale and reach of crime control and the criminal justice system have been substantially facilitated by the failure of American public health to provide adequate access to mental health treatment. Today, roughly 40 percent of prison and jail inmates have a diagnosable mental illness, and 80 percent have a substance use disorder. Nearly 60 percent of prison inmates have had at least one traumatic brain injury, commonly leading to neurocognitive impairment, including executive dysfunction, which involves the inabil- ity to appropriately plan, analyze, respond to, interpret, and control behavior and impulses. Our failure to provide sufficient capacity and access to treatment puts the justice system in the position of being the repository for a large number of disordered offenders.

Today, approximately 44 million Americans, or 19 percent of the population, have a mental illness. Ten million of these 44 million have a serious mental illness. The majority of adults with a mental illness (56 percent) did not receive treatment in the past year. There is consider- able variation across states in untreated mental illness, from lows of 41 percent in Maine and 44 percent in Vermont and Minnesota to 64 percent in Hawaii and Alaska and 66 percent in Nevada. Nearly two- thirds of youth with major depression received no treatment. New Hampshire had the lowest percentage (42) and Arkansas the highest (77).[33]

Access to mental health treatment is compounded by the lack of insurance coverage on the part of 17 percent of adults with a mental illness (7.5 million). Again, there is substantial variation by state in the percentage of uninsured mentally ill, from a low of 3 percent in Massachusetts to a high of 28 percent in Nevada. Substantial lack of a mental health care workforce aggravates the situation. There are more than 5,000 designations of mental health professional shortage areas.[34] These consist of geographic areas, populations, or facilities. These 5,000 designations affect 123,800,000 people. The current number of mental health care professionals can meet 33 percent of the need. It is estimated that an additional 5,900 mental health care professionals would be required to remove the shortage designations. The workforce shortages also vary considerably by state. Massachusetts, the District of Columbia, Maine, and Vermont have a ratio of population to providers of 260:1 or below. Alabama, Texas, and West Virginia have ratios of 1,200:1, 990:1, and 910:1, respectively.[35]

Added to these constraints is the fact that only about 50 percent of psychiatrists in the United States accept insurance (compared to 89 percent for other medical specialties).[36] That requires many patients who can afford it to pay out of pocket for professional services, creating another substantial barrier to access.

Public mental health treatment is more limited still. Most states restrict eligibility for the poor to publicly funded mental health treatment. While the rules vary by state, many impose restrictions by diagnosis and/or level of functional impairment. Moreover, fewer than 45 percent of psychiatrists who take insurance take Medicaid.

Medicaid is a federal and state program of health insurance for low-income individuals, children, the elderly, and people with disabilities. Medicaid currently pays for health care for nearly 75 million people in the United States. While all states provide coverage under Medicaid and must meet minimum standards, the coverage varies considerably by state. One of the primary reasons for such differences is whether states have expanded Medicaid beyond the minimum federal requirements. Thirty-one states have expanded Medicaid under the Affordable Care Act, eight are in the process of expansion, and nineteen have not. One consequence is that states that have not expanded Medicaid have significantly higher rates and numbers of uninsured.[37]

Recent research shows that there is a link between Medicaid expansion and crime rates.[38] Using county-level data, the researchers find that Health Insurance Flexibility and Accountability waiver expansion (the initiative that provides states with federal matching Medicaid funds) results in significant reductions in robbery, aggravated assault, and theft. They also show that the reduction in crime is likely due to increases in treatment for substance use disorders provided through the waiver expansion. A separate analysis looks at the county-level impact on crime of opening and closing substance abuse treatment facilities. The research reveals that the presence of substance abuse treatment facilities reduces violent and property crime, with a particularly strong effect on relatively serious crimes.[39] A third paper published recently also shows a significant crime reduction at the county level associated with expansion of Medicaid coverage under the Affordable Care Act.[40] The logic of the results makes sense—poverty is associated with a higher risk of crime as well as a lower likelihood of having health care coverage. Under Medicaid expansion and the parity provisions (equal coverage for physical and mental health) of the Affordable Care Act, individuals have greater access to mental health care, substance abuse treatment, and treatment for physical health conditions.

Limited access to health care, including mental health treatment and substance abuse treatment, is a major contributor to crime and the prevalence of mentally ill individuals in the criminal justice system. Failure to provide adequate behavioral health treatment to justice-involved individuals is a major contributor to recidivism.[41]

Evidence provided by the U.S. Department of Justice indicates: (1) that individuals in the nation's prisons and jails who are mentally ill are more likely to have prior convictions than those without a mental illness and that their sentences are longer, and (2) that only a relatively small percentage of prison and jail inmates who had mental health problems received any treatment while incarcerated. One-third of state prison inmates with a mental health problem received treatment while in prison. The comparable figure for federal prison is one-quarter. Fewer than one in five jail inmates in need of mental health treatment received any while in jail. The most common type of treatment for state and federal prison inmates and jail inmates was medication (between 27 and 15 percent, respectively). Smaller numbers received professional mental health therapy (between 7 and 22 percent for state and federal inmates, respectively).[42]

While the evidence indicates that diversion of mentally ill offenders is preferred in many situations, there are only 300 or so mental health courts in the United States, and only eighteen states have laws that authorize them.[43] There are very few well-designed, evidence-based, adequately funded mental health treatment options for offenders in prison and jail as well as those diverted to community supervision and/ or mental health courts and similar diversion programs.

There has been a mix of motivations and mechanisms that played key roles in the expansion of American criminal justice. It is the coincidence of changes to sentencing law and procedure, expansion of the criminal law, drug policy, failures of public health, the broad and extensive discretion of prosecutors, lax enforcement of criminal intent, retribution as a primary motive for punishment, and the extensive reliance on plea negotiation that have facilitated the great punishment experiment. Moreover, many of these factors continue to exert substantial influence in sustaining tough-on-crime policies today.

We now briefly turn to what all of this investment in punishment cost and what was accomplished.

COST AND RETURN ON INVESTMENT

The cost of crime control is stunning. We have spent $1 trillion at the local, state, and federal levels over the past forty-five years on being tough on crime. We have spent another $1 trillion on the war on drugs. Another way to look at it is that we spend $1 trillion *annually* on criminal justice as well as the collateral social, economic, crime-related, and victimization costs.[44]

So what is the return on investment? Many have suggested that the expansion of correctional control is responsible for the decline in crime during the 1990s, resulting in historically low crime rates today. While that may be a logical conclusion, the evidence indicates that it's not that simple. Crime rates increase and decrease for a variety of reasons. Incarceration and control policies are only one factor.

So what is the relationship between the massive expansion of correctional control, especially incarceration in the United States, and declines in crime rates? Modest at best since dozens of Western nations experienced similar (in scale and timing) crime declines during the 1990s without implementing anything like U.S. crime control policies. The evidence indicates that, at the most, crime control policies are responsible for 10 to 15 percent of the crime decline during the 1990s and the essentially historically low crime rates we have today.[45]

Another measure of the impact of punishment is recidivism, or reoffending. There are several ways to measure recidivism, such as rearrest, reconviction, and reincarceration. Here is what we know. Three-quarters of inmates released from prison are rearrested within three years. More than 50 percent are reincarcerated. Moreover, these statistics tell only part of the story since they are based on those who are caught. Fifty percent of crimes are never reported to the police, and of those that are reported, about 50 percent of violent crimes and 20 percent of property crimes lead to an arrest.[46] As a result, the actual recidivism rate is a good bit higher than the official measure.

The picture is more distressing when we consider reoffending of disordered offenders. Jacques Baillargeon and colleagues reported that Texas prison inmates with serious mental illness (major depression, bipolar disorder, schizophrenia, and nonschizophrenic psychosis) had a much higher risk of prior multiple incarcerations over a six-year time frame of their study.[47] The recidivism rate for mentally ill offenders and those with a substance use disorder is as high as 70 to 80 percent.[48] The recidivism rate for juvenile offenders is 80 percent (75 percent of juvenile offenders have a mental health problem and/or a neurodevelopmental disorder). This is statistical confirmation of the revolving door of the prison system, especially regarding disordered offenders.

The vast majority of the resources expended on the war on drugs are used for trying to control the supply of illicit substances. Supply control includes international interdiction in countries that produce illegal drugs as well as trying to prevent drugs from entering the United States and being distributed and sold once they are in the country. One would be hard-pressed to find an informed observer who believes that our approach to drug control has been successful. The evidence clearly supports the conclusion that it has been a resounding failure.[49]

An obvious question is why we have such a miserable report card for forty-five years of a very concerted effort to reduce crime. The simple answer is that punishment does nothing to change many of the underlying crime-related circumstances, situations, disorders, impairments, and deficits that many criminal offenders bring into the justice system. There is nothing about incarceration that makes one mentally healthy or addresses a substance addiction (abstinence is not treatment). Prison does not add IQ points to those with intellectual deficits,[50] nor does it fix the neurocognitive impairments, such as executive dysfunction, commonly associated with physical and emotional trauma, among other causes. Punishment does not make one employable, nor does it provide housing once released. In fact, criminal justice involvement makes employment and housing more difficult to obtain.

It is ironic and unfortunate, despite all of the effort and resources expended, that we have created the ultimate recidivism machine. Not only does punishment not mitigate underlying crime-related conditions, circumstances, and disorders, the evidence indicates that incarceration actually increases recidivism. The metaphor of the revolving door is a very accurate descriptor of the American criminal justice system.

THE CURRENT STATUS OF CRIME CONTROL

Crime control policies have created a massive criminal justice system that routinely operates at or over capacity. Police resources are stretched, court dockets are unreasonable, prosecutors and public defenders have unmanageable caseloads, jails and prisons are full, and probation and parole officers have caseloads that often far exceed professional standards.

Despite recent discussions at the national, state, and local levels about criminal justice reform and smart crime policy, the vast bulk of the criminal justice system remains in place. There have been quite modest reductions in prison populations, driven largely from state-level financial concerns triggered by the recession beginning in 2008. Some jurisdictions have placed more emphasis on diversion and rehabilitation programs, but those largely remain piecemeal, with very limited capacity. Punishment is still the primary response that the U.S. criminal justice system has for crime.

Momentum that was gained by broader discussions of reform and being smart on crime over the past five or six years is potentially in question due to the election of Donald Trump, who ran as a "law-and-order" candidate. And, apparently, the Trump administration is attempting to deliver on that promise. Trump criticized Democrat Doug Jones, who ran against and beat Republican Roy Moore for the Alabama U.S. Senate seat, as weak on crime. Trump provided no evidence to back up his claim. Jeff Sessions, the U.S. attorney general, is breathing new life into tough on crime and the war on drugs with the new charging directives given to federal prosecutors. There is no mistake— all of this is straight out of the tired, old 1980s and 1990s punishment playbook that ignores the scientific evidence that clearly shows that punishment does not reduce recidivism but actually increases it. The revival of tough on crime is not surprising given that the Trump administration is at least science agnostic if not antiscience. Moreover, the current opioid crisis is resurrecting not only tough rhetoric but also tough criminal sanctions. The reform-minded governor of Kentucky, Matt Bevin, recently signed a bill that calls for doubling the prison sentence of individuals caught possessing less than two grams of heroin. An article by Vox reporter German Lopez documents at least sixteen states that as of September 2017 have enhanced the criminal penalties for possession of opioids, including heroin, painkillers, and fentanyl.[51]

GOING FORWARD

While legislators have been the architects of tough on crime, prosecutors have been the implementers in chief. Prosecutors have served as the gatekeepers to criminal prosecution, conviction, and punishment of felony and misdemeanor defendants in state and federal court, aided by much discretion, little oversight, and extraordinary reliance on plea negotiation. While plea negotiation is a defining characteristic of American criminal justice and the keystone of tough on crime, it is, in a very real sense, a black box of criminal prosecution, typically occurring behind closed doors, in courthouse hallways, and in local jails.

To borrow another metaphor, plea negotiation is the elephant in the room. There are a number of significant concerns that have been raised about it, such as lack of due process protections; essentially unfettered discretion by prosecutors; little judicial and appellate review; the risk that a confession, which serves as the basis for a plea, can be coerced; issues regarding assistance of defense counsel; pretrial detention practices; very limited provision of evidence to the defendant; excessive caseloads for prosecutors and public defenders; the fact that large numbers of defendants with a variety of disorders, deficits, and impairments are routinely convicted and incarcerated rather than diverted; and the conviction of innocent individuals, among others. Most of these problems and concerns associated with plea negotiation don't get the attention they deserve from policymakers or the courts, except for occasional hand-wringing, and they remain largely without remedy.

Plea negotiation has played a primary, fundamental role in the massive expansion of correctional control and punishment. As such, it also plays a critical role in criminal justice reform, especially how it fits into the development of a more effective system for reducing crime, recidivism, victimization, and cost.

We spend time in subsequent chapters developing how plea negotiation works, the concerns and problems associated with it, the role it has played in the expansion of American criminal justice, and, importantly, how it needs to change in order to accomplish meaningful criminal justice reform. There are many moving parts to comprehensive reform of the American criminal justice system. Changing plea negotiation is paramount.

What we propose here are fundamental changes to the process of criminal prosecution and conviction, including the practice of plea negotiation and the environment in which plea negotiation takes place, namely, the pretrial system. The goal is to develop a more balanced approach to dealing with criminal offending, an approach that preserves the selective use of retribution and the use of incarceration to incapacitate or separate certain dangerous individuals from society and that at the same time provides the opportunity for meaningful diversion, behavioral change, and recidivism reduction for many, many other offenders. We argue that this cannot be achieved under the current policies of prosecution, conviction, and punishment of the vast majority of criminal offenders entering the justice system.

Much of our analysis and discussion is on criminal prosecution and the practice of plea negotiation. As such, a primary focus of this book is on prosecutors. Sentencing reform largely succeeded in limiting the discretion of judges. At the same time, it transferred discretion to prosecutors, discretion that is largely unfettered. Statistical evidence of the impact of prosecutorial discretion is the research cited previously regarding the role of prosecutors' charging and plea decisions in the massive expansion of incarceration in the United States. Since prosecutors are the key players in achieving tough-on-crime policies, they need to be key players in criminal justice reform.

The analysis that informs our discussion and policy recommendations consists of research conducted by a variety of academics and policy researchers from a number of disciplines, including law, public policy, sociology, criminology, political science, psychology, psychiatry, neuroscience, public health, and epidemiology. Moreover, we have conducted numerous face-to-face and telephone interviews with prosecutors, judges, and public defenders in a variety of jurisdictions to get their perspectives on plea negotiation, the concerns associated with it, and the role of plea bargaining in the bigger picture of criminal justice reform. We also rely on all of that evidence as we develop strategies for change.

2

PLEA BARGAINING IN PRACTICE

A SHORT HISTORY OF PLEA BARGAINING

John Langbein said it twenty-five years ago: "jury trials are about as representative of the criminal courts of New York City as the hippopotamus in the Bronx Zoo is representative of wildlife in New York. They both are curious, anomalous spectacles."[1]

Someone from a foreign country reading our Constitution, especially the Bill of Rights, would come away with a version of American criminal justice that emphasizes a variety of due process protections and guarantees for criminal defendants. Our visitor would assume that criminal defendants routinely enjoy the right against unreasonable searches and seizures (Fourth Amendment); protection against a coerced or compelled confession to a crime and deprivation of life, liberty, or property without due process of law (Fifth Amendment); and the right to a trial by a jury, the right to defense counsel, and the right to confront and cross-examine witnesses (Sixth Amendment).

What our visitor would see by spending a day or two in our criminal courtrooms is not the theoretical version of due process provided in the Bill of Rights or the Hollywood version of long, in-depth investigations of the facts and the eventual, proper discovery of the truth. Rather, what they will see is an administrative process where the priority is to move as many people as quickly as possible through an extraordinarily overburdened system. An obvious conclusion that our guest might draw from observing the evidence is that when we fail to provide adequate resources for handling the numbers of people entering the criminal justice system, one of the consequences is sacrificing constitutional principles and protections that serve as important pillars of our democracy.

Plea bargaining or plea negotiation is the method used to adjudicate and convict the vast majority of felony and misdemeanor defendants in both federal and state criminal justice systems. Today, more than 95 percent of all criminal convictions are arrived at by an admission of guilt and the simultaneous waiver of a variety of protections, including the right to a trial, the right to confront and cross-examine witnesses, the privilege against self-incrimination, and the right to appeal. As two astute observers of the criminal justice system concluded, "[Plea bargaining] is not some adjunct of the criminal justice system: it is the criminal justice system."[2]

Plea negotiation is not new. Evidence indicates its use before the Civil War. It began to increase in use at the turn of the twentieth century, and by 1925 it had an established foothold in many jurisdictions. For example, in the 1920s, plea deals were the basis for 85 percent of felony convictions in Chicago, 76 percent in Denver, 81 percent in Los Angeles, 78 percent in Detroit, and 90 percent in Minneapolis.[3]

There are three ways in which plea deals are made: charge bargaining, sentence bargaining, and sentence recommendations. Charge bargaining involves pleading guilty to a lesser charge—say, from an original indictment for of aggravated robbery to a lesser charge of simple robbery or felony theft to misdemeanor theft—which in turn translates into lesser punishment. Charge bargaining can also involve dismissal of charges in situations where there are multiple counts. Sentence bargaining is more directly what plea bargaining is all about—negotiating how much time, such as time in prison or jail or time on probation. A somewhat less certain form of plea bargaining is the prosecution agreeing to make a particular sentence recommendation. As it sounds, a recommendation is just that, a recommendation, which the judge may or may not follow.

Plea bargaining exists for several reasons.[4] The most obvious is that it is an efficient way to move huge caseloads. This serves the interests of and is an advantage to prosecutors, judges, and public defenders. It is also an effective way to resolve cases where there are no factual or legal issues to litigate. It makes no sense to hold a criminal trial if there is agreement on the facts. A third reason is that plea deals provide an opportunity for witnesses and codefendants to provide information to the government in exchange for lesser charges and lesser punishment. For example, this is institutionalized in the federal sentencing guidelines with the "substantial assistance" departure. A fourth reason that plea negotiation exists is that it provides opportunities for creativity, innovation, and flexibility in the adjudication of criminal matters. As such, plea deals can result in more just outcomes, as prosecutors can create results that better fit the circumstances of the case if they are so inclined.

We add a fifth reason for plea negotiation, one that has been absent from discussions of its purpose. The premise of this book is that plea negotiation has, either wittingly or unwittingly, played a central part in accomplishing the crime control objectives of U.S. criminal justice policy over the past fifty years. Not only does it expedite criminal prosecution and conviction, but it does so primarily with a simple, harm-focused, just deserts approach. When the culture is tough on crime, putting the discretion and authority in the hands of prosecutors helps ensure accomplishing that agenda. We briefly discussed this in chapter 1 and expand on it considerably in subsequent chapters.

The legal framework of plea negotiation is sparse. Plea bargaining is a process that is governed by few rules and regulations, a free market of sorts. What does exist has been provided largely by case law rather than statute, and even that constitutes a relatively light hand by the U.S. Supreme Court. Some basic due process protections afforded defendants in criminal trials have not yet been applied to plea negotiations.

The decision to negotiate as well as the specifics of the deal are essentially at the discretion of the prosecutor. It is the option of the defendant to reject the deal and/or make a counteroffer. Moreover, just because the prosecutor does not offer a deal does not mean the case necessarily goes to trial. The defendant may plead guilty in court and rely on any goodwill from the judge in getting a more favorable sentence. This is known as a "blind plea" since the defendant does not know the sentence outcome when entering the plea.

How Did We Get Here?

Anyone who observes a felony or misdemeanor court for an hour or two (when there is not a criminal trial occurring) typically comes away with a bewildered look. What they see is a nearly constant parade of prosecutors, defendants, and defense lawyers and then some discussion about something, and then the next set of lawyers and defendants appear. What's going on here? The answer is case or docket management—the expedited processing of people and cases. Why do we have such an emphasis on moving people as quickly as possible? Simply put, there are too many people and too few resources to handle them. Nearly fifty years ago, Warren Burger, the chief justice of the Supreme Court, noted the necessary changes to court resources as a consequence of reducing the plea negotiation rate:

> The consequence of what might seem on its face a small percentage change in the rate of guilty pleas can be tremendous. A reduction from 90 per cent to 80 per cent in guilty pleas requires the assignment of twice the judicial manpower and facilities—judges, court reporters, bailiffs, clerks, jurors and courtrooms. A reduction to 70 per cent trebles this demand.[5]

All of the key players, particularly prosecutors, public defenders, and judges, face the same challenges of wholly unrealistic caseloads and dockets, and that pressure has created and sustained plea bargaining as the first choice for adjudicating and convicting criminal defendants. An obvious question is, why so many people?

Part of the answer is demographic. The population of the United States has risen consistently over time. In 1860, there were 31.4 million. By 1920, it was 106 million, a 240 percent increase. That pace continued throughout the decades. By 1980, there were 236.5 million, and as of 2016, it is 323 million. All else equal, the greater the population, the greater the number of people coming in the criminal justice system.

Another factor driving greater numbers of individuals in the justice system is urbanization. Crime tends to be concentrated in urban areas; thus, all else equal, as more people live in cities, more crimes occur and more individuals are arrested and thus enter the justice system. In 1860, 20 percent of the population lived in urban areas. By 1920, that had risen to 51 percent. By 1980, 74 percent lived in cities. Today, 81 percent live in urban areas.

Crime trends played a significant role in the evolution of plea deals. While bargaining was prevalent in American courtrooms in the 1920s, the unprecedented rise in crime in the 1960s and 1970s, the growing use of illicit drugs in urban areas and college campuses, and the official response to both of these trends resulted in a substantial increase in criminal cases on prosecutors' caseloads and court dockets.

Enforcement of minor misdemeanor crimes also comes into play here. "Broken windows," zero tolerance, and order maintenance policing, which target petty, quality-of-life crimes often committed by the homeless, have been responsible for significant increases in offenders in misdemeanor courts, aggravating already substantial caseload problems there.

Overcriminalization, or the expansion of the criminal code over time, is an important factor in the increase in people in the justice system. As Congress and state legislatures have added thousands of crimes and regulations with criminal liability, the number of people entering the criminal justice system has increased dramatically.

There is also the increased complexity of criminal prosecution and adjudication as a result of landmark decisions of the Supreme Court of the 1960s and 1970s. Cases like *Mapp v. Ohio*, *Escobedo v. Illinois*, *Miranda v. Arizona*, *Gideon v. Wainwright*, and many more required trial courts, prosecutors, and public defenders to spend more resources on due process matters, further magnifying the burden of increased caseloads.[6]

Another very important consideration in explaining why the criminal justice system is so crowded and thus needs to rely on such high plea rates is the failure to reduce recidivism. About 65 to 70 percent of convicted offenders reoffend within three years of release from the justice system. For certain subgroups of offenders, like those with significant mental health problems, the recidivism rate is 80 percent.[7] As we noted in chapter 1, the actual recidivism rate is higher than the 65 and 80 percent since recidivism is an official statistic of known reoffending.

On any given day, the clear majority of defendants on court dockets and on prosecutors' and public defenders' caseloads have been there at least once before. Many have been there multiple times. The inability of the criminal justice system to effectively reduce recidivism is one of the key reasons that there is so much caseload and docket pressure and, in turn, why such a high rate of plea negotiation is essentially guaranteed. It is indeed rather circular—high recidivism requires high plea rates, and high plea rates, we argue, are a major contributor to high recidivism.

There are a number of very important facilitators of plea bargaining that provide prosecutors with critical leverage to motivate plea deals. One such facilitator is sentencing reform, the name given to the dramatic rewriting of sentencing laws in the states and the federal system. Sentencing reform shifted law and procedure from indeterminate statutes (where judges had broad discretion) to sentencing schemes characterized by determinate sentences, mandatory sentences, and mandatory minimums. These determinate and mandatory sentences are closely tied to the conviction offense. Changing sentencing accomplished a number of things, including the dramatic reduction of judicial discretion and the displacement of that discretion upstream to the prosecutor's office. The end result is that prosecutors' charging decisions dictated the potential punishment exposure a defendant faced since the conviction offense, not the judge, largely determined the punishment. In turn, the certainty and severity of the potential punishment could be effectively used as leverage in the plea process. Pleading to a lesser charge could take a mandatory sentence off the table. Sentencing reform gave prosecutors a tremendous advantage in the plea negotiation process and further amplified their role as the most important decision makers in the criminal justice system. "Truth-in-sentencing" laws were implemented to reduce the gap between sentence imposed and time served. It was considered dishonest when the judge imposed a sentence of ten years but the offender was paroled after serving three years. The result of truth-in-sentencing laws was a substantial increase in punishment and, again, considerable leverage in a plea deal if the agreement excluded being subject to a truth-in-sentencing law.

Overcriminalization also gave significant leverage to prosecutors in the plea process. Broadening of the criminal code provided prosecutors with more, often overlapping offenses with which to charge a defendant. Charge stacking, or charging multiple offenses for the same criminal conduct, gives prosecutors flexibility to dismiss some of the charges in exchange for a guilty plea. As the late Harvard Law School professor William Stuntz explains it,

> Suppose a given criminal episode can be charged as assault, robbery, kidnapping, auto theft, or any combination of the four. By threatening all four charges, prosecutors can, even in discretionary sentencing systems, significantly raise the defendant's maximum sentence, and often raise the minimum sentence as well. The higher threatened sentence can then be used as a bargaining chip, an inducement to plead guilty. . . . Substituting an easy-to-prove crime for one that is harder to establish obviously makes criminal litigation cheaper for the government. And the cost saving is large, since guilty pleas are much cheaper than trials, and defendants often respond to easily proved charges by pleading guilty. Charge-stacking, the process of charging defendants with several crimes for a single criminal episode, likewise induces guilty pleas.[8]

At least one expert observer suggests that overcriminalization and plea bargaining have a symbiotic relationship: "plea bargaining and over-criminalization perpetuate each other, as plea bargaining shields over-criminalization from scrutiny and overcriminalization creates the incentives that make plea bargaining so pervasive."[9]

In the end, what made plea negotiation the overwhelmingly preferred method of criminal adjudication and conviction is that it met the needs and interests of the key actors in the justice system. As George Fisher tells us in his history of plea bargaining, "Plea bargaining's triumph was manifestly the work of those courtroom actors who stood to gain from it."[10] Prosecutors benefit by the efficiency of plea deals and the certainty and ease of conviction. High conviction rates are the metric by which many prosecutors are evaluated. Defense counsel (primarily public defenders and assigned counsel since the majority of criminal defendants are indigent) benefit because the weight of excessive caseloads would make their jobs impossible without the expediency of plea negotiation. Judges benefit because plea negotiation is essential for moving and managing impossible dockets and because it provides judges protection from reversal since most plea deals involve a waiver of appeal. Criminal defendants benefit by eliminating the uncertainty associated with a trial and by avoiding more severe punishment if they take their case to trial. Fisher also sees the criminal justice system as a beneficiary of plea negotiation:

> To the extent plea bargaining delivers a verdict that onlookers acknowledge truthful, it protects the jury and the system that sponsors it from the risk of issuing the wrong verdict . . . despite all the criticism heaped upon plea bargaining by those who think it deprives defendants of their trial right or the public of its right to uncompromised punishment, when it comes to the apparent accuracy of outcomes, plea bargaining helps protect the system's legitimacy.[11]

PLEA BARGAINING CASE LAW

A number of factors have played key roles in sustaining the use of negotiated pleas in American criminal justice. The power of the prosecutor to exercise broad discretion and access considerably greater resources than the defendant and the use of a variety of inducements and tactics to leverage or motivate defendants to accept plea deals have ensured that plea negotiation retains its prominent place in American jurisprudence. The courts have also played a fundamental role in preserving the centrality of plea negotiation.

Plea negotiation has been endorsed by the Supreme Court on numerous occasions (in 1970 in *Brady v. United States* and *North Carolina v. Alford*, in 1971 in *Santobello v. New York*, in 1978 in *Bordenkircher v. Hayes*, in 1982 in *United States v. Goodwin*, in 1995 in *United States v. Mezzanato*, and in 2012 in *Lafler v. Cooper* and *Missouri v. Frye*). The Court declared plea bargaining constitutional in 1970 in *Brady v. United States*:

> we cannot hold that it is unconstitutional for the State to extend a benefit to a defendant who in turn extends a substantial benefit to the State and who demonstrates by his plea that he is ready and willing to admit his crime and to enter the correctional system in a frame of mind that affords hope for success in rehabilitation over a shorter period of time than might otherwise be necessary.[12]

The *Brady* Court also declared that adequate advice of counsel would prevent errors and miscarriages of justice, such as innocent defendants falsely pleading guilty. Presumably, the Court also saw adequate defense counsel as the remedy for a variety of other risks to defendants associated with plea bargaining. More on this in subsequent chapters.

The Court held in *Santabello* that plea bargaining is an essential and desirable part of the adjudication of criminal defendants, that it is quicker and less expensive than trials, and that it is to be encouraged. In particular, the *Santobello* Court held,

> The disposition of criminal charges by agreement between the prosecutor and the accused, sometimes loosely called "plea bargaining," is an essential component of the administration of justice. Properly administered, it is to be encouraged. If every criminal charge were subjected to a full-scale trial, the States and the Federal Government would need to multiply by many times the number of judges and court facilities. [13]

A few years earlier, the American Bar Association stated that plea bargaining benefits the court system by reserving scarce resources for "'real disputes' and reducing the need for additional funding and personnel required for criminal trials." [14] Moreover, the Court has yet to hold that plea bargaining presents a constitutional problem. [15]

Nearly four decades ago, the Supreme Court in *Bordenkircher v. Hayes* held that tough bargaining by a prosecutor, in the form of threats of harsher punishment if the defendant refused the plea deal, was permissible. In *Bordenkircher*, the defendant was indicted for forgery. The prosecutor told him that if he refused a plea deal, he would be charged under the state's habitual offender law, which would invoke a mandatory life sentence. The defendant refused the offer, and the defendant, Bordenkircher, was convicted under the mandatory law and sentenced to life. The prosecutor later testified that he pursued the habitual offender indictment strictly to motivate the defendant to waive his right to a jury trial and take the plea deal.

The *Bordenkircher* Court essentially embraced the state's interest in avoiding trials: [the Court has] "necessarily accepted as constitutionally legitimate the simple reality that the prosecutor's interest at the bargaining table is to persuade the defendant to forgo his right to plead not guilty." [16] The Court also offered a rather sweeping dismissal of potential constitutional issues with the practice:

in the give and take of plea bargaining, there is no such element of punishment or retaliation so long as the accused is free to accept or reject the prosecution's offer . . . defendants advised by competent counsel and protected by other procedural safeguards are presumptively capable of intelligent choice in response to prosecutorial persuasion and unlikely to be driven to false self-condemnation.[17]

Both the *Bordenkircher* and the *Mezzanato* decisions rely on assistance of counsel as the remedy for things like the power and resource imbalance between the defendant and the state, tough bargaining tactics, and duress. Moreover, both cases seem to make the presumption that defense representation is adequate.[18]

The landmark decision *Gideon v. Wainwright* gave significant force to the Sixth Amendment right to counsel. *Gideon* established the requirement that in any felony prosecution, the state shall provide defense counsel to those defendants who are indigent. This provision was later applied to some misdemeanor defendants who faced a sentence of jail time on conviction. While certainly a fundamentally important decision, *Gideon* unfortunately was silent regarding quality of counsel. In 2012, the Supreme Court decided two cases that dealt with the effective assistance of counsel in the context of plea negotiation.

Missouri v. Frye involved a failure of defense counsel to inform his client of a plea deal offered by the prosecutor before it expired. The original plea deal was for a misdemeanor charge. As a result, the defendant pled guilty to a felony charge in a subsequent plea offer and was sentenced to three years in prison.

In *Lafler v. Cooper*, bad defense lawyering resulted in more serious consequences. The defendant was charged with multiple counts, including attempted murder. The victim had been shot several times in the hip, rear, and lower abdomen. The prosecutor offered a plea deal, but the defense lawyer advised against accepting it on the argument that the government could not prove intent to commit murder because the victim had been shot below the waist. The rejected offer involved four years and three months to seven years in prison. The case went to trial, and a jury convicted him. He was sentenced to fifteen to thirty years in prison.

The importance of *Lafler* and *Frye* was the acknowledgment by the Court that plea negotiation is how the vast majority of criminal convictions are achieved and that the Sixth Amendment assistance of counsel applies to plea bargaining just as much as a criminal trial. They further provided relief to defendants who, because of poor defense representation, declined favorable plea deals.

Unfortunately, the Court did not address what competent counsel looks like. In *Frye*, the majority opinion declared,

> Bargaining is, by its nature, defined to a substantial degree by personal style. The alternative courses and tactics in negotiation are so individual that it may be neither prudent not practicable to try to elaborate or define standards for the proper discharge of defense counsel's participation in the process.[19]

There is another way in which the Supreme Court has had a very important hands-off policy. *Brady v. Maryland* imposes a duty on prosecutors to disclose exculpatory evidence to the defense. *Brady* is a trial-based right. If the government has discovered evidence that indicates that the defendant may not have committed the crime for which he is on trial, in the interest of justice, the defendant should be informed of that. Failure to do that is a violation of the due process protections under the Fifth and Fourteenth Amendments.

However, the Court has not applied the *Brady* rule to plea negotiation. Such exculpatory evidence could be materially important in deciding whether to accept a plea deal if, for example, it renders the testimony of a key witness invalid. However, in *United States v. Ruiz* (2002), the Court held that a defendant could not reverse a guilty plea just because the prosecutor failed to divulge impeachment evidence. To add to the problem, some federal appellate circuits allow defendants to raise a *Brady* issue to challenge a guilty plea, and others do not. As things stand, there is no clear guidance on this matter from the Supreme Court.

In very important respects, plea negotiation is a due process stepchild of American jurisprudence. The reluctance of the Supreme Court to afford the plea negotiation process the same protections as the trial process is puzzling, especially when we consider that the vast majority of criminal convictions, both misdemeanor and felony, are plea deals.

In this era of historically low crime, the administration of criminal justice is based on a procedure developed to deal with the consequences of the ever-expanding reach of criminal justice and the consequent flood of individuals into the nation's misdemeanor and felony courts. In the end, the one key factor that guarantees the extraordinary reliance on plea negotiation into the foreseeable future is the failure of the American criminal justice system to accomplish what it presumably was designed to do: reduce recidivism.

3

GOING TO THE SOURCE

Interviewing Prosecutors, Defense Counsel, and Judges

INTRODUCTION

The goal of this book is to understand how plea negotiation works, what concerns there are about the process of plea bargaining, how to address those concerns, and how to change plea negotiation in ways consistent with meaningful criminal justice reform. To better understand these issues, we interviewed key individuals involved in plea negotiation: public defenders, prosecutors, and judges.

METHODOLOGY

Personal telephone interviews were conducted with defense counsel, prosecutors, and judges. The interviews were structured and were based on interview guides developed for each of the three segments. The interviews took approximately forty-five minutes to an hour to complete.

The interview methodology did not involve random sampling. The jurisdictions we ended up sampling from were areas where we had access through personal contacts or recommendations and referrals. The individuals we interviewed were those who district attorneys and chief public defenders provided to us. Our intention is for the interviews to be illustrative, not representative.

We did attempt to interview from jurisdictions that varied in size, so we spoke with interviewees from large metro areas, moderate-size towns, and rural areas. Nearly all of the interviews were conducted in Texas, with the exception of a few from Louisiana. Per the confidentiality agreement and what interviewees were told, we cannot reveal the particular jurisdictions where the interviewees practiced. They were selected from a total of eight jurisdictions, seven counties and one federal judicial district. There were a total of eighty-nine interviews conducted. We obtained forty-four completed interviews with defense counsel, thirty-three with prosecutors, and twelve with judges.

We had no difficulty obtaining interviews with defense counsel other than significant challenges with scheduling. Prosecutors, however, were not eager to be interviewed. We had a number of requests for interviews with district attorneys that were declined. We sought to interview assistant U.S. attorneys but did not receive a reply to our request to the U.S. Justice Department. Interviews with judges included mainly state felony and misdemeanor judges. A few federal judges were interviewed.

We present some general findings about the plea process and a top-line summary of the rest of the results below. Most of the interview results, including verbatim comments, are presented in subsequent chapters when we discuss the relevant subject matter to which particular findings pertain. Copies of the interview guides are provided in the appendix.

HOW PLEA NEGOTIATION WORKS

When the negotiation process begins is variable. Some indicated that it can begin as early as around the time of arrest. Some jurisdictions and some prosecutors negotiate before indictment, which can provide advantages to the government by avoiding indicting a case. Much of the negotiation occurs after indictment:

> I usually try to have my recommendations on the case set by arraignment.

> It starts as early as arraignment and as late as the day of trial.

Starts right after indictment.

Most state-level plea negotiation is characterized as back and forth, with the state making an offer from which negotiation proceeds. Below are illustrative comments from public defenders:

> Usually more back and forth. I take the initial offer recommendation to my client but still talk about other options with my client.

> Generally it's a lot of back and forth. I'll go to the state saying "Can I get a recommendation?" And they'll give me an initial estimate, but they normally don't write their bottom line. So if I'm looking at an aggravated robbery and they give me fifteen, it lets me know what the case is worth to them. If the client says they're willing to do five and the state wants fifteen, then we may do eight to ten years—keeping in mind that the client probably lowballed you as well, five is what they're okay with, but they'll probably stand for a little more.

> It is usually back and forth. A lot of factors can come into play. In my experience, it depends on the DA, my client's criminal history, and the offense.

> Sometimes it's take it or leave it, sometimes it's back and forth.

Federal public defenders describe a process involving less negotiation and more of a take-it-or-leave-it approach:

> In federal courts, it's more the prosecutor makes an offer and we take it.

> I would say there's not a whole lot of negotiation. We get standard plea agreements and a lot of resistance from prosecutors as to changes to those standard terms. That's not a negotiation, just our client accepting the terms.

Defense counsel indicated that nearly all of the leverage involves threats of worse outcomes. These threats include mandatory sentences, charge and sentence enhancements, the trial penalty, and pretrial detention. Incentives are mainly dismissal of charges. Some prosecutors put short time lines on offers. All of this illustrates broad prosecutorial discretion.

Many prosecutors said that the incentives were reduced time in prison or on probation or the option of probation over incarceration. Some also said that they negotiate probation conditions, presumably easing some of the restrictions:

> I might start off with a little bit higher of an offer than what I want to give. So, if I'm looking to have the final plea be five years, I will start off at seven or eight and let the defense attorney negotiate with me a little. Then in the end, it looks like they got something.

> Number of years of probation. . . . Also, working with the fine because most people don't have money to be spending on court costs.

> Prison time, some charges come with lifetime registration, we negotiate the kinds of charges with registration in mind.

> Probation versus confinement, or deferred adjudication versus final conviction.

> Reduced time, probation conditions, not filing enhancements and letting them plea to a lesser charge.

At the state level, the prosecutor routinely makes the sentence a part of the plea deal. While it is a recommendation to the court and as such is not binding, the vast majority of the time the judge concurs with the sentence:

> It happens nearly all the time in my experience.

> I think it happens in the majority of cases. It is usually a recommendation.

> It's almost always a part of the deal.

> Pretty routine. . . . It's not binding, the judge can refuse to accept. . . . I can tell you I have never seen that happen in felony court.

> There are times that they'll [judges] bust a plea, but it's pretty rare.

It is rare that a sentence is part of the plea deal in federal prosecutions. The federal public defenders we interviewed indicated it happened perhaps 5 or 10 percent of the time.

TOP-LINE OVERVIEW OF INTERVIEW RESULTS

Concerns with the Plea Process

The interviews with prosecutors, public defenders, and judges provide support for what critics of plea negotiation have been saying for some time. Overall, public defenders have serious due process concerns about plea negotiation as well as the use of pretrial detention and limited access to the government's evidence. Not unexpectedly, prosecutors do not generally share those concerns. A couple of the judges had problems with plea negotiation being hidden.

Defense counsel identify use of pretrial detention, the trial penalty, threats of mandatory sentences, charging enhancements, and imposing time lines for accepting open offers as tactics to motivate acceptance of plea deals. Prosecutors state that they typically threaten harsher punishment as leverage. The perspectives of defense attorneys and prosecutors diverge considerably on the question of coercion. The defense is clear that their clients are often pressured into taking deals. A couple of the prosecutors expressed concern over coercion in the plea process, but the rest were silent on that matter.

Several prosecutors indicated that they had significant questions about the competence of defense counsel. A few judges also have reservations about the quality of defense representation.

Prosecutors are commonly in charge of determining the appropriate punishment since, at least in state prosecutions, prosecutors either stipulate the sentence in the plea agreement or provide sentencing recommendations. In the jurisdictions we included in this research, state judges routinely affirm the stipulated sentence or recommendation. It is a rare circumstance when a judge "busts" a plea deal. Prosecutors' descriptions of how they determine appropriate punishment is fairly vague—some combination of the offense, criminal history, experience, and victim input, among others. Both defense counsel and prosecutors indicate that the outcomes of cases, the "going rate" in terms of punishment, depend on things like the seriousness of the offense, strength of the evidence, criminal history, personal experience, and victim input.

Screening, Assessment, Diversion, and Recidivism

Prosecutors and defense counsel agree that screening and assessment of defendants are infrequent and, when done, are of questionable quality. There apparently is no routine screening of offenders for mental health, substance abuse, and/or neurocognitive disorders. The evidence indicates that at least in the jurisdictions in which we interviewed, it is often up to the defense attorneys to request an assessment. In those cases where disorder is known, whether and how that information is used in a plea deal varies considerably.

Judges stated that screening is adequate but that capacity for diversion is lacking. They also noted that better assessment is warranted for individuals who may be mentally ill.

Prosecutors believe that recidivism reduction is typically out of their control; some said that the primary tool they have to reduce reoffending is punishment. This is consistent with the perception of public defenders—they believe that the prosecutors with whom they work are tough on crime. A few indicated that the circumstances that are related to criminal involvement should be better addressed both by prosecutors and by the justice system more broadly. Judges were mixed in terms of their perceived ability to impact recidivism. What is interesting is that neither prosecutors nor judges generally believe that recidivism reduction is their responsibility.

4

PLEA BARGAINING'S CRITICS

Stephanos Bibas, a law professor and critic of plea negotiation, pointedly summarizes the due process concerns many have expressed about plea bargaining:

> Juries and especially jury trials were supposed to ensure fair process, accurate outcomes and checks on abuse of power. . . . Our legal system put its faith in adversarial proceedings that culminated in vigorously fought trials, at which the collision of truth and error would ensure that factual, legal and moral justice won out. . . . While the shell of the adversarial system remains, the core has been hollowed out. Plea bargaining began as a way for a few indisputably guilty defendants to resolve their cases quickly saving everyone the time and expense of getting to a foreordained conclusion. But the exception has swallowed the rule.[1]

The realities of modern American criminal justice require the procedural mechanism of plea deal making in order to expedite the processing of too many criminal cases and criminal defendants. What we end up with is a far cry from the ideal of the litigation of evidence based on criminal procedure and rules of evidence. Rather, as Douglas Guidorizzi, a trial attorney at the U.S. Department of Justice puts it, the finding of guilt is an "administrative determination by the prosecutor. . . . Additionally, the purposes served by the rules of evidence and procedure become secondary."[2]

Despite the necessity for and ubiquity of plea negotiation, many have raised significant concerns with the practice. We discuss these issues in this chapter, relying on the research and observations of others as well as the interview results with prosecutors, public defenders, and judges that we reported on in chapter 3. We begin with general due process concerns with plea negotiation and then turn to more specific problems.

GENERAL CONCERNS

One of the defining characteristics of American criminal jurisprudence is the emphasis on due process. Well-established case law and codes of criminal procedure elaborate a variety of procedural safeguards that are afforded criminal defendants. For example, the law provides how the police may search, seize, and interrogate; protection against coerced self-incrimination; the right to a jury trial; protection against discrimination in jury selection; confrontation and cross-examination of witnesses; rules of evidence; requirements that the government provide the defense with exculpatory and impeachment evidence; and that the government prove its case in chief beyond a reasonable doubt.

In theory, the conviction of a criminal defendant requires an investigation of the evidence by the government and the defense, indictment, presentation of the government's evidence before an impartial jury or judge, cross-examination and presentation of evidence by the defense, deliberation of the evidence, and a verdict. The trial occurs in open court, it is adversarial, and it follows clearly articulated rules of procedure. Similar protections apply in the sentencing hearing as additional evidence is litigated and the government generally tries to aggravate the sentence and the defense tries to mitigate it. Moreover, there is a judge who oversees this process to ensure that all proceedings follow the law. If that is disputed afterward, there is usually the opportunity to appeal. While criminal trials are public affairs occurring in the light of day, plea deals occur in courtroom hallways and jails and on cell phones.

The reality is that most of these due process protections are enjoyed by only a tiny minority of criminal defendants. That is because due process is reserved largely for criminal trials. The right to a trial by jury or judge and the right to confront and cross-examine witnesses are waived as part of a plea agreement. In fact, in many cases, waiver of these rights and protections is a precondition to the plea bargaining process, and at least one expert calls it the "price" paid by the defendant for the privilege of plea bargaining.[3] As one legal scholar puts it, "[T]he judiciary articulates great principles that govern the determination of guilt at trial, but then the executive branch [prosecutors], with the approval of the judiciary, bargains with criminals to purchase these procedural entitlements."[4]

The defense counsel we interviewed expressed a number of concerns about the lack of due process protections for defendants who accept a plea deal:

> It's true. Due process protections don't apply to defendants who plea deal.

> The system is not set up to protect defendant's rights [when they plea negotiate].

> I don't think it's widespread, but these protections are lacking.

> You can get protections at trial but not much when you plea.

Several expressed the concern in terms of a lack of fairness:

> Plea negotiation is not representative of a fair process.

> You have it all the time where people with similar crimes, similar history, getting wildly different plea deals.

> More needs to be done to ensure that clients do receive protection from unfairness whether they plead or not.

Although both prosecutors and judges have concerns about plea negotiation, neither group specifically identified a due process issue when asked.

One may assume that certain protections apply regardless of whether a defendant pleas or goes to trial. For example, *Weeks v. United States* and *Mapp v. Ohio* provide for the exclusion of evidence that is searched and seized in violation of the Fourth Amendment protection against unreasonable searches and seizures. Despite this protection, it is problematic whether an illegal search would interfere with the plea agreement conviction of a criminal defendant. As Albert Alschuler, one of the preeminent legal scholars of our time, puts it, "[E]xclusionary rules are less likely to deter the police from engaging in illegal investigative activity (such as warrantless searches), if the police know that defendants' procedural rights can be treated as bargaining chips and compromised in the negotiation of a guilty plea."[5]

There are well-established rules that govern what evidence may be used in a criminal prosecution. These relate to things such as relevance of evidence, witness testimony, expert opinion, hearsay testimony, authentication of evidence, and privileged evidence, among others. These rules play a central role in what can be used to prosecute and convict someone at trial, and it is the responsibility of the judge to ensure that these rules are followed. However, they do not necessarily apply to the prosecution and conviction of defendants in a plea deal. Evidentiary rules generally forbid the jury from considering the defendant's criminal history. The theory is that past behavior is generally not relevant in determining whether the defendant committed the instant offense. While the jury would not be allowed to know about inadmissible evidence, the prosecutor knows about all of the evidence and can, in theory, consider inadmissible evidence in determining if a defendant is guilty as well as what to negotiate in a plea deal:

> The prosecutor's access to evidence is not limited like the jury's. The prosecutor can evaluate inadmissible evidence in considering whether it is likely that the defendant is guilty, whether to pursue the prosecution, and whether to offer a plea bargain. Even if the evidence is inadmissible, the prosecutor can use it as leverage over the defendant in plea bargaining by bluffing that the evidence is admissible.[6]

Juries are also provided with instructions by the court that identify how they are to consider the evidence provided, deliberate, and reach a verdict. Juries are also instructed to determine either innocence or guilt, a binary outcome. However, it appears that prosecutors may sometimes consider guilt a relative concept. The interview data indicate that prosecutors may charge bargain by offering a plea deal with lesser charges when the evidence is weak or some key evidence is inadmissible. It is unclear how weak the evidence needs to be before prosecutors would dismiss a case. The obvious question, for which we have no answer, is how often a jury would acquit a defendant in those cases where the prosecutor simply offers a better deal (relative guilt) because the evidence is problematic.

Obviously, defense counsel plays an important role in advising a client about the admissibility of evidence as well as whether he or she should take a plea deal. Substantial caseload constraints as well as limited access to investigators and experts present substantial challenges to public defenders and assigned counsel (as opposed to retained counsel) in providing adequate counsel. More on this later.

Some have compared plea bargaining to mediation and settlement in civil litigation. The comparison holds to the extent that both are forms of settlement of a case. However, the comparison ends there when one considers, among other things, that a civil case settlement is based on broad discovery and sharing of evidence, including through deposition of witnesses and experts. Such extensive sharing of evidence is rare in criminal prosecution.

One would assume that in order to make an informed, voluntary decision about a criminal plea agreement, the defendant should have knowledge of the evidence against him. That is not often the case since there is no constitutional right to the government's evidence and prosecutors are not required to provide all of the evidence to the defendant.[7] Even in states where the government is required to provide evidence, many are not required to provide it in a timely manner, meaning that defendants engage in plea negotiation ignorant of the evidence against them. In New York, the limited discovery rules are referred to as the "blindfold law" since the evidence is effectively kept from defendants.[8]

Limited discovery rules keep defendants ignorant of the scope and strength of the state's case and at a clear disadvantage in the plea negotiation process.[9] Limited discovery may also facilitate overcharging by prosecutors since the defendant does not have all of the evidence necessary to effectively refute charges. Overcharging or bringing multiple charges may serve as a bargaining strategy if, for example, the prosecutor agrees to dismiss some of the charges in exchange for a guilty plea to one or some of the charges.

In 1986, Michael Morton's wife, Christine, was brutally murdered in their home in Williamson County, Texas. Michael testified that he had left for work that morning at 5:30. Her body was discovered later that morning. Michael was arrested for the murder, indicted, prosecuted, convicted, and sentenced to life in prison. Morton was convicted despite the fact that the prosecution provided no witnesses or physical evidence linking him to this crime. He spent nearly twenty-five years in prison before he was exonerated in 2011.

The criminal justice system consists of humans making decisions within a structure of laws and procedure. However, those decisions are usually based on judgment and probabilities. There are no hard metrics for things like probable cause or reasonable doubt. Because humans make decisions based often on imperfect evidence, mistakes happen. Unfortunately, sometimes those mistakes are deliberate and dishonest. That was the case with Michael Morton. The police and prosecutor's investigation of the murder revealed key exculpatory evidence that indicated Morton's innocence. The jury did not hear about it because the prosecution deliberately withheld the evidence from the defendant.

Brady v. Maryland (1963) and subsequent cases have established the requirement that the prosecution provide exculpatory evidence to the defense in a timely manner. This requirement holds regardless of whether the defense requests such evidence. The reality, however, is that compliance with *Brady* is highly variable. Some states have broad provisions for disclosure, and others barely comply. It is also variable within the federal system. That is the situation regarding exculpatory evidence for cases that go to trial.

Public defenders whom we interviewed were pretty clear regarding their concerns about access to the government's evidence:

> When you've got a bad prosecutor, it's a five [on a one-to-five scale] because although we have the Michael Morton Act in place, they will get things to you much later than they should, which hurts your case and defense.

> Michael Morton [Act] has been amazing with proving evidence, but there are still some DAs that don't comply.

> The Michael Morton Act states that I am supposed to get everything. We are supposed to have an open file policy. The problem is the "timely" manner in which we receive the evidence. I should be getting it sooner than I do.

It is also absurd that the prosecutor decides what is work product because what they consider work product may yield meaningful evidence in helping my client.

We don't get discovery, so we have to rely on the client.

If we want to see discovery, fine, but the deal's gone.

You'd think the rules would give us the state's evidence, but more often than not it doesn't play out that way.

While providing exculpatory evidence to the defense may seem like an important provision for leveling the playing field when knowingly and voluntarily entertaining a plea offer from the prosecutor, the extent to which it happens is problematic: [10]

> The Supreme Court's decision in *Brady v. Maryland* requires the prosecution to disclose evidence that establishes the defendant's factual innocence during a trial. Some courts apply this rule during plea bargaining and require the disclosure of material exculpatory evidence before the entry of a guilty plea. Other courts have held or suggested that the prosecution may suppress exculpatory evidence during plea bargaining, forcing the defendant to negotiate and determine whether to accept a plea offer or proceed to trial without it. Substantial disparities therefore exist in the bargaining power and decision-making ability of criminal defendants, depending on where they are charged. [11]

New York State has fairly restrictive discovery laws, requiring prosecutors to provide exculpatory evidence only thirty days before trial. Because prosecutors are not complying sufficiently, a new law requires judges to remind prosecutors of this obligation. That is all well and good for those who go to trial, but the discovery law in New York does essentially nothing for those who plea negotiate. Plea deals are typically consummated well before the thirty-day window prescribed by New York law; thus, many pleas take place without the state providing any exculpatory evidence.

Plea negotiation is a process that generally does not involve a judge, or, if it does, the judge's role is after the fact. The Federal Rules of Criminal Procedure prohibit judges from involvement in plea negotiation; that is also the case in many states.[12] Once a plea deal has been agreed on by the prosecutor and the defendant, the judge's role is to ask a series of boilerplate questions to determine if the plea was entered into voluntarily, if the defendant understands the constitutional rights and protections he or she waived, and if there is a factual basis for the plea. However, judges have no access to discovery in the plea cases and do not have access to independent evidence pertaining to the factual guilt of the defendant, so they must rely on the prosecutor's and defense counsel's versions of the facts. The docket pressures that the courts face highlight the need to move cases. In all likelihood, this results in judges generally "rubber-stamping" plea deals before them.[13]

All of the judges whom we interviewed acknowledged that their roles are very limited. State judges can reject a plea deal, but that is extremely rare:

> You are forced to accept pleas because of the volume of cases you receive. You're forced to rely on the prosecutors' information because you don't have the time and information they do. You have about five minutes to decide an outcome and minutes to review evidence.

> My role is very limited.

> I usually don't have much of a role. However, if there is something they are not agreeing on, then I might waive some fine in lieu of something else.

It is even more restricted in federal cases:

> It's very minimal on the federal side. The federal rules and case law prohibit us from getting involved, and a judge participating would be reason to strike an agreement.

It should be troubling that the primary way that misdemeanor and felony defendants are prosecuted, convicted, and punished is through an essentially informal process that grew neither out of the values and foundations of American adversarial jurisprudence, procedure, and trial law nor from any premise that this is a better way to administer justice but rather out of the interests and motivations of the parties involved and out of the pressure for expediency. It also reflects public officials' funding priorities by failing to provide the resources required for sufficient numbers of courtrooms, judges, prosecutors, and public defenders necessary to hold any more trials than is currently the case.

As one of the nation's leading critics of plea negotiation, Bibas put it, "It is astonishing that a $100 credit-card purchase of a microwave oven is regulated more carefully than a guilty plea that results in years of imprisonment."[14]

We now turn to more in-depth discussion of what we consider to be the key concerns and criticisms of plea bargaining.

SPECIFIC CONCERNS

The Standard of Proof Problem

Reasonable doubt is required under the due process clause of the Fifth Amendment in order to convict someone of a criminal act. Reasonable doubt is the highest standard of proof in American jurisprudence. The U.S. Supreme Court has explained the need for this higher standard for criminal conviction based on "a fundamental value determination of our society that it is far worse to convict an innocent man than to let a guilty man go free."[15]

Beyond a reasonable doubt is generally understood as proof of such a convincing character that one would be willing to rely and act on it without hesitation in the most important of one's own affairs. The term "firmly convinced" is also used in definitions and jury instructions regarding beyond a reasonable doubt. Below is some language about reasonable doubt excerpted first from the U.S. Courts of the Ninth Circuit and then from the state of New York jury instructions.

The jury instructions from the Ninth Circuit regarding reasonable doubt state:

> Proof beyond a reasonable doubt is proof that leaves you firmly convinced the defendant is guilty. It is not required that the government prove guilt beyond all possible doubt. A reasonable doubt is a doubt based upon reason and common sense and is not based purely on speculation.[16]

The jury instructions for New York State:

> A reasonable doubt is an honest doubt of the defendant's guilt for
> which a reason exists based upon the nature and quality of the evi-
> dence. . . . Proof of guilt beyond a reasonable doubt is proof that
> leaves you so firmly convinced of the defendant's guilt that you have
> no reasonable doubt of the existence of any element of the crime or
> of the defendant's identity as the person who committed the crime.[17]

Probable cause is the standard of evidence or proof that is required to
lawfully arrest someone, issue a search warrant, or indict someone for a
crime. It is generally defined as a belief by a reasonable individual,
based on the totality of the evidence, that there is a fair probability that
a crime has been committed and a fair probability that this particular
individual committed that crime.

Probable cause is a rather low standard compared to reasonable
doubt or even preponderance of the evidence. Preponderance of the
evidence, which means more likely than not, or, statistically, 50.1 percent, is the standard used in civil litigation. Although there is no agreement regarding what probable cause means statistically, most agree that
it is a lower standard than preponderance of the evidence.[18]

The rather substantial difference between beyond a reasonable
doubt (firmly convinced) and probable cause (fair probability) is the
concern. The vast majority of felony and misdemeanor convictions are
plea deals. Since these cases are never litigated in a courtroom before a
judge or jury, we really do not know what standard of proof is used for
conviction. While we have the lofty requirement of proof beyond a
reasonable doubt, we really have no idea how often that threshold is
actually achieved. There is only limited research that examines the evidence after the fact of a plea to determine the veracity of the evidence
relative to the plea. Even if we had more extensive analyses, there is
always the issue that the evidence and the decision of innocence or guilt
is in the eyes of the beholder, the prosecutor.

There is reason to believe that many individuals who are convicted
pursuant to a plea deal are convicted based on a standard that is lower
than reasonable doubt. Probable cause is the relevant standard for the
key up-front case processing decisions that prosecutors make, such as
who to charge and what charges to bring. Recommendations regarding
detention or pretrial release can be based on probable cause. The in-

dictment is the formal charging of an individual and the go-ahead to prosecute a case. The evidence presented to a grand jury is done so in an ex parte presentation by the prosecutor, often heavily relying on the arrest report filed by the police.

Because of substantial caseload and workload pressure and lack of resources, many prosecutors likely face significant challenges conducting additional investigation and gathering additional evidence beyond that provided by law enforcement. Additional evidence may allow additional charges or more serious charges, and the lack of some evidence may require more compromise on the prosecutor's part in the plea offer. However, if the prosecutor believes that he or she can secure a reasonable plea deal with the evidence at hand, there may be little incentive for further investigation and gathering of evidence.

Gerald Lynch, a Columbia University law professor and expert on American criminal jurisprudence, concludes, "Most commonly, in all likelihood, the prosecutor simply accepts the results of the police investigation, and any process of independent adjudication occurs at the instigation of defense counsel."[19]

This conclusion is generally confirmed by what the public defenders told us in response to our questions about standard of proof in plea negotiation. Several defense attorneys believe that many plea deal convictions are based simply on probable cause:

> I believe it, I believe that's what everything is being based on until we really talk about getting to trial. Not many DAs look past probable cause.

> Absolutely. I think DAs look at a probable cause affidavit and think that the client is guilty.

> If you're in a conservative county, all you need is to get an arrest, and then the case is decided.

> It is so easy to make an arrest, and the prosecutors will usually refer to the arrest report and automatically take it as true since the defendant was arrested. A lot of times they don't look deeper.

> The courts and prosecutors believe that as long as probable cause exists, they'll try to get a conviction. Now when you point out that

reasonable doubt exists, they'll push back and say that's for the jury to decide, so they won't worry about that.

I'm not quite sure how to answer that. I think there's a good chance that lawyers want to defend our own jobs and say, no, beyond a reasonable doubt is the standard no matter what. But in the context of 95 percent plus result in pleas, then we very rarely have a view of what beyond a reasonable doubt means for a jury, and so I think that we get a lower standard for conviction.

Several said that what the prosecutor believes regarding guilt is key in how the case is resolved:

Once the prosecutor believes you're guilty, that's gonna carry the day. Sometimes they may see evidence that they can't admit in trial, my kid gave a confession, and even though it's inadmissible, the prosecutor feels it in their gut "that son of a bitch is guilty" and that will drive the case and offer.

There is always "you're accused, so you're guilty."

A couple defense lawyers stated that it is up to defense counsel to require reasonable doubt for conviction. One stated,

A good lawyer will argue for the difference [between probable cause and reasonable doubt], so if probable cause is the standard for conviction, it's because you didn't do your job.

The reality is that an admission of guilt doesn't require a standard of proof beyond probable cause. It just requires a willing defendant.[20]

The Power and Discretion of the Prosecutor

Jed Rakoff is a U.S. district judge and an outspoken critic of American criminal justice. Plea bargaining and the impact it has had on the relative power and roles of prosecutors and judges has been a concern of his:

[P]rosecutors [are] increasingly being thrust into the role, not of advocates, but of rulers—with very unfortunate results. The plea bargain is the ultimate source of this ever-increasing prosecutorial power. . . . The net result is that prosecutors, rather than judges, now effectively determine the sentences to be imposed in most cases. They do this in plea bargains hammered out in the prosecutors' offices in unrecorded conversations with defense counsel—sessions in which, because of the pressure on defendants to reduce their sentencing exposure, the prosecutors effectively hold most of the cards. Furthermore, not only are these sessions secret, one-sided, and lacking judicial oversight, but also the results vary materially from prosecutor to prosecutor.[21]

All the prosecutors we interviewed agreed that their discretion is very broad. There are some circumstances when they consult with superiors, such as murder cases. But, for most situations, their decision making is pretty unfettered:

> We have broad discretion.

> From my standpoint, it is very broad.

> Pretty much up to me.

> I have wide latitude, with some exceptions like murder cases or domestic violence.

> It's usually my decision.

Not surprisingly, public defenders view prosecutorial discretion as largely unencumbered. Their comments indicate that the power and discretion of prosecutors allow them to essentially control the plea process. This one quote summarizes well how defense attorneys experience prosecutorial discretion in the context of plea negotiation:

> Prosecutors really have control over the whole system. The prosecutor gives ultimatums—either take my deal or go to trial.

A couple prosecutors raised the issue of lack of consistency in outcomes across courts as a consequence of prosecutorial discretion:

> Consistency. A person who commits a criminal offense in one court receives a different outcome in a different court when committing a similar offense.

Most judges that we interviewed indicated that they believe prosecutors have considerable discretion. The downside of that discretion is that decision making is dependent on the beliefs of individual prosecutors and inconsistent outcomes:

> If you get the wrong prosecutor you will get a plea recommendation that is way out of sync with what's appropriate.

> You are dependent on the personality or beliefs of a particular prosecutor.

> Prosecutors that are fair-minded lead to an okay system. If you have prosecutors that are not fair minded and are only looking to promote themselves into higher office, that isn't good.

> The downside is lack of consistency.

Some judges see discretion as a positive:

> I do think there is [broad discretion], and I know that is a bad connotation because certainly some prosecutors do abuse their power. However, a lot of times, it is used to benefit the defendant, and it helps a lot.

> I can't speak for all, but we are lucky to have prosecutors with a fair amount of discretion. It's good because it allows them to decide not to file a certain charge that may seem unfair.

There is probably little doubt among even casual observers that prosecutors are the most important people in the administration of American criminal justice. They possess and exercise the most discretion, influence, power, and leverage. Part of their power derives from the role of the prosecutor—those individuals responsible for assessing evidence and then making decisions about who to indict and prosecute, what charges to bring, what evidence to use to support the charges, what to offer in a plea deal, and what sentence to recommend.

The power and influence of prosecutors is also a result of the substantial imbalance in resources that favors prosecutors over defendants and defense counsel. The vast majority of criminal defendants are indigent and thus lack resources to retain counsel, get out of jail, and hire experts, among other things. These defendants are represented by public defenders or assigned counsel, lawyers generally with quite limited resources and, at least in the case of most public defenders, extraordinarily high caseloads. Granted, many prosecutors have very high caseloads that place substantial constraints on their day-to-day functioning. However, state and federal prosecutors have access to resources that typical criminal defendants lack.

There have been several changes to criminal procedure, policy, law, and jurisprudence that have further expanded the discretion and power of prosecutors. The shift to crime control and the emphasis on punishment has resulted in substantial changes to sentencing laws. Specifically, the implementation of determinant, fixed, and mandatory sentences has limited the discretion of judges and shifted it to the prosecutor's office. As sentences often depend on the conviction offense, what the prosecutor decides the charge is largely determines the sentence. The expansion of the criminal law as we discussed earlier (overcriminalization) has given prosecutors broader discretion in charging options, such as charge enhancements and multiple charges.

The nature of plea bargaining in the United States, specifically the fact that the evidence is not litigated in the traditional sense of a jury or bench trial, places the prosecutor in the position of being the trier of fact: the judge and the jury. It is up to the prosecutor to determine who is guilty and the crimes for which they are guilty. It is then up to the prosecutor to proceed to negotiate a plea deal based on his or her presumptions about the defendant's guilt. It is also up to the prosecutor to determine the sentence either explicitly by attaching punishment to the plea deal or through a recommendation regarding the appropriate punishment in each case. In reality, plea bargaining is negotiating time: years in prison or jail or on probation. It depends on the ability of the prosecutor to deliver the agreed-on consequences for the guilty plea.

Prosecutors are human, and, as such, they bring to the decision-making process certain perspectives, opinions, beliefs, attitudes, presumptions, and biases. The question is the extent to which such factors influence decision making in any systematic way. Recent research indicates that they do.

Defendant characteristics, particularly race/ethnicity, age, gender, prior criminal record, and pretrial detention, all predicted poorer negotiated outcomes. Minorities had worse charge and sentence outcomes, as did those who are younger and male, those with more extensive criminal histories, and those who were detained in jail awaiting disposition of their cases.[22] Interestingly, the research shows a more limited than expected impact of the evidence in the case on plea outcomes.[23] These dispositions are tied to the substantial discretion prosecutors have in determining the specifics of plea deals and sentences.

A public defender's perspective of prosecutorial discretion, based on personal experiences and observations, confirms to a large extent what the statistical analyses cited above have to say. Angela Davis, currently a law professor and prior to that a public defender in the District of Columbia, describes conviction-driven prosecutors and significant disparities in case outcomes:

> During my years as a public defender, I saw disparities in the way prosecutors handled individual cases. Cases involving educated, well-to-do victims were frequently prosecuted more vigorously than cases involving poor, uneducated victims. The very few white defendants represented by my office sometimes appeared to receive preferential treatment from prosecutors. . . . At times it simply appeared that two similarly situated people were treated differently. . . . If there were a difference in prior criminal history or some other relevant factor, the disparate treatment would be explainable. But without a difference in the legitimate factors that prosecutors are permitted to consider in making these decisions, the disparities seemed unfair. Yet I saw such disparities all the time.[24]

There is a bit of an irony here. Sentencing reform, which paralleled the shift to crime control and tough punishment over the past fifty years, involved moving from indeterminate sentencing, where judges had wide latitude or discretion, to determinate sentencing, where the role of the judge was substantially restricted. Under determinate sentencing, which includes mandatory sentences and mandatory minimums as well as set or fixed sentences, the conviction offense largely drives the sentence. Determinate sentencing removed discretion from judges and pushed it upstream to the prosecutor's office. The motivation for the change in part was that judges had too much sentencing discretion, often leading to sentencing disparity. One is hard-pressed to conclude that sentencing reform did anything to reduce the effects of discretion.

What it did was to keep that discretion underground, much less visible than when it was exercised on the bench.

Controlling Prosecutorial Power and Discretion

The reality is that prosecutors are in charge of criminal prosecution, conviction, and punishment. As much as some may lament that, it is how the American court system runs. At least one observer of the transition to a nearly exclusively plea-based system notes that we have by default the executive branch of government determining who is guilty and how much punishment they should receive. Moreover, he observes that what has arisen in terms of the process of plea negotiation is an informal system, void of many rules and written procedures:

> This process is rarely governed by formal legal standards, other than the basic definitions of offenses, and the procedures by which it operates are not usually written down anywhere. . . . Because our governing ideology does not admit that prosecutors adjudicate guilt and set punishments, the procedures by which they do so are neither formally regulated nor invariably followed.[25]

Prosecutorial discretion is substantial. Equally substantial is the absence of statutory, judicial, or procedural regulations of the decisions that prosecutors make.[26] The Supreme Court has held that "so long as the prosecutor has probable cause to believe that the accused committed an offense defined by statute, the decision whether or not to prosecute, and what charges to file . . . generally rests entirely in his discretion."[27]

As noted above, judges have a quite limited role in plea negotiations. When judges are involved, it is after the fact. While there is an expectation that judges will, among other things, assess the factual basis of the plea, they rarely have access to independent information to determine the defendant's culpability and guilt.[28] Moreover, many cases involve no judicial review, and when there is a review, it is a rare circumstance when a judge rejects a plea bargain agreement.[29]

Prosecutorial discretion has enjoyed relative immunity from court review. As Chief Justice Warren Burger wrote in *Newman v. United States* in 1967, "[F]ew subjects are less adapted to judicial review than the exercise by the Executive of his discretion in deciding when and whether to institute criminal proceedings, or what precise charge should be made, or whether to dismiss a proceeding once brought."[30]

Nevertheless, prosecutorial discretion is not entirely unlimited or unregulated. The Supreme Court has held that there are constitutional restrictions on discretion, such as prohibiting selective prosecution based on race, ethnicity, religion, or gender. However, what limits have been set by the Court are often difficult to invoke because of the high threshold of proof required in cases of excessive or improper prosecutorial discretion. The reason is that in most situations, the complainant must prove improper motive or purpose on the part of the prosecutor, something that is very difficult to do.[31]

A 2011 Supreme Court case, *Connick v. Thompson*, involving a wrongful conviction and the death penalty, was the latest guidance from the Court regarding prosecutorial power, discretion, and misconduct. John Thompson was convicted of capital murder and sentenced to death. The problem was that the prosecutor withheld exculpatory evidence from the defense, evidence that proved he did not commit the murder. This was a clear violation of *Brady v. Maryland*, in which the Court held that the prosecution must turn over all exculpatory evidence that may exonerate the defendant.

Thompson's conviction and sentence were overturned, and he sued the district attorney for monetary damages. He won $14 million. The Supreme Court overturned the verdict and award. They argued that legal education, professional ethics, on-the-job supervision, and existing oversight mechanisms were sufficient to control prosecutorial discretion and misconduct.[32]

The Supreme Court recognized more than eighty years ago the powerful position that prosecutors are in. They declared that the prosecutor is "in a peculiar and very definite sense the servant of the law, the twofold aim of which is that guilt shall not escape nor innocence suffer. . . . It is as much his duty to refrain from improper methods calculated to produce a wrongful conviction as it is to use every legitimate means to bring about a just one."[33]

While this is a lofty ideal, we seem to have few mechanisms in place to effectively address some of the issues regarding prosecutorial discretion.

The Punishment Market Problem

Juries serve a number of functions in criminal trials. One is as the independent evaluator of the evidence, then weighing that evidence against the evidentiary threshold of reasonable doubt. Juries also reflect the standards—the market—for punishment when prevailing law allows jurors discretion in determining the sentence. One of the concerns of the disappearing criminal trial is that we (and, in particular, judges and prosecutors) lose important guidance on the "going rate" for a particular crime.

There is another, related issue. While juries deliberate the evidence and determine if someone is guilty of the offense charged, a prosecutor will determine what someone pleads guilty to based on cooperation and convenience. Consider that the prosecutor presumably makes some evidence-based determination when a defendant is indicted. Then, as a result of the process of plea negotiation, the actual offense that the defendant is convicted of and the amount of punishment he or she receives are often a function of how cooperative the defendant is and how much time and effort the defendant saves the prosecutor.

The Assistance of Counsel Problem

The Sixth Amendment provides, "In all criminal prosecutions, the accused shall . . . have the Assistance of Counsel for his defense." That's it. Nothing about when, how, who, or how well. Some of those questions have been addressed by the Supreme Court. For example, the landmark 1963 case *Gideon v. Wainwright* established that the state shall provide defense counsel to any indigent defendant being prosecuted for a felony. It was a unanimous decision that declared it an "obvious truth" that defense counsel are "necessities, not luxuries."[34] Over time, this right has been expanded to misdemeanor cases where the defendant is facing the possibility of incarceration on conviction (primarily in *Argersinger v. Hamlin* [1972]).

At issue here is providing counsel to those too poor to retain a private attorney. This is a substantial matter, as between 80 and 85 percent of criminal cases involve indigent defendants who require either a public defender or appointed counsel.

While the question of who shall be provided counsel has been addressed, many questions still remain, such as when counsel should be provided (at what stage of processing a criminal defendant), what is a reasonable caseload for a public defender or appointed counsel, and what qualifies as adequate representation.

Our interviews with prosecutors echo concerns about representation that indigent defendants receive from defense counsel:

> The skill level of attorneys can be a problem.

> Incompetence of the defense attorneys.

> The level of representation someone may have.

> I'm worried, like most prosecutors, that most defense attorneys are not doing their due diligence.

> I worry about how well defendants are defended.

One prosecutor indicated that defense attorneys sometimes just try to get their clients off rather than considering longer-term options like treatment, options that may produce better longer-term outcomes:

> It used to be that defense attorneys would approach plea bargaining in ways that would improve clients' lives, and now it seems that they are trying to just reduce their client's sentence and not worry about other factors, such as seeking treatment and helping reduce recidivism.

A couple of the judges also expressed concerns about adequacy of defense representation:

> Defense attorneys accepting plea deals because it's the easiest and quickest way to deal with their case when they're not in the best interest of their client.

> The system is premised on a competent defense attorney and a reasonable prosecutor, and when those two things don't happen, you have problems.

The headline from the *Kansas City Star* for October 19, 2017, reads, "KC Public Defenders Say High Caseloads Mean Losing Their Licenses, Going to Jail, or Quitting." This was in reference to what many public defenders in the state characterized as excessive, untenable caseloads and the refusal to take new cases by the chief public defender in Kansas City. The response by the Missouri Supreme Court was to put a public defender on probation for failing to provide adequate counsel for clients. "The [Court] action put public defenders across Missouri on notice that they were stuck in a Catch-22: If they take on too many cases, they could lose their law license to an ethics complaint. But if they refuse to take more cases, they can be held in contempt of court and jailed."[35] An American Bar Association study of the Missouri State Public Defender System caseloads concluded that the number of public defenders needed to be increased by 75 percent in order to provide basic services.[36]

The situation in Missouri may be worse than in many other states since Missouri ranks forty-ninth in funding public defenders. Nevertheless, the public defender system is under tremendous strain across the nation as caseloads and workloads are extraordinary and funding is limited.

In Caddo Parish, Louisiana (Shreveport), because of severe funding shortfalls for public defenders, judges were randomly assigning lawyers to criminal cases. The problem is the courts were assigning attorneys without criminal expertise, such as tax attorneys and real estate, personal injury, and adoption lawyers. The training they received was a three-hour course on the do's and don'ts of providing effective assistance.[37]

In some jurisdictions, the right to counsel is ignored. Investigations reveal failure to provide counsel in Nashville, Tennessee, and Miami, Florida, as well as several cities in South Carolina.[38] A recent report shows that in Utah, nearly two-thirds of misdemeanor defendants have no access to counsel.[39]

Recently, the Louisiana legislature cut public defense funding by 62 percent, making an already dire situation critical. The New Orleans public defender's office resorted to a crowd-funding campaign to raise $50,000 to keep operating. The chief public defender in New Orleans stated, "It's ridiculous and absurd that one of the original 10 Amendments of the Constitution relies on crowdfunding for its guarantee."[40]

Another issue is that thirteen states leave it up to local counties to fund, administer, regulate, and evaluate indigent defense representation, as opposed to state funding and regulation. Four other states have limited state-level structures.[41] Counties typically labor under greater revenue restrictions than states, making it more difficult to adequately fund let alone administer and regulate indigent defense.

The realities of public defender caseloads are stark. In Kentucky, the average caseload for a public defender is 448 per year.[42] In New Orleans, public defenders carry 385 cases.[43] In Maryland, about 380 public defenders are doing the work required of 530 lawyers.[44] Even in Colorado, which has the best-funded indigent defense counsel system in the nation, the public defender offices operate at a 10 percent staffing deficit.

Overall, 73 percent of county-operated public defender systems (in twenty-seven states) were operating above the recommended average caseload.[45] Another way of looking at it is that, on average, a public defender in the United States today would need 3,035 hours (1.5 years) to do the work required of current annual caseloads.[46] Still, another troubling perspective is a Bureau of Justice Statistics report that concluded that only 27 percent of the nation's public defender offices had enough full-time equivalents to meet caseload guidelines (which are 190 misdemeanor cases or 125 felonies). The situation is worse in the largest metro jurisdictions, where only 12 percent had enough employees to cover the guideline caseloads.[47]

There is agreement from many sources that current funding and caseload realities for public defenders prevent them from providing adequate, effective assistance of counsel.[48] A Department of Justice brief in support of a lawsuit challenging excessive caseloads and lack of resources observed that insufficient resources "is tantamount to the system's failure to appoint counsel."[49]

There are obvious reasons why excessive caseloads and limited resources place indigent defendants in very precarious positions. Clearly, the complexities of a criminal trial as well as all of the procedural and evidentiary issues that arise in preparation for trial require legal expertise. It is no less the case just because a charge is resolved by a negotiated plea. The requirement that a proper plea is voluntary and informed should not simply be a matter of a defendant being offered a deal. Caveat emptor is nowhere close to living up to the spirit of the Sixth

Amendment. Legal expertise is required to understand the totality of the evidence, any procedural issues that should be weighed in a plea deal, whether a prosecutor's offers are reasonable and whether the trial alternative (the trial penalty that the prosecutor is threatening) is realistic, whether the deal is fair in terms of the "going rate" in that jurisdiction, and what the waivers of rights required in most plea deals mean. Importantly, it is necessary to clarify that what we just described is not expertise that judges can and should be involved in providing. That is the role of defense counsel.

The matter of when counsel should be provided has been addressed by the Supreme Court in *Brewer v. Williams* in 1977 and more recently in 2008 in *Rothgery v. Gillespie County*. The Court determined that right to counsel attaches when judicial proceedings have begun, including a formal charging, indictment, or arraignment. More recently, in *Rothgery*, the Court declared that the right attaches at the initial appearance where the defendant is made aware of the charges and the court deliberates detention or release pending further disposition. The American Bar Association maintains that counsel should be provided to an indigent defendant prior to any appearance before a judge or magistrate, including the initial appearance. The initial appearance (sometimes called magistration, initial appearance, or arraignment) is when a decision about pretrial detention or release is made. Some defendants may plead guilty at that point to avoid remaining in jail. Such matters benefit from assistance of counsel in terms of explaining all of the options and providing advice about pleading guilty at that point.

Despite the holdings of the Supreme Court regarding when counsel should first be present, there is considerable variation across states when defense counsel are provided to indigent defendants. For example, in Michigan, there is no requirement that defendants are represented at an initial appearance. A 2015 survey revealed that less than 10 percent of district courts in Michigan required defense counsel to be present at the initial appearance.[50] This is not atypical of the situation in other states. A 2009 survey found that only ten states provided indigent defendants defense counsel ahead of arraignment or initial appearance.[51]

While excessive caseloads for indigent defense counsel play a role in promoting plea deals in order to move cases, pay structures for appointed counsel also motivate plea deals.[52] Many assigned counsel are paid flat fees for cases. For example, in Texas, assigned counsel in misdemeanor driving while intoxicated (DWI) cases are paid $240. In Virginia, it is $140. Felonies in Texas bring between $500 and $600. The incentive is obvious: Case volume and quick disposition increase revenue.

The Sixth Amendment right to counsel for indigent defendants has a theoretical version laid out by a series of Supreme Court decisions and then has the actual, day-in-and-day-out, in-the-trenches version that reflects the realities of indigent defense in this country.[53] There is often a fairly substantial divide between the two. As one careful observer noted more than thirty years ago, "[T]he severity of the underfunding of those agencies providing defense counsel to the indigent seriously endangers the Sixth Amendment guarantee to effective assistance of counsel."[54] Moreover, there is nothing new here. Experts have been voicing concern about indigent defense for decades.[55]

One of the ironies associated with the state of indigent defense is that by design or default, the primary problems of excessive caseloads and underfunding have the consequence of further perpetuating such extraordinary rates of plea negotiation. When public defenders have minutes rather than hours to devote to clients, the only realistic resolution to cases is a negotiated plea.[56] This characterization is supported by decades of surveys of indigent defendants represented by public defenders or assigned counsel: The primary if not exclusive focus of counsel is pleading guilty.[57]

This situation becomes even more troubling when we consider that the majority of criminal defendants have a variety of disorders, impairments, and deficits that can have significant negative impacts on their decision-making abilities. Adequate defense counsel is even more important for this segment of the offender population.

The Voluntary Confession Problem

Judge Jed Rakoff is an outspoken critic of various aspects of plea negotiation, including the presumption that plea deals are entered into voluntarily:

> The Supreme Court's suggestion that a plea bargain is a fair and
> voluntary contractual arrangement between two relatively equal par-

ties is a total myth: it is more like a "contract of adhesion" in which one party can effectively force its will on the other party.[58]

Plea bargains are about confessions, the defendant confessing guilt to whatever crime or crimes the prosecutor has offered in the deal. Offering incriminating evidence and confessing to a crime is legal and proper as long as the confession or plea is knowing, informed, and voluntary.

The Supreme Court declared in *Brady v. United States* (1970) that a confession that is coerced or compelled is unconstitutional, a violation of the Fifth Amendment right against self-incrimination. This decision has been seen as a significant shift in the Court's tolerance of plea bargaining, representing a conditional acceptance of this form of justice. The vision the Court laid out in *Brady* was one where plea negotiation was acceptable in situations where the evidence supporting the guilt of a defendant is overwhelming, leading to a low probability that the defendant would prevail at trial.[59] It was seen a bit like expediting a forgone conclusion where both parties could benefit.

However, *Brady* also stipulated that plea negotiation was not to be used for cases where guilt was uncertain and the government overwhelmed an innocent defendant into pleading guilty.[60] "[T]he agents of the State may not produce plea by actual or threatened physical harm or by mental coercion overbearing the will of the defendant." The Court went on to declare their discomfort if the plea negotiation process caused or pressured innocent defendants to plead guilty. "We would have serious doubts about this case if the encouragement of guilty pleas by offers of leniency substantially increased the likelihood that defendants, advised by competent counsel, would falsely condemn themselves."[61]

The Supreme Court's remedy for an involuntary plea appears to be *McMann v. Richardson* (1970). In *McMann*, the Court held that any coercion imposed by the prosecutor would be neutralized by consulting with defense counsel prior to a plea. However, we know from our previous discussion that defense counsel is not always in a position to provide optimal time and advice due largely to tremendous caseloads and workloads and lack of resources for things like investigation of cases.

It is extremely difficult to know when a set of circumstances may have compelled a defendant to enter into a plea agreement. Nevertheless, the potential for coerced confessions is troubling to many critics of plea bargaining. One prominent observer states, "In the context of plea bargaining, however, the Court has placed very few limitations on the types of inducements that prosecutors may use to obtain guilty pleas."[62]

We asked public defenders if they believe that their clients are ever coerced into accepting a plea deal. Some defense attorneys were quick to call the tactics used by prosecutors coercion. Many were reluctant to use the term "coercion," relying on words like "pressured" and "bullied":

> Absolutely, it happens more in misdemeanors than felonies. I think they're afraid of losing at trial and they want to get out of jail. Coercion is absolutely the right word.

> Yes. People plea to stuff they don't like all the time. They will do it to avoid greater punishment all the time. And coercion carries a lot of weight, but I think it's appropriate.

> The entire system is coercive, but it's nothing explicit.

> Yes. Absolutely. 100 percent. By holding them in the county jail until they take a deal.

> It would depend on the client and circumstances. Some might feel it's coercive.

> I think some clients feel that way. . . . I wouldn't call it coercion, it's just how they play their cards.

> I think they are bullied into pleading guilty.

> There are times when our clients will accept offers that are not in their best interest and prosecutors know that but they know clients will bite at it so they can get out of jail. It's probably 30 to 40 percent of cases.

> I'd say squeezed. If they're indicted on a drug charge and the affidavit says it was in a drug-free zone, then they have to reindict the case [and] they are looking at more time. They threaten in this manner.

> I'd call it pressured, extremely pressured.

Almost always pressured.

One prosecutor raised a concern with coercion. Another mentioned a concern with innocent defendants pleading guilty:

> I think there's a coercive factor in plea bargaining, and that should never be our job. We're supposed to seek justice, not throw a low offer just to save face and get a conviction.

> I think sometimes innocent people plead to minimize their risk of going to trial.

While the courts have not been particularly clear about what too much pressure looks like or when a defendant is overwhelmed, the real acid test in *Brady* is when innocent defendants plead guilty. This is referred to as the innocence problem and is discussed shortly.

There are many ways in which prosecutors can induce or motivate a plea. We briefly discuss some of the more common ones below.

Overcharging or Charge Stacking

Overcriminalization, which we discussed earlier, is the expansion of the criminal law, the creation of many new laws involving a broad array of crimes. This has been a consequence of congressional legislation extending the scope of federal law as well as state legislatures creating new laws that give states expanded criminal jurisdiction over behavior. Both federal and state criminal codes have grown at the felony and misdemeanor levels. The expansion of administrative regulations with criminal liability is also an important component.

One consequence of overcriminalization, in combination with wide prosecutorial discretion, is the facilitation of what is called charge stacking. Charge stacking involves bringing multiple charges against a defendant. Often, these charges are overlapping. Consider the following example. An intoxicated driver hits another car, and the occupant of the other car is badly injured. The intoxicated driver flees the scene of the accident and in so doing is evading arrest, speeding, and driving recklessly. The police catch up with him in a school parking lot. It also turns out that he has a crack pipe, a nearly spent marijuana joint, and an open bottle of vodka in his car, which the police find when they arrest him. The primary offense and the primary harm done to the victim is the intoxicated driver hitting the victim's car. However, it is entirely possible that our drunk driver could be charged with DWI, intoxication, assault (perhaps aggravated assault, depending on how badly the victim was injured), resisting arrest, fleeing the scene of an accident, speeding, reckless driving, possession of drug paraphernalia, possession of a controlled substance, possession of an open container of alcohol in the car, drug possession in a drug-free zone (the school parking lot), and probably several other offenses.

The result of charge stacking is increased criminal liability, which in turn gives prosecutors more leverage in a plea negotiation (more charges mean more punishment) as well as more bargaining room since they can dismiss charges if the defendant agrees to a plea deal. While we really do not know how often charge stacking occurs, it is a relatively safe practice for prosecutors because whether the charges are supported by the evidence is rarely tested at trial.

The Trial Penalty

The trial penalty is the presumed greater punishment associated with taking a case to trial compared to agreeing to a plea deal. The trial penalty can be due to the defendant facing more serious charges at trial (charges that may be reduced in the plea deal, so-called charge bargaining; charges, for example, that have a mandatory and more severe sentence) and/or the prosecutor recommending a more severe sentence after conviction at trial.

Public defenders mentioned threats of lengthy prison sentences:

> Usually it's the hammer of a lengthy prison sentence.

> What they're looking at [punishment] if they go to trial.

> They'll take a guy and offer him twenty-five to life at trial or six months with a deal, so if you lose, you lose big.

Recent research demonstrates that the trial penalty is real. Many studies show that, after controlling for the conviction offense(s), those who go to trial receive a significantly harsher punishment than those who plea.[63] Another comparison shows the stark difference in sentences for federal drug offenders who take a plea rather than go to trial. The average sentence for the plea deal defendants is 5.3 years; for trial defendants, it is sixteen years.[64]

The threat of the trial penalty is one of the key elements that makes plea bargaining possible. Avoiding trial is accomplished by providing a substantial disincentive.

The Supreme Court has addressed the trial penalty matter as we saw earlier. In *Bordenkircher v. Hayes* and *United States v. Goodwin*, the Court held that just presenting the defendant with the implications of going to trial (harsher punishment) or adding charges when the defendant refused a plea deal is not a due process violation.

Enhancements and Upcharging

Enhancements are typically statutory provisions that increase the severity of the charges and thus expose the defendant to more punishment. Upcharging refers to the practice of charging a more serious crime.

Public defenders told us that threats of enhancements and upcharging are pretty common:

> Threaten to refile as a felony.

> Enhancements. Threaten more time.

> They'll hold enhancement paragraphs over their head, or they threaten to file additional charges.

> Threaten to upcharge, threaten consecutive sentencing.

Exploding Offers

Exploding offers are a way to speed up the plea process. The logic is that once the deadline has passed, the next offer will not be as favorable to the defendant or the case goes to trial. We asked prosecutors and defense counsel about imposing such deadlines on plea offers. Prosecutors:

> There's no incentive given, I give deadlines because we want to move the docket . . . plea negotiation is supposed to efficiently and fairly move the case, and if the defense attorney dallies or delays or if they set for trial several times, that number [years in prison] is going up because that's not the point.

It's not really an incentive. . . . You offer XX years, it expires sixty days prior to trial, and the offer goes up if you don't take it.

Defense counsel:

Take it now, or it's off the table.

This is only good today.

This offer is valid for the next two hours.

It is interesting that the outcome of a case—the charges a defendant is ultimately convicted of and the amount of punishment imposed on a defendant—can be substantially influenced by extralegal factors such as how long one takes to decide on a plea deal. The fact that the "offer goes up if you don't take it" really underscores the focus on expediency of the process. The amount of punishment one receives is to a significant extent driven by how quickly a defendant cooperates and how a defendant helps or hinders the bottom line, which is moving cases.

Mandatory Sentences

Mandatory sentences are triggered by the conviction offense. Federal mandatory minimums and mandatory sentences tend to focus on drug crimes and gun crimes, among others. State mandatory sentences apply to many drug crimes, certain sex crimes, and crimes against children as well as habitual offenders and violent offenders. Mandatory sentences provide substantial leverage to prosecutors in the charge bargaining process. The government can threaten to charge a defendant, triggering a mandatory sentence, but then offer a lesser offense that avoids the mandatory.

The Supreme Court recognized the pressure on defendants to accept plea deals under the threat of a mandatory sentence:

Because there is no judicial check on the enhanced mandatory minimums prosecutors can inject into a case, they can put enormous pressure on defendants to plead guilty. In many cases, only a daring risk taker can withstand that pressure. Most people buckle under it.[65]

Defense attorneys concur that the threat of a mandatory sentence is commonly used by prosecutors as a way to motivate a plea:

> These days mandatory minimums. They will basically threaten us.

> The federal sentencing guidelines.

> Three-strikes law, mandatory minimums, multiple charges.

> Definitely imposition of mandatory minimums, not bringing additional charges.

> Threaten a mandatory sentence.

A couple of prosecutors acknowledge using mandatory sentences as leverage:

> Mandatory minimums for delivering over 400 grams, then that's fifteen years. I have no problem saying to the defense attorney that I'll give them ten or twelve and that's a gift than if they come back guilty.

The courts have generally approved other forms of persuasion in plea negotiation such as threatening to indict family members. Also permissible is the requirement that multiple defendants all plea. That way, each defendant will convince the others to plea.[66]

The Supreme Court has acknowledged that plea bargaining involves the exertion of pressure on a defendant but has generally held that such pressure is simply motivation. On the other hand, others see this exertion of pressure as a due process problem.[67] "Since American courts do not seriously scrutinize the voluntariness of guilty pleas, the Due Process Clause effectively does not apply to the vast majority of criminal proceedings in the United States." That sentiment is shared by a large number of experts of criminal procedure and plea bargaining.[68]

The Pretrial Detention Problem

Local jails are increasingly being used for pretrial detention, the practice of detaining individuals awaiting disposition of their cases. Over the past forty-five years, pretrial detention grew more than five times. In 1993, about one-half of individuals in local jails were being detained pretrial.[69] Today, it is more than two-thirds. Approximately 450,000 individuals are pretrial detainees on any given day. The price tag for this practice is $14 billion per year.[70]

Admissions to jail far outpace those to prison. There are roughly 12 million individuals admitted to jails each year, which is nineteen times the number admitted to U.S. prisons.[71] When we hear the terms "mass incarceration" and "warehousing offenders," we tend to think of prisons. The reality is that jails are much bigger warehouses than prisons.

Pretrial detention is not reserved only for urban counties. A recent report by the Vera Institute demonstrates that while rural jails account for 20 percent of all individuals in jail, the population-adjusted rate of pretrial detention is highest in rural jurisdictions.[72]

Pretrial detention, as the term implies, is detaining individuals in jail before they have been convicted of the arrest charge, when they are presumed to be innocent of the charge. The decision to detain someone or release him or her on bond involves balancing several considerations, including public safety, flight risk, and maximizing liberty.

In rare circumstances, a court can deny release because of the perceived dangerousness of the individual or the perceived flight risk he or she poses. However, most are given the opportunity to be released on bond if they are able to post the required amount or the fee charged by a bail bond company. In many instances, income becomes a deciding factor for release. For example, research by the Prison Policy Initiative shows that the median bail bond amount required for release comprises eight months of income for the typical defendant who is detained.[73]

The issue of income-based disparity or discrimination in the money bail system has moved into the courts. In April 2017, a federal judge issued a ruling finding that the Harris County, Texas (Houston), money bail practices were unconstitutional. The ruling ordered the release of nearly all misdemeanor defendants within twenty-four hours of their arrest whether or not they could afford the bail amount set by the court. In January 2018, indigent inmates in the Dallas County jail sued the county, arguing that the bail system is unconstitutional because it discriminates based on ability to pay.[74]

There are a variety of negative consequences associated with pretrial detention. An obvious one is being deprived of liberty in an unpleasant environment. Often, detention can lead to lost income, a lost job, lost housing, debt, family stress and disruption, medical problems, and psychiatric and psychological problems, among others.

While motivating a plea deal is not one of the three considerations in making the detention decision we discussed above, it is a significant issue in the bigger picture of the use of jail detention. Being detained in jail awaiting disposition of the case can and does have substantial negative consequences for defendants. Moreover, the evidence shows that 60 percent of jail detainees have a mental illness and that the vast majority receive no treatment while incarcerated in jail.[75] The experience of being in jail, as well as the collateral negative consequences, can cause a defendant who is detained in jail to agree to a plea.

Several recent studies have provided evidence empirically linking pretrial detention and guilty pleas. These studies find that detention is significantly related to the probability of a criminal conviction, largely through increases in guilty pleas. This is the case at both the felony level and the misdemeanor level.[76] As Gerald Lynch put it, "Pleading guilty at the first opportunity in exchange for a sentence of 'time served' is often an offer that cannot be refused."[77] A scenario is that the prosecutor argues someone should not be released pretrial because he or she is too dangerous or that the court should set a high bond amount. The defendant remains in jail and as a consequence accepts a plea deal and is sentenced to time served.

The public defenders we interviewed agreed that the use of pretrial detention is the number one way that the government motivates a plea:

> It's the biggest motivating factor.

> Jail is the biggest one. . . . A motivated client will wear out.

> That's the best motivator prosecutors have.

> Oftentimes, this is what forces people to accept a deal they would not have otherwise accepted.

> I think that's the reason people are pleading out.

> A major, major, major issue is pretrial detention. It is completely unfair and absurd.

When people can't get out of jail, and their number one priority is to get out of jail, you're not going to wait for trial.

It's easier for the government to negotiate when the defendant is in jail.

Most people can't afford bail, so we often see pleas just to get out.

They'll ask for a bond increase and put the client back in jail if he's out.

If a lot more defendants were out on bond, then there would be a lot more trials.

Lots of my clients are in jail and want to fight but have to get back to their families.

They [prosecutors] will fight bond reduction and keep clients in jail. Prosecutors are opposed to bond reduction, and judges are elected. So, most judges are not impartial.

And they remain in jail. . . . I have a lot clients who feel they have no choice but to plea.

Drug tests, then use the results to raise the bond.

Several public defenders noted that it involves the court setting bond amounts beyond the ability of defendants to pay rather than an outright denial of release:

It's less a matter of the state than it is judges detaining people pretrial. I think there's more coercive measures from the judge or court as a whole.

Our bonds are set too high without any consideration of the defendant's ability to pay the bonds.

They also identified a variety of negative impacts that pretrial detention can have, such as loss of a job:

When you hold somebody's freedom, you limit their ability to hold a job, pay their bills . . . they'll make the deal pretty much no matter what.

I see a lot of clients in holdover [pretrial detention]. There is a lot of pressure for them to get out of jail from their family and job. And they can't afford to bond out, so the next best thing is to take a deal and leave immediately.

There are additional significant downstream consequences associated with the pretrial detention decision. Whether someone is detained because of a realistic, risk-based determination that he or she is dangerous or because the prosecutor argues for detention to facilitate a plea deal, research shows that the incarceration experience significantly increases the likelihood of recidivism. It is not just the fact of pretrial detention but the length as well that is predictive of worse short-term and longer-term outcomes. First, pretrial detention is related to a greater likelihood of being convicted and sentenced to incarceration and for longer periods of time. In addition, the two-year recidivism rates among low-risk detainees increased substantially by length of pretrial detention.

There is a good bit of controversy surrounding pretrial detention and the decision-making process involved in determining who is released and who is detained. Our concern in the moment is the extent to which pretrial detention is used to persuade individuals to accept a plea. The broader consequences regarding sentencing and recidivism outcomes are very important in the bigger picture of criminal justice reform. We return to this later.

The Innocence Problem

The National Registry of Exonerations is a collaboration among the Newkirk Center for Science and Society at the University of California, Irvine; the University of Michigan Law School; and the Michigan State University Law School. Exonerations are findings of innocence of previously convicted individuals based on new evidence. That evidence includes DNA, but exonerations are also based on incorrect eyewitness testimony, false or misleading forensic evidence, false confessions, perjury, and official misconduct. The Registry has tracked criminal exonerations since 1989.

Innocent people do plead guilty. In 1992, Troy Mansfield was convicted of molesting a four-year-old girl in Williamson County, Texas. Mansfield faced life in prison if his case went to trial, and that trial penalty was made clear to him. He was offered a plea deal of 120 days in jail and ten years on probation, which he accepted. He also had to register as a sex offender. As a registered sex offender, he "faced being shamed, threatened and humiliated, to being run out of towns, communities, and churches, to not being able to participate in his two children's lives fully, to being deported at gunpoint from Mexico because he was a registered sex offender."[78]

Mansfield was exonerated, and his conviction was set aside in 2016. He is suing Williamson County because the district attorney and three assistant prosecutors withheld exculpatory evidence from the defense, evidence that proved he did not commit this crime. He also claims that the prosecutors lied to his defense counsel.

The relevance of the National Registry for our purposes is that it establishes empirically that innocent defendants do plead guilty. It also provides rough estimates of the extent to which that happens. Here is what we know from the Registry:[79]

- Fifteen percent of known exoneree convictions were based on a guilty plea.
- Six percent of those exonerees who pled guilty were convicted of murder; 50 percent were convicted of manslaughter.
- Two-thirds were convicted of drug crimes.

This information is not representative of all innocent individuals who accept a plea deal since it is based on cases that someone pursued to the point of uncovering sufficient exculpatory evidence and/or procedural violations. The actual number of felony and misdemeanor defendants who plead guilty when in fact they are innocent is unknown.

Only a couple of our interview respondents mentioned the problem of wrongful convictions of innocent defendants. One prosecutor and one judge mentioned the innocence issue in relation to concerns with plea negotiation.

One may think that an innocent individual pleading guilty is irrational. However, it is certainly possible to envision a variety of circumstances where an innocent defendant pleading guilty is in the best interests of the defendant based on the circumstances at the time. For example, if it is a relatively minor crime and the defendant is being detained pretrial and already has prior convictions, the marginal consequences of another conviction may be relatively low and the benefits—getting out of jail—high.

A lawful guilty plea is one that is voluntary and intelligent. The obvious concern here is a coerced admission of guilt, an involuntary plea. The Supreme Court in *McMann v. Richardson* (1970)[80] held that any coercion exercised by the prosecutor is removed by effective assistance of counsel. This presumption of voluntariness in the presence of effective defense counsel is problematic as we understand the constraints on public defenders and assigned counsel that we discussed previously.

Interestingly, the Supreme Court has created the opportunity for a defendant to plead guilty in a negotiated plea deal while at the same time maintaining his or her innocence. This is known as an Alford plea (*North Carolina v. Alford* [1970]). The Alford plea, thought of by some as "evidence of the criminal justice system's addiction to guilty pleas (even in cases where the defendant might be innocent),"[81] applies to all levels of felonies and misdemeanors and is permitted in the vast majority of states.

The logic of the Alford plea is a bit of a curiosity: plead guilty but maintain innocence. It may be a way for guilty defendants to save face with family or friends by being able to officially enter an Alford plea. However, some believe that Alford pleas in effect increase the likelihood that innocent defendants will plead guilty since a plea may be the best alternative under the circumstances but they can still maintain their innocence.[82]

Judges exercise considerable discretion in deciding whether to accept an Alford plea. In theory, the judge is supposed to be convinced of the guilt of the defendant based on sufficient evidence supporting that conclusion. However, the courts have not provided much guidance on what is sufficient evidence, and as a result there is considerable variation among judges in accepting Alford pleas. Moreover, some courts have relaxed the evidentiary requirements regarding guilt.[83]

Mens Rea Ignored

We hypothesized that in the course of plea negotiation, the priority for the prosecutor is obtaining a confession pertaining to the criminal act, with much less consideration given to the state of mind of the offender. In essence, if a defendant is willing to confess to the crime, the deal is done. The interviews with defense counsel provided confirmation of this view:

> I think mental capacity of the defendant is put on the back burner and the action is what is focused on.

> Most of the time they [prosecutors] don't care [about mens rea].

> They usually just worry about whether the act occurred without considering the intent.

> It's not very important to them [prosecutors] because they don't fear the lack of intent. They feel like they can usually still win without it.

> There's a tendency for the state to only look at the crime and the criminal history, so they might not consider the mental state of the defendant.

> Especially with drug possession—sometimes people were in the other room in the house and had no idea.

> Mens rea takes a back seat in my experience.

Several indicated that when intent is even an issue, prosecutors tend to infer or assume it without independent proof:

> The prosecutors have an opinion [rather than proof of intent].

> I think they're [prosecutors] more likely to infer mens rea.

> Prosecutors just assume they can prove the element needed to be proved. Offender has dope in his pocket. Prosecutor can prove defendant knew about drugs in pocket. The prosecutor assumes the same about all cases.

I have mentally ill and intellectually disabled defendants that didn't know what they were doing. It is a problem.

The Evidence Is Not Litigated in a Plea Deal

Several expressed concern that the evidence that is used in a plea deal is not really litigated, at least in the sense of a third party, like a jury or judge, hearing the evidence from both sides and then offering an opinion:

> Whether we are not putting in mitigating evidence or whether we are letting the state get away with weak cases because our client doesn't want to fight it, the evidence isn't being litigated, so that is a problem.

> If you look at it that way, every case that is plea bargained has this problem. The DAs may have little or no evidence, and my client will still take the deal.

> It's a big deal not to litigate it out. You don't get that confrontation and cross-examining and get that information out.

The Misdemeanor Justice System

While the preceding discussion applies to concerns with plea negotiation generally, a good bit of research has focused on the particularly troubling situation at the misdemeanor level. For that reason, we want to spend some time highlighting the observations and conclusions of experts who study misdemeanor plea bargaining.

The scale of the misdemeanor justice system is ten times that of the felony system. Every year, there are approximately 1 million felony convictions. In that same year, there are more than 10 million misdemeanor convictions. Although misdemeanors are less serious than felonies, they have important consequences for individuals.[84] These include jail time (both pretrial detention as well as postconviction incarceration), which can have substantial impacts on employment, housing, and family; hefty fines that many lower-income defendants cannot pay (recall that the vast majority of criminal defendants are too poor to retain counsel); criminal convictions that can impact employment opportunities (65 percent of employers say they would not hire someone with a criminal conviction[85]); and eligibility for occupational licenses, public assistance, student loans, public housing, and health care, among others. So, while it is often called petty crime, the consequences are not petty.

Not only does the misdemeanor system handle many more cases than felony courts, but misdemeanor courts are the typical entry point for the majority of offenders. Most felons were originally misdemeanants. What happens to them while in the misdemeanor system can have profound impacts on longer-term outcomes, such as the probability of recidivism and graduation to the felony level.

Alexandra Natapoff has written extensively on the misdemeanor justice system. Her characterizations of misdemeanor court processes are troubling:

> In comparison to felony adjudication, misdemeanor processing is largely informal and deregulated, characterized by high-volume arrests, weak prosecutorial screening, an impoverished defense bar, and high plea rates. Together, these characteristics generate convictions in bulk often without meaningful scrutiny of whether those convictions are supported by evidence. . . . Massive, under funded, informal, and careless, the misdemeanor system propels defendants through in bulk with scant attention to individualized cases and often without counsel.[86]

Analyses by a variety of researchers[87] all pretty much portray the misdemeanor system as one of often inadequate or nonexistent screening of cases by prosecutors, absence of defense counsel, or, if present, public defenders and appointed counsel who are overwhelmed with cases; a system of fast pleas with little regard for evidence and due process; and excessive use of pretrial detention.

Paul Heaton and colleagues investigated the use of pretrial detention in misdemeanor cases and found that those who are detained are 25 percent more likely than similar released offenders to plead guilty. Moreover, the detained misdemeanants are 43 percent more likely to be sentenced to incarceration in jail after conviction.[88] Also, pretrial detention of misdemeanants increases the likelihood of subsequent reoffending—a 30 percent increase in the probability of committing a new felony and 20 percent increase in the probability of committing a new misdemeanor. Thus, it appears that an important determinant of moving from a misdemeanant to a felon is pretrial detention for a misdemeanor.

Senator Charles Grassley, the Republican chair of the Senate Judiciary Committee, recently stated at a hearing, "The Supreme Court's Sixth Amendment decisions regarding misdemeanor defendants are violated thousands of times every day. No Supreme Court decisions in our history have been violated so widely, so frequently and for so long."[89] Part of the issue is the all-too-common failure of some misdemeanor courts to provide counsel to indigent misdemeanants and/or prosecutors engaging in plea negotiation without advising defendants of a right to counsel. There are no large-scale studies of this matter, but case studies indicate that, at least in some misdemeanor courts, this is business as usual.[90]

Another part of the Sixth Amendment issue in misdemeanor courts is the overwhelming caseloads of indigent defense counsel. The National Association of Criminal Defense Lawyers conducted a fairly comprehensive analysis of the misdemeanor justice system and reported their findings in 2009 in "Minor Crimes, Massive Waste: The Terrible Toll of America's Broken Misdemeanor Courts." Their conclusions paint a difficult picture of criminal defense. They found, among other things, defender caseloads that are routinely six to seven times the national standards, a situation considerably worse than the challenging situation at the felony level. By way of example, they report that in Chicago, Miami, and Atlanta, defenders carry more than 2,000 cases per year, amounting to, at best, one hour per case.

What we take away from many of the descriptions of the misdemeanor process is one of wholesale justice, where there is less regard for individual culpability and more attention paid to mass conviction of defendants:

> Misdemeanor defendants are identified, processed, convicted and punished in large numbers based on generalized characteristics through procedures that are insensitive to individual evidence or circumstances . . . misdemeanor processing is lackadaisical about individual guilt . . . [and] liability should be based on actus reus and mens rea. . . . Instead, the process tends to select and convict people en masse without the standard procedural checks that ask whether individual defendants actually did what they are accused of doing.[91]

SUMMARY

The practice of plea negotiation, especially on the scale that it is currently used, provides a stark contrast between the ideals of American jurisprudence and the realities of the day-to-day administration of the criminal courts. A justice system founded on principles of due process, fairness, and objectivity (consider the blindfold on the Lady Justice statue) routinely plays out in what most would consider a dramatic departure from our foundational values.

All of the evidence indicates that plea bargaining was born of necessity, a procedural and dispositional shortcut that allows the criminal courts to operate within the budgetary constraints that characterize much of the administration of criminal justice (prisons perhaps serving as the exception). In that sense, plea negotiation is no different than the civil side of the docket. The vast majority of civil lawsuits are resolved through settlement, rendering the civil trial as much an anomaly as its criminal counterpart. However, the similarities between the two generally end there.

Our analysis of plea bargaining revolves around two major sets of concerns. The first involves the large number of widely held criticisms of the practice of plea negotiation. These include unfettered discretion of prosecutors, the potential for coercion and involuntary confessions, pretrial detention, general due process concerns, the fact that many defendants are convicted based on probable cause rather than reasonable doubt, the conviction of innocent defendants, and severe constraints on public defenders and assigned counsel that may and do jeopardize the quality of representation. Any one of these problems is troubling. Taken together, they serve as a serious indictment of plea bargaining. Nevertheless, the plea process churns on, and plea bargaining remains the elephant in the room that few seem willing to confront. We turn to potential remedies in chapters 5 to 7.

The second broad concern with plea negotiation is that it is a key facilitator of crime control. It does this in part by expediting the prosecution and conviction of offenders. Perhaps more important, since punishment is the primary currency that is negotiated (how many years in prison or months in jail or years on probation), it keeps punishment the central focus of how the criminal justice system does business. Both the speed of prosecution and the focus on punishment place diversion and treatment/rehabilitation in the backseat. The end result is recidivism rates of 65 to 70 percent. It is for this reason that serious discussions of meaningful criminal justice reform must confront plea negotiation head on. That is in part the subject of chapter 6.

5

PLEA BARGAINING'S REMEDIES

We argued in our recent book *From Retribution to Public Safety: Disruptive Innovation of American Criminal Justice* that, by design or default, the U.S. criminal justice system is the nearly perfect recidivism machine. The front door is wide open, willing to accept all of the individuals who come to the doorstep. Their numbers have dramatically increased by the expansion of criminal codes; the failures of institutions, such as public health, public education, and affordable housing (there was a 60 percent reduction in affordable housing stock in the United States between 2010 and 2016);[1] zero-tolerance and broken-windows policing strategies; and a variety of other factors. Once they are in, we then apply the one remedy for crime that has defined criminal justice policy for decades: punishment. Not just punishment but more and longer punishment, much of which continues well after someone has left the justice system, such as restrictions on employment and housing.

The logic of this fifty-year punishment binge seems to be partially tied to the oversimplification of crime as largely a matter of making bad decisions. Punishment, so the argument goes, should make an offender think twice next time (specific deterrence), and the risk or threat of punishment keeps the rest of us from engaging in crime (general deterrence). The unfortunate reality is that many offenders suffer from circumstances, disabilities, deficits, and disorders that mitigate any deterrent effect of punishment and impair their ability to make good decisions. This is not an apology or excuse; it is just the reality of the situation.

While there are many circumstances that played important roles in the expansion of correctional control in the United States (discussed in chapter 1), one that we feel deserves detailed attention, especially in terms of meaningful criminal justice reform, is plea bargaining. It is our contention that plea bargaining has been the *great expediter* of tough on crime. This is a result of a number of characteristics of plea bargaining, characteristics or features that make it fairly simple to prosecute, convict, and punish large numbers of individuals in fairly short periods of time. These include but are not limited to the relative lack of due process protections for defendants; the use of a variety of strategies to motivate acceptance of a plea by a defendant; the coercive or pressured nature of the plea process, including, for example, the trial penalty and the excessive use of pretrial detention; the challenges associated with adequate defense representation for the vast majority of defendants who are indigent; and the fact that prosecutors have an inordinate amount of power and write the script for how each plea will play out, a script that is usually only modestly modified by defense counsel and typically promotes tough-on-crime values and outcomes. On top of all that, there is little judicial oversight of the plea negotiation proceedings, in part because judges are restricted or are effectively discouraged from participating. Colorado, Arkansas, North Dakota, South Dakota, West Virginia, Tennessee, Pennsylvania, Utah, the federal system, the District of Columbia, Georgia, Mississippi, New Mexico, Virginia, Texas, Wisconsin, Alaska, Kansas, and Nevada prohibit judicial participation in the plea process by statute, rules of procedure, or case law.[2] Twelve more states that have not explicitly prohibited judicial involvement in plea negotiation nevertheless discourage it. A result of limited judicial participation in plea deals is minimal interference in moving as many cases as quickly as possible. When judges are involved in approving a plea deal, it is often a pro forma ritual of questions regarding whether the defendant entered into the plea knowingly and voluntarily, after which the defendant provides the properly rehearsed answers that then allow the court to move on to the next case.

All of these characteristics of plea bargaining conspire to facilitate expedited criminal conviction and punishment, often at the expense of careful consideration of individual circumstances and situations and informed strategies for reducing recidivism. The result again is the nearly perfect recidivism machine.

It is no secret that the criminal justice system has become the landing place for many of the nation's mentally ill, especially those with serious mental illness (schizophrenia, bipolar disorder, and major depression). The Cook County (Chicago) jail and the Los Angeles County jail are the largest mental health facilities in Illinois and California, respectively. It is not uncommon that 25 to nearly 50 percent of calls for service to local police departments are for mental health–related incidents.[3] The unfortunate reality is that the critical shortage of local emergency psychiatric facilities, which provide short-term stabilization, typically through use of medication, often results in booking these individuals into jail. The bottom line is there is nowhere else for them to go. Even when such emergency facilities exist, large numbers nevertheless get booked into jail. As Michael Biasotti, the former chief of the New Windsor, New York, Police Department and past president of the New York State Association of Chiefs of Police puts it,

> We wait hours for psychiatrists to evaluate them [individuals in mental health–related situations that police respond to] only to find the doctor overrules us and refuses to admit the patient. . . . The easier solution for our officers is to take people with serious mental illness to jail, something we are loath to do to sick people who need help. But the mental health system gives us little choice.[4]

The most recent systematic analysis of the prevalence of mental illness in the American criminal justice system shows that 56 percent of state prisoners, 45 percent of federal prisoners, and 64 percent of jail inmates have a mental health problem. The vast majority of those with one mental illness have at least one comorbid disorder, which is often a substance use disorder.[5] Approximately 400,000 of the seriously mentally ill in this country are in our jails and prisons. More than 750,000 are on probation or parole. Absent significant treatment, the vast majority will reoffend, and those who do will likely reoffend multiple times.[6]

The return or recidivism rate of offenders with mental illness is more than 70 percent. Moreover, it is important to remember that the recidivism statistic is an official measure of those who have been caught. Actual reoffending is arguably a good bit higher.

A common entry point into the criminal justice system for the mentally ill is misdemeanor court. Over the past forty years as broken-windows and zero-tolerance policing have focused substantial attention on so-called quality-of-life or public order crimes, local law enforcement has increasingly arrested many mentally ill individuals, who are often homeless as well, for low-level misdemeanors. Many of the nation's mentally ill cycle in and out of the misdemeanor justice system, typically receiving limited, if any, services and incurring substantial cost each time they return.

A variety of factors, many of which we discussed earlier, facilitate criminal conviction for these low-level crimes, setting up a typically long-term process of cycling in and out of the justice system. Absent effective intervention to address mental health issues, in combination with the impacts of criminal convictions on things like employment, public assistance, and eligibility for public housing, we have a nearly endless supply of individuals who take considerable amounts of law enforcement time and resources, clog misdemeanor courts as well as the caseloads of prosecutors and defense counsels, populate jails, and require substantial expenditures of public money every time they cycle through.

Eighty percent of individuals in the U.S. justice system have a substance use disorder, consisting of varying levels of severity of addiction, dependence, and abuse. In 2014, 83 percent of all drug arrests were for possession, and 40 percent were for possession of marijuana.[7] We have been relentlessly trying to punish the drug problem away. We see even more of that at the federal level in response to the opioid crisis. The U.S. attorney general has called on federal prosecutors to charge the maximum in drug cases. We also see it at the state level, including many states that have otherwise passed criminal justice reform legislation. Being tough on the opioid crisis seems to be the hard-to-refuse solution. Kentucky recently passed punitive opioid legislation, as did Indiana, Florida, Illinois, Ohio, Delaware, Pennsylvania, and Rhode Island, among others.[8]

All of this comes at a time when the evidence could not be clearer that tough drug policies have been ineffective. As recently as June 2017, the Public Safety Performance Project at the Pew Charitable Trusts sent a letter to Governor Chris Christie in his capacity as chair of the President's Commission on Combating Drug Addiction and the Opioid Crisis. The letter documented the failure of incarceration policies to reduce state drug problems. "These findings reinforce a large body of prior research that casts doubt on the theory that stiffer prison terms effectively deter drug use, distribution, and other drug-law violations."[9] It is time to raise the white flag and get serious about alternatives.

Large numbers of offenders in the justice system have serious cognitive impairments due to physical and emotional trauma, exposure to environmental toxins, poor parenting, mental illness, substance abuse, and a number of other sources. Moreover, individuals with cognitive impairments can present with comorbid mental illness and substance use disorders.

Whether we focus on violent and nonviolent felonies or lower-level misdemeanors and quality-of-life crimes, a common denominator is the presence of extraordinary numbers of disordered offenders. It doesn't matter whether we are talking about the felony or the misdemeanor system: neither are appropriate venues for much of that population. Moreover, the justice system is ill equipped and lacks the expertise and funding to effectively treat many of these disordered offenders.

One of the defining characteristics of the U.S. criminal justice system is crowding: too many offenders on court dockets, in jails, and on prosecutors' and public defenders' caseloads. One would think by looking at the numbers that we have been experiencing a major crime wave for decades. The reality is that the primary reason there are so many people filing through the court systems in the United States is the failure of criminal justice policy and practice to effectively reduce recidivism. Another very important reason is that the justice system has become the de facto dumping ground for many disordered individuals who arguably do not belong there.

We suggest that a key facilitator of all of this is plea negotiation. The plea negotiation process is designed and functions to fast-track criminal convictions and bargain length or severity of punishment. There is little focus on individual circumstance beyond what is relevant for negotiating punishment. Because of the institutional value of expediency, there is little motivation to break the pattern of conviction and punishment.

So where do we go from here? We have identified two broad sets of concerns related to plea negotiation. First, there are those issues directly associated with plea bargaining, such as due process concerns, coercion, innocence, effective defense counsel, standard of proof, discovery, the power and discretion of the prosecutor, and pretrial detention. The second is the role that plea negotiation plays as the facilitator or expeditor of tough-on-crime policies. It is our contention that plea bargaining is a key piece of equipment in the nearly perfect recidivism machine. A related matter is that of the disordered offender and the extent to which plea negotiation simply keeps this segment of the offender population cycling in and out of the justice system.

In the next section, we review and assess what others have proposed for reforming plea bargaining. As we will see, this is an important step in the right direction. However, we believe it misses the bigger picture of reforming plea negotiation within the context of broader criminal justice reform. In chapter 6, we identify evidence-based changes to the plea negotiation process that address procedural concerns and that can effectively reduce recidivism. In chapter 7, we take on changes to the broader context in which plea negotiation occurs: the pretrial process, including things like pretrial detention and pretrial diversion. We also discuss changes to criminal defense for indigent defendants, which is one of the glaring deficiencies in the American criminal justice system.

REFORMING PLEA NEGOTIATION: A REVIEW

There is no shortage of recommendations for reforming plea negotiation. They range from abolishing it to a variety of fine-tuning measures that address specific concerns, such as discovery, prosecutorial discretion, and judicial involvement in the plea process. We have organized this discussion by specific recommendations. We then discuss the merits of these before turning to the changes to plea negotiation and associated pretrial processes and procedures that we believe are necessary in order to bring about meaningful criminal justice reform.

Abolish Plea Negotiation

A radical approach is to eliminate plea bargaining altogether.[10] Stephen Schulhofer notes that plea bargaining harms the public's interest in maximizing deterrence through maximizing punishment (plea deals result in reduced punishment) and society's interest in minimizing the risk of convicting innocent individuals (the innocence problem we discussed earlier). We know from imperfect statistical evidence that at least 15 to 18 percent of plea-bargained criminal convictions (which by definition are obtained by a confession) are of innocent individuals.

These problems—and many more identified in chapter 4—presumably can be mitigated by abolition. As John Blume and Rebecca Helm suggest, many European nations do not permit the practice of plea negotiation, and they appear to be able to manage dockets.

Others have suggested that, short of total abolition, there is a compelling argument to be made that in many cases, where there are no disputed issues of fact or law and where a defendant voluntarily admits guilt, a trial is unnecessary. If the evidence is solid and there are no procedural issues that cannot be addressed by a hearing, a trial would be a waste of resources. As a confession and a plea deal make absolute sense in such situations, why not give the defendant something in return?

Bench Trials

If plea negotiation were abolished, how would courts process the crushing number of cases in an efficient manner? An alternative proposed by several abolition advocates is bench trials where the judge serves as judge and jury.[11] The argument is that bench trials are much quicker than jury trials and that, if certain adjustments are made, such as relaxing some trial-related rules of procedure, this approach could be efficient. An obvious impediment to this approach is the fact that, at least in felony and other serious cases, a jury trial is guaranteed by the Sixth Amendment.

Limiting Prosecutorial Discretion

A variety of concerns revolve around prosecutors' broad power and discretion. The remedies largely involve limits on prosecutorial decision making. Several call for limiting the size of plea discounts. One way to do this is to cap the plea discount or fix the plea discount to some percentage of the expected penalty if convicted at trial. Another way to limit the size of the trial penalty is by requiring prosecutors to bring the maximum charges up front so that the defendant knows that additional charges will not be brought up later.[12] This also communicates to the defendant what the prosecutor believes is provable, and therefore the defendant has more information on which to base any plea decision made. Related to this is requiring that prosecutors justify any additional charges they may bring later in the process and require that they are based on new evidence. This is designed to prevent bringing new charges out of retribution for refusing to accept a plea deal.

Written Plea Deals

Several critics believe that an important step toward improving the plea process is to require that plea deals are in writing and placed in the record of the proceedings.[13] This preserves the essentials of the negotiation and adds protections for the defendant regarding things like the specifics of the agreement and any promises made by the government. It is argued that written agreements help inform the defendant of the specifics of the deal and thus may help the defendant make a more informed decision. Written plea deals also shine a light on the process that is largely in the dark and off the record today.

Defense Counsel

A common concern with plea negotiation is the adequacy of counsel for indigent defendants. Most point to extraordinary caseloads for public defenders as the primary cause. Greater funding for public defenders and assigned counsel, including resources for things like investigators and experts, is the primary remedy.[14] Taking it a step further is a program implemented in Texas that gives defendants choice of defense counsel by providing vouchers for indigent defendants so they can retain their own counsel from either a private firm or a public defender.[15]

Open Discovery

Many critics of plea negotiation have recommended expanded access to the defendant of the evidence against him or her.[16] One of the significant handicaps that defendants have in a plea negotiation is not knowing what evidence the state has and how compelling it is. Unlike civil litigation, criminal defendants are not generally entitled to see all of the government's case. The one exception in the law is exculpatory evidence, although there certainly are examples of violations of that requirement.

The situation for criminal defendants is particularly problematic in New York State, which has what is called the "blindfold law." This permits prosecutors to wait until trial before providing the state's evidence to the defendant. This is a particular problem for defendants who plea negotiate since those cases do not make it to trial; thus, many defendants agree to a plea deal without knowing what the case is against them. There are ten states, including New York, that currently permit prosecutors to lawfully withhold discovery evidence from the defense until trial, and defendants who plea have similar disadvantages as those in New York regarding evidence against them.[17]

The logic behind open discovery is that access to the state's evidence can go a long way in helping the defendant make a knowing and informed decision about whether to accept a plea deal. Open discovery can help the defendant know about the risk of conviction at trial and whether the deal offered by the prosecutor is reasonable. Absent open discovery, the defendant and defense counsel are largely in the dark about important aspects of a plea negotiation. In response to the blindfold law in New York, Governor Andrew Cuomo is advocating for changing the law to permit more open discovery and speeding up the time line during which prosecutors are required to provide discovery evidence.

Limiting Due Process Waivers

A significant concern of many experts is the waiver of due process protections that is typically required in a plea deal. This is common in federal plea negotiation. It is less common in state prosecutions, and in fact some states forbid it is as a matter of public policy.[18] Limiting or eliminating waivers of claims of ineffective assistance of counsel, appeal of conviction and sentence, and discovery, it is suggested, enhance fairness and accuracy of the outcome.

Increase Judicial Participation

As we mentioned earlier, judges are largely restricted from direct participation in plea negotiation. The typical judicial role is what has been described as a rather passive, perfunctory review of the plea deal at case disposition. The concerns some have expressed about greater judicial involvement in the plea process is that it may potentially impose even greater pressure on defendants to accept a plea deal. Defendants may be more intimidated by a judge's pronouncements, pressuring them as much, if not more, to accept a plea deal. Moreover, effective judicial involvement may require judges understanding details of cases, such as the veracity of the evidence and potential due process violations. These activities would likely require more time by judges and thus may interfere with the efficient management of dockets. In essence, judicial neutrality may be compromised by the need to move cases.

On the other hand, greater involvement by the judge in the actual negotiation process, a role that is supervisory, providing oversight, is seen as a way to inject neutrality into the process and counter some prosecutorial discretion and potential coercion. It is also viewed as a method for docket management, increasing the speed and efficiency of case processing, largely by resolving plea negotiations sooner.[19] It is argued that greater judicial involvement in the process should enhance fairness and accuracy of the outcome.[20] Connecticut, Florida, and Maryland currently permit judicial involvement in the plea process, and the evidence suggests that the outcomes appear fairer.[21]

A related recommendation is to prohibit prosecutors from sentence bargaining—preventing prosecutors from stipulating a particular sentence, preserving that for the judge. That policy was adopted in Alaska. The result is that Alaskan courts hold sentencing hearings in plea cases much like sentencing hearings after conviction at trial. Some commentators believe that having the judge impose the sentence can produce better case screening and charging decisions since prosecutors would know that the court would be reviewing the case in some detail in order to impose the sentence.[22]

A modification of this approach of greater judicial involvement has been proposed that utilizes specially assigned magistrates or judges without trial dockets who would preside over what are called settlement dockets.[23] The role of such magistrates is to review evidence and make plea recommendations as well as mediate and provide oversight of the process. This recommendation appears to avoid the issue that trial court judges have significant interest in moving cases due to substantial docket pressure. More on this in chapter 6.

Extrajudicial Review

Several have recommended external review procedures that utilize individuals outside of the prosecutor's office and outside of the judge's chambers to assess plea deals. The nature of these oversight teams varies, but the idea is the same: independent groups charged with the responsibility of reviewing various aspects of plea deals.

One proposal puts the states' offices of the attorney general in the position of being an external oversight entity (external to the charging authority) responsible for addressing prosecutorial overcharging.[24] Another assigns citizen panels the responsibility of reviewing guilty pleas in cases where defendants maintain innocence (e.g., in Alford plea situations).[25]

Still another related proposal involves the use of plea juries. The concept is using lay juries to determine if guilty pleas have a factual basis and are knowing and voluntary.[26]

Caveat Emptor

Stephanos Bibas, a law professor and vocal critic of plea negotiation, suggests that criminal defendants should have protections, much like consumer regulations for things like medications, motor vehicles, loans, and child toys. He suggests that we should extend the logic of consumer protections to the plea process, thus putting the defendant in a more informed position to make good decisions.[27] Part of Bibas's consumer protections involve issues like written plea agreements, a "cooling-off" period for plea deals, requiring a waiting period between the plea offer and consummation of the agreement, certain disclosures by prosecutors regarding considerations such as sentencing implications of a plea deal, and better defense representation through bar associations developing best practices for plea deal procedures.

Plea Negotiation in Other Countries

The use of plea bargaining in other countries has grown dramatically in the past twenty-five years. In 1990, fewer than twenty nations used some version of negotiated guilty pleas. Today, sixty-six countries use it.[28] Essentially all European nations have some type of plea waiver system, as do Canada, Australia, New Zealand, most of Latin America, and China. Canada, England and Wales, Ireland, Scotland, Italy, Austria, and Spain were early adopters along with the United States, with systems in place prior to 1990.

The specifics vary by country, but the U.S. model has been influential in the adoption of plea negotiation internationally. While no nations embrace plea bargaining as extensively as the United States does with its 97 percent plea rate, several nations convict the majority of defendants with plea deals. These include Georgia (88 percent), Scotland (85 percent), England and Wales (70 percent), the Russian Federation and Estonia (64 percent), and Australia (61 percent).[29]

International comparisons of U.S. criminal procedure, especially with regard to plea negotiation, highlight important differences in the plea process as well as differences in the roles and responsibilities of the key individuals involved.[30] Arguably the most important difference is the broad, essentially unfettered discretion of U.S. prosecutors. Prosecutors in European nations do not have nearly the power or autonomy as in the United States to pressure a plea deal or force defendants to cooperate. There are several mechanisms in place to reduce the risk of coercion. European sentencing laws do not provide for sentences as harsh as U.S. laws do. The result is that European prosecutors do not have such draconian punishment to threaten defendants with to motivate a plea deal. European criminal procedure provides much broader pretrial discovery compared to the United States. Criminal investigations in Europe focus on compiling both incriminating and exculpatory evidence. That evidence is then made available to the defendant, helping the defendant make a more informed decision about a plea deal and preventing the prosecutor from making empty threats about additional charges.[31]

European law and criminal procedure give judges a much greater role in controlling prosecutorial discretion. For example, in France and Germany, a component of the plea process is a trial where the judge examines the evidence in open court to determine whether there is a factual basis for the charges and whether the evidence is sufficient to support a plea. In Italy, there are rather strict requirements for judges to scrutinize prosecutorial decision making to keep discretion in check.

OUR TAKE ON THESE REFORMS

There certainly has been a good bit of thought put into identifying concerns with plea bargaining as well as a wide variety of strategies for fixing many of these problems. Some of the ideas put forward definitely have merit. Others are not as practical as is probably necessary to ever see the light of day. Many do not go nearly far enough and seem piecemeal rather than wholesale reforms of a troubling process of criminal conviction and sentencing.

The problems with abolition are monumental. Many commentators have observed that if the plea rate were reduced significantly, let alone abolished, the court system as currently configured and resourced would likely collapse. That risk is particularly acute in the misdemeanor courts, where caseloads are extraordinary. One irony that is important to point out is that much of the caseload problem in both our misdemeanor and our felony courts is of our own making due to our decisions about crime and punishment, a result of our penchant for punishment. The broad failure of the criminal justice system to effectively reduce recidivism is the primary reason that court dockets and prosecutor and public defender caseloads are so high.

The necessity of adding courts, prosecutors, judges, court staff, and public defenders as well as the expansion of infrastructure for all of these new positions would place tremendous financial pressure on local jurisdictions and state government. Court systems in the United States are generally funded by the combined contributions of local county government and state government. Federal courts are funded by Congress and face similar financial pressures that state systems face.

Another challenge in abolishing plea bargaining is changing the current culture of the court system. Settlement is how both civil and criminal dockets are managed. Plea deals have been the established way of doing business for many decades, and while there are legitimate concerns, plea negotiation is deeply embedded in the culture of the courts, prosecutors, and the defense bar.

Abolishing plea negotiation does nothing to address the issue of disordered offenders in the criminal justice system. If anything, it may harm the longer-term outcomes of these individuals if, as seems necessary, tremendous amounts of money are allocated to expanding the court system, likely resulting in fewer resources for things like assessment, diversion, and treatment. It seems safe to conclude that abolishing plea bargaining is a tough sell to state legislatures and county government and in all likelihood is not viable.

The concept of bench trials is also problematic. Bench trials are still trials and thus would require significant reorganization of court systems and prosecutor and public defender offices and reallocation of resources. It would also require a waiver of the Sixth Amendment right to a jury trial. While bench trials may address some of the concerns with plea bargaining—for example, counterbalancing prosecutorial discretion—it is unclear how this addresses other concerns, such as the adequacy of defense counsel and pretrial discovery, among others. There is also the concern that a primary objective of the bench trial process is, in reality, moving cases and managing dockets and caseloads. That pressure is what has caused many of the problems with plea negotiation. It is unclear how many procedural shortcuts would be necessary in order to make the bench trial process viable and the extent to which those shortcuts place defendants in vulnerable positions.

Judicial oversight seems like a good idea. As the plea process currently works, it is largely a negotiation between the prosecutor and defense counsel with the judge having a rather perfunctory role at the end. However, judicial oversight can pose significant caseload problems. If trial court judges are those who provide judicial oversight, they will be functioning under the same if not greater caseload pressure and will have incentives to move cases as quickly as possible. That seems to be one of the primary outcomes of greater judicial involvement in the plea process.[32] This raises concerns about how well such proceedings will address the variety of problems identified with plea bargaining.

Oversight by magistrates or lower-court judges or even trial court judges with restricted oversight dockets could be a plausible modification to the process, depending on what issues are assessed in the oversight process. Settlement dockets could also be a productive path forward, depending on how they are operated and how well they address primary concerns.

Extrajudicial review by citizen panels, state attorneys general, or plea juries could be a step in a positive direction, depending on what type of authority they have. The goal is to mitigate the problems with plea negotiation. If such review panels had broad investigatory authority and the power to reject plea deals, they could serve as a deterrent to some concerns. However, it is unclear how their review function could address inadequate defense representation or prosecutorial charging decisions. Perhaps a primary shortcoming of this idea is that it is a review after the fact rather than something like a magistrate who participates directly in the process from the beginning.

What extrajudicial review, oversight by magistrates or lower-court judges, and oversight by trial judges all share in common is the concept of introducing a third party into the plea process. We believe there is considerable merit to this idea, though we offer a variation on the concept in the next chapter in the form of what we call a plea mediator.

Open discovery is a worthwhile feature of plea negotiation and should provide defendants with important information. It also gives defense counsel the opportunity to challenge the state's case. Limiting due process waivers sounds like a reasonable idea. However, it is important to appreciate that waivers are a key part of the exchange that serves as the basis for plea negotiation. If that is limited, the parties will need to find other things to bargain.

As it stands, plea bargaining is simply a very effective tool for expediting mass conviction and punishment with little regard for individuals and their circumstances, especially the large numbers of mentally ill and otherwise disordered offenders who flood our courts, jails, and prisons. As such, plea negotiation is the key ingredient for the revolving door—the unfortunate metaphor that has come to accurately describe the American criminal justice system.

There are important changes that can be made to the plea negotiation process to enhance its fairness and constitutionality. Some of them have been proposed by others and were discussed in this chapter. We expand on some of these in the next two chapters. But the larger agenda is developing a workable, constitutional, fair system of case disposition that focuses less on the question of "how much punishment?" and more on the question of "how do we reduce the likelihood that this person will reoffend?"

6

PLEA NEGOTIATION AND MEANINGFUL CRIMINAL JUSTICE REFORM

We are assuming that plea negotiation is here to stay. It was born of necessity and appears to be the only way currently to manage the enormous number of cases and offenders that flood the felony and misdemeanor courts in this country. The interviews with prosecutors and judges confirm this common wisdom.

No one said that plea negotiation is a fairer or a more just way to dispose of cases. Rather, the typical reason prosecutors gave for plea bargaining is caseload pressure and thus expediency:

> Because it's the easier thing to do, easier on everyone.

> We really don't have much choice with the number of cases we have.

> Because that's the most efficient way to dispose of cases due to the volume of cases.

> Even with eight [felony] courts, at most we could be looking at the ability to try 192 jury trials a year. Currently, there are over 12,000 [felony] cases filed every year.

Judges concur that the benefits include handling huge caseloads in an expedient way. One judge had a very interesting take on it by calling plea negotiation "a rough form of justice":

It disposes of a huge number of cases quickly and inexpensively. And it is a rough form of justice.

Extremely important because our court systems would stop if we didn't have plea negotiation.

Expediency.

We can't do it any other way.

It [to do away with plea negotiation] would be overwhelming and catastrophic. Absolutely catastrophic.

Our goals here are twofold: first, to change plea bargaining in order to address the major concerns that have been identified and discussed in prior chapters, and second, to identify relevant, comprehensive changes to plea negotiation and the related processes and procedures in the pretrial system that allow all involved to make better, more informed decisions with the primary objective being reducing recidivism. Part of this involves ensuring that defendants receive appropriate defense counsel, enjoy due process protections, and are able to make informed, voluntary decisions regarding plea deals offered by the government. It also involves providing key decision makers, such as prosecutors, judges, and defense attorneys, with accurate, clinically derived information regarding defendants' circumstances, disorders, and impairments so that they can make better decisions regarding things like diversion, intervention, and rehabilitation.

There are two parallel outcomes that we hope these recommendations can achieve: leveling the playing field for criminal defendants in plea negotiation regarding due process protections, defense representation, and counterbalancing the discretion and power of prosecutors, and at the same time effectively and cost efficiently reducing recidivism. The recidivism focus specifically targets offenders with mental health problems, substance use disorders, cognitive impairments, and intellectual disabilities, as they characterize the majority of individuals who continuously cycle in and out of the justice system and in so doing consume vast amounts of resources. However, what we propose can apply to offenders without such impairments and disorders by identifying changeable, crime-related circumstances and providing appropriate, evidence-based rehabilitation services. The point is to make better decisions about punishment versus rehabilitation, retribution versus behavioral change.

Our analysis of plea negotiation—including extensive review of the research and expert opinion, case law, recommendations for reform, public opinion about the criminal justice system, our interviews with the key players in the process, and a broader understanding of the pretrial system within which plea negotiation occurs—led us to four primary targets of reform. We discuss two of them in this chapter: (1) transforming plea negotiation in order to effectively reduce recidivism, and (2) mitigating the due process concerns about plea negotiation and the largely unfettered discretion of prosecutors. In the next chapter, we: (1) address the excessive reliance on pretrial detention and other counterproductive aspects of the pretrial system that precede and impact plea negotiation, and (2) discuss reforms for the crisis in public defense.

TRANSFORMING PLEA NEGOTIATION TO REDUCE RECIDIVISM

We presume that the purpose of a criminal justice system is to enhance public safety and reduce recidivism and victimization and to do so cost efficiently. It is clear that American criminal justice policy has failed to accomplish these objectives. It is also evident that plea negotiation has played a central role in promoting crime control policies by expediting the prosecution, conviction, and punishment of millions of misdemeanor and felony offenders, especially over the past five decades of pronounced tough-on-crime policies. It has done so principally by placing extraordinary power and discretion in the hands of prosecutors—those who decide whom to prosecute, who is guilty, what they are guilty of, and what is the appropriate punishment.

Our concern here is that this system of adjudication, conviction, and punishment may not result in the best decisions and, in turn, the best outcomes. We have convincing evidence in the form of recidivism rates that the outcomes are poor for most involved. We believe that one of the primary reasons for poor outcomes is that prosecutors lack the appropriate information and expertise to make informed decisions about who should be prosecuted and punished on the one hand and who should be diverted and treated on the other. We also suggest that many prosecutors work in environments and cultures that perpetuate the punishment-focused resolution of cases. Many criminal offenders arrive at the justice system with complex comorbidities as well as a variety of negative experiences such as trauma and growing up in an environment of poverty. These are challenging situations without one-size-fits-all solutions and certainly are not situations for which punishment is likely to change behavior in a positive direction.

The end game for us is fundamental, comprehensive criminal justice reform, meaning policies and procedures that identify and mitigate why individual offenders are involved in crime and, in turn, that significantly reduce recidivism. We cannot propose meaningful criminal justice reform without considering the prime role that plea bargaining has played in getting us where we are today and, much more important, the ways in which plea negotiation needs to change in order to produce meaningful reform.

We begin by reiterating the fact that the criminal justice system is flooded with offenders with a variety of disorders, impairments, and deficits and that the recidivism rate for disordered offenders is in the neighborhood of 70 to 75 percent. We maintain that one of the key reasons that the justice system is flooded with disordered offenders is that plea bargaining provides a very quick, easy, and efficient means to prosecute, convict, and punish large numbers of offenders in a relatively short period of time. Plea bargaining is all about speed. Prosecutors and public defenders' caseloads and judges' dockets place extraordinary pressure on the primary players in this process to move cases and people. This method of doing business is in part a result of state legislatures' and local governments' refusal to properly fund and staff prosecution, public defense, and courts to handle the crushing volume of cases. As one observer of misdemeanor plea processing put it, "I felt I was watching justice dispensed at the pace of speed dating."[1]

What is typically negotiated in a plea deal is time—length of punishment, such as years of incarceration or probation. How much punishment is generally determined by some measure of harm perpetrated—the seriousness of the instant offense and prior criminal involvement. That is the currency of the exchange. It is largely a harm-based system of punishment. Punishment is what most prosecutors and defense counsel understand and barter day in and day out. That, in turn, reinforces our nearly unilateral reliance on punishment.

One of the results of this relentless focus on speed and efficiency is loss of the consideration of the individual offender and his or her circumstances. What is often considered are categories or aggregates of offenders—drug offenders, domestic violence offenders, or habitual offenders. Sentencing laws, we suggest, perpetuate the focus on categories rather than individuals. Consider the federal sentencing guidelines' emphasis on putting offenders into essentially two categories: the offense level (a score) and the prior criminal history category (a score). Offenders are assigned to these categories with little opportunity for consideration of individual differences. In fact, consideration of individual differences is for the most part precluded by law by the identification of factors "not ordinarily relevant" for consideration in sentencing, such as age, education, employment, mental health status, or presence of a substance use disorder. Those factors that allowed judges to differentiate among offenders before the guidelines were put in place were made illegal by the Federal Sentencing Commission. Mandatory sentences, such as mandatory minimums or habitual offender laws, work in a similar way by stipulating that the only consideration is the instant offense and/or prior offenses. Truth-in-sentencing laws, which are designed to require offenders to serve longer percentages of the sentence imposed before they are eligible for consideration for release, are triggered by a particular offense, such as certain violent crimes. What is lost with the focus on aggregations and categories in addition to the consideration of individual circumstances is mitigation of sentences, which, in turn, promotes tough-on-crime policies.

It is arguably worse at the misdemeanor level because of greater case pressure, but there is little reason to think the situation is much better in felony prosecution. It appears that when prosecutors differentiate among defendants, it is generally in terms of offense-related factors and prior criminal involvement. It is noteworthy that only one or two of the dozens of prosecutors we interviewed suggested that when considering a case, they looked for or sought out evidence of mitigation. It was typically strength of the evidence, seriousness of the offense, and criminal history that drive the specifics of the plea deal:

I look at the strength [of the evidence], the seriousness, and I look at criminal record.

Type of offense, the facts, the criminal history, cooperative witnesses.

Strength of the case, looking at prior history, talking with victims, figuring out other mitigation, are there treatment concerns.

My twelve years of experience.

Public defenders pretty much confirm what prosecutors said:

Prior convictions of my client.

Strength of the prosecutor's case.

The nature of the offense, the facts of the particular case, criminal history, victims involved, and how they feel determine a plea offer.

If it's a murder case, they'll probably offer twenty to forty on their initial, and you'll need a compelling argument or mitigating evidence to bring down that offer. If it's a drug case, then they'll offer closer to the minimum. You'll also look at the priors; more priors means the higher sentence.

On the other hand, some prosecutors did say that when there is clear evidence of a mental health problem, many would consider that a mitigating factor. One public defender stated that sometimes mental health, addiction, and other individual characteristics are considered, but that is more the exception than the rule:

Depends on the prosecutor, your client's criminal history, age, drug addiction history, treatment history, type of offense, mental health history.

Observers describe a system that convicts en masse and moves so quickly that there is little time to consider matters such as "individual evidence or circumstances . . . individual guilt."[2] It is also a system that is often insensitive to considerations of culpability, criminal intent, and mental health, as our interviews with defense counsel and prosecutors confirmed. Caseload and docket pressure in conjunction with too few resources preclude much consideration of criminogenic circumstances and situations. Coupled with the broad discretion afforded prosecutors and plenty of tools to leverage or motivate a plea, it should be no surprise that the system is set up to convict and punish.

It is no wonder that individual characteristics are often left out of the calculus since there is relatively little emphasis on collecting relevant information about offenders' circumstances. Our interviews with public defenders and prosecutors affirmed our concern that screening and assessment of offenders are rare to nonexistent and that, when they do occur, they are of questionable quality. Many indicated that it was often up to defense counsel to raise an issue of a mental disorder in order for a defendant to receive any screening and assessment. Prosecutors and defense attorneys agreed that the quality of screening and assessments can be problematic.

Defense Counsel Interviews

Screening and assessment are nonexistent or rare:

> Not really.

> Rarely.

> I would say no, not at all.

> No they are not [screened]. Not at all. Prosecutors don't care about impairments or recidivism.

> Very rarely [screened].

> Some might get a quick screen in jail. If it's [a mental illness] not obvious, nothing shows up.

> It [the process] is just not set up to do that.

Any screening and assessment that is done is of questionable quality:

> Probation officers do the screening. There is probably room for improvement.

I think they miss a lot of things. Most of the assessment is self-reported, until they are acting so strange that someone else takes notice.

I wouldn't bet on their [those doing the assessments] experience.

Not really. They aren't properly screened according to any standard for proper care.

They get screened, but it's not something the scientific community would sign off on. . . . So I think it's rare that they will get a good screening.

They are not always the brightest bulbs, so I make sure to do my own screening.

You've got the jail who does the screening; a nurse might be doing it if you're lucky.

It's the police who do a really basic screening.

Several defense attorneys indicated that screening and assessment are often up to them to do:

A huge amount of it falls on the lawyer.

I usually have to bring it up, but I'm no expert. I'm not a psychiatrist.

We do that in investigating, talking to family members.

The defense initiates any screening and assessment. Prosecutors don't give a shit. Pretrial services work for the government, and I have no faith in them. It's up to the defense to do this.

Only a quick screen is done in jail if a person shows signs of a disorder. The screening would mostly come from us [public defenders].

Prosecutor Interviews

The short answer is that screening and assessment for disorders is not very common:

> It's not broadly done.

> It doesn't happen very often as far as I know.

> I don't deal with that too much, but I don't see it happening much.

> It's not automatic.

Several prosecutors stated that it is typically up to the defense attorney to raise the issue:

> They are usually only screened after the defense attorney has brought up the issue of a disorder. It isn't an initial and immediate process that is conducted.

> Their defense attorney will bring it up to us if they feel that their client has a mental illness or a disorder. . . . I do not think we screen everybody coming through the door.

> A lot of that is done by the defense attorney.

> I think once the defense attorney brings up the issue, then they are screened.

> It only happens if it's obvious and someone brings it up.

> I don't know how or when because it's up to the defense attorney.

Or, when a mental health problem is obvious, the prosecutor may request an evaluation:

> When we see that [indication of a mental health problem], we request a psych evaluation.

> I know it's obviously done in obvious cases.

One prosecutor expressed concern that the screening and assessment system is inadequate, resulting in at least some disordered offenders "slipping through the cracks":

> I think that there're a lot more people with some level of mental impairment that are probably slipping through the cracks, only because I imagine that the screening can't be lengthy enough to make great observations apart from what is obvious at the surface.

Judicial Interviews

Judges generally believe pretrial screening is adequate, at least in terms of how many individuals are routinely screened. They were not asked about who does the screening and how well it is done. They believe that while there are a good number of diversion programs for offenders, the limited capacity of these programs is a serious concern:

> We always need more. We are always working on a shoestring budget.

> No. It's growing and it's better than it ever has been, but it's not adequate.

> No. I would say substance abuse and mental health are huge. That's where the volume [of cases] is. There's certainly a gap there.

> In the federal system, Congress provides a lot of resources to monitor those that have been released. The state doesn't have anywhere near those resources. It's not perfect, but it's much better than the state system. However, the mentally ill are a problem in the federal system.

The fact that defendants are not routinely screened for important causes, correlates, or facilitators of criminal offending prevents serious consideration of mitigating circumstances and disorders. It may also be a matter of when any screening is done. If prosecutors do not have relevant information at the time of plea negotiation, that information obviously cannot be reflected in a plea deal.

Some of the circumstances that many criminal defendants present with, such as significant mental illness, an acute addiction, serious neurocognitive impairment, or a combination of all of these, can certainly provide important information about why some individuals engage in crime; they may speak to the culpability of certain individuals and can point to circumstances that may need to be addressed in order to reduce the likelihood that someone will end up back in the criminal justice system. It's simple: If we don't know about it, we can't fix it.

Public defenders were asked how disorder (mental illness, substance abuse, or neurocognitive impairment) is considered in a plea negotiation. It is remarkable that many defense counsel stated that they do not believe prosecutors think or care about offenders' disorders:

> State doesn't care.

> I don't find that prosecutors care.

> Not considered. Prosecutors in this county don't care.

> Not so much for prosecutors.

> It depends on the prosecutor.

> It is the exception.

> Very rarely. The government doesn't care.

> It's the exception. If I could get one prosecutor to give a shit about a mental illness. They just don't care.

> Only if the defense attorney makes it a consideration.

> Prosecutor doesn't think it [mental illness] is mitigating.

> On the felony side they consider it [mental illness (MI)] to be an aggravating factor rather than mitigating. MI makes them [defendants] scarier.

A few defense lawyers said it is used for mitigation and to speak to the matter of criminal intent:

> I use it to mitigate culpability or reduce punishment.

It could bear on an issue of mens rea in trying to negotiate to a lesser charge.

We use it to mitigate culpability, reduce sentences, and to clear up whether there was mens rea.

Many prosecutors indicated that mental illness could be a mitigating factor, resulting in leniency in terms of punishment:

If we find evidence of a mental illness, usually we are more lenient.

It's not a get-out-of-jail card, but we take that into consideration, and we won't go as hard on that individual.

It can be mitigation.

I might change my mind on an offer [after documentation of a disorder] with a lesser sentence, probation, or another diversion option.

It could be mitigating conduct, mitigating punishment; it could also be used to aggravate the punishment.

It [screening] can be done sometimes before the plea so we will have the information before negotiations.

Minimizing punishment.

Others considered mental illness more in terms of competency than of mitigation. Competency is the mental ability to assist in one's defense:

The defense, judge, or I can bring it up and check competency.

If someone is not competent, there can be no plea.

One was less amenable to considering disorders, especially substance use disorders:

It's not that big a consideration. I disagree that substance use offenders fall in the same category as mental illness and cognitive disorders. That [substance use] is a choice which is quite different from mental illness.

The fact that attempts to identify problems that defendants may have is not systematically done or is a low priority speaks volumes about efforts to reduce recidivism. It should be no surprise that many prosecutors do not think that reducing recidivism is up to them or, if it is, that the primary way to accomplish that is through punishment. While some jurisdictions around the country may have significantly different policies and approaches regarding these issues of disorder and assessment, a fair conclusion is that it is rarely systematic and comprehensive. In part, this is a consequence of our long-term focus on tough on crime and punishment. That priority does not automatically or often lead to mitigation.

There is no consensus regarding the prosecutor's role in reducing recidivism. The responses to the question of what your role is in terms of reducing recidivism fell into four primary categories: no role, limited role, more punishment as the way to reduce recidivism, and addressing the determinates of criminal involvement.

Several prosecutors do not believe they play any role:

> I'm not sure we play a role.

> We don't look at recidivism; we just look at the case before us.

> Reducing recidivism is a great thing, but I don't see that as my job.

Prosecutors commonly believe that recidivism is up to the offender:

> I'm jaded, but I just don't think people change. . . . People just don't give a crap anymore. They don't care about going back to jail.

> I don't know . . . I think it's up to the defendant.

> We are here to punish people for conduct. Whether or not someone chooses to reoffend after they have been punished is up to them. . . . They reoffend because it is their choice.

> I think people make choices. I can't do much about that.

Several think that they do play a role and that the primary tool they have available to reduce recidivism is punishment:

We play a huge role because if someone is going to be a repeat offender, then we will increase the punishment.

I think the best way to prevent recidivism is a long prison sentence. People can be rehabilitated, but too many times it's way too late in the game. Out of 100, we can save maybe three or four from being a repeat offender.

I think it's a big role. I think we need to look at the risk of recidivism, and if the risk is high, then we need to be more severe on the punishment.

Our general philosophy is that if we hold them accountable, then they won't want to do it again.

A significant number of prosecutors do not have any constructive ideas on how to reduce recidivism:

If there was a magic wand for it, we would've done it a long time ago.

I have no idea.

Even if I did think I had a role, I have no idea what to do.

That's the $10 million question, and I don't have an answer.

I would not be the right person to ask. I feel like we're ill equipped as prosecutors to handle that.

I definitely think that is one thing I do not know the answer for.

Then there are prosecutors who think that not enough is done to reduce recidivism. They understand that there are many factors that drive recidivism and that many of those factors are not being addressed:

If you have defendants with mental illness and homelessness, we have to do more for them because without help, they'll recidivate forever. Prison and jail. That's punishment. Probation is rehab, but it's limited. They need real treatment.

> Recidivism is a driver for making my plea offer. I take it into account so I can try and predict what their best option is and what will keep them away.

> We as prosecutors have to look at whether we are actually addressing someone's needs and the cause for the crime happening. Once someone gets into the cycle of committing offenses, just sending them to prison or jail will not fix the problem.

> We can play a role . . . in giving them tools to prevent them coming back into the system.

> The justice system seems to be obsessed in just moving cases and not listening to the needs of those offenders.

Many prosecutors do not believe they have many options beyond punishment. Those who do recognize that treatment is necessary, especially for mentally ill defendants, do not think that what is available is adequate. Several prosecutors expressed concern that the criminal justice system has become the dumping ground for many mentally ill:

> I don't think we are the right system for dealing with them [mentally ill].

> Many of the mentally ill don't belong here.

The judges we interviewed varied considerably in terms of whether they believe they play much of a role in reducing recidivism. In theory, one would assume that judges consider recidivism when they impose sanctions. However, since most case dispositions are plea deals in which the prosecutor effectively sets the sentence, judges usually do not have a direct impact.

One judge thinks that recidivism reduction is a very challenging proposition:

> We have a raft of programs we use in the hopes of reducing recidivism. If you haven't graduated from high school, we'll make you get a GED. We have dozens of programs. But it's a battle, and I don't know what the solution is. These people grew up in poverty and have substance abuse problems. It's difficult to rehabilitate them because

they have never been habilitated. We do the best we can with limited resources.

Another said she had no responsibility for reducing recidivism:

Recidivism to me is based on how you were raised. By the time I'm involved, a whole lot of decisions have been made by the defendant. So, my quick answer is that I'm not.

Another said it is generally up to the individual judge:

It's really individualized as to how cynical you are and how proactive you are with trying to improve things.

One judge offered that they have a broader responsibility to reduce recidivism:

I think we have an obligation to improve the criminal justice system across the board with recidivism in mind. I feel like judges have a responsibility to work holistically on reducing recidivism.

Several stated that they can play a role when dealing with offenders on probation:

I see them throughout their probation. That accountability and relationship they have with me is extremely important to their success.

For me, that's the hand holding on the probation end in giving them skills. We don't want them to come back.

Those in charge of making the decisions about whom to prosecute, convict, and punish are lawyers. Prosecutors know the law and criminal procedure. The same is true for defense counsel (most typically public defenders/appointed counsel) and judges. These individuals are not behavioral health experts. They do not generally have expertise in psychiatry, psychology, neuroscience, or addiction medicine, and as a result, they are ill equipped to make determinations about offenders' mental or cognitive health. Unfortunately, there is often no one else in the process who is responsible for making such determinations. As we learned from the interviews, it is largely up to these individuals, more often defense counsel, to initiate any screening and assessment for a disorder. Again, the situation does not appear systematically better across the country.

These factors, in combination with a largely punishment-focused system of justice, are the essential ingredients for the revolving door that characterizes the American criminal justice system. Routinely prosecuting, convicting, and punishing offenders who have a variety of behavioral, cognitive, and intellectual disorders (as well as employment and financial problems, educational deficits, family problems, medical conditions, and homelessness, among others) and expecting them to respond positively to punishment is simply naive. Recidivism data leave little doubt. So where do we go from here?

Where we go first, it seems to us, is the prosecutor's office. There is little doubt that prosecutors conduct the essential business of the criminal justice system. While there are many actors and agencies that deal with criminal offenders, at the end of the day, one would be hard-pressed to find anyone who has more influence on case outcomes than prosecutors. Those decisions set the stage for what happens to offenders once they are processed through the court system. It is prosecutors who typically provide the opportunities for diversion and alternatives to traditional prosecution, conviction, and punishment, as limited as they often are. But it is also prosecutors who have carried the tough-on-crime torch for decades. As we described in chapter 1, prosecutors are the primary implementers of crime control policies.

The evidence distinctly indicates that what can reduce recidivism for many is diversion from traditional criminal prosecution, conviction, and punishment.[3] Diversion, when properly designed and operated, can minimize the negative, often criminogenic consequences of exposure to the criminal justice system and provide a combination of intervention, treatment, and rehabilitation while effectively managing the risk of re-offending.

What this tells us is that these key decision makers in the criminal justice system should be those who assume primary responsibility for reducing recidivism. As it currently stands, no one appears to be in charge of recidivism. If we are serious about meaningful criminal justice reform, it is time that recidivism reduction be the primary goal and that prosecutors accept that responsibility—but not without considerable assistance, which in part involves helping prosecutors make better decisions.

In our book *From Retribution to Public Safety: Disruptive Innovation of American Criminal Justice*, we proposed a comprehensive renovation of the criminal justice system. It begins with acknowledging that our legacy of tough on crime has its roots in retribution or just deserts, with little regard for individual circumstances and little regard for whether such punitive efforts can and do enhance public safety. Prosecutors and judges have for decades seemingly engaged in anger- or morality-based decision making and when it comes to sentencing often have posed three questions: how much harm has an offender done in committing the instant offense, how much harm has he or she perpetrated in the past, and thus how much punishment does he or she deserve as a result? This response to crime has been largely automatic or reflexive with ostensibly little regard for longer-term outcomes. We propose

> a model based on outcomes, particularly recidivism reduction, not blameworthiness and just deserts. The approach shifts the focus from a largely exclusive assessment of moral responsibility and harm done, which usually leads automatically to how much punishment, to an emphasis on what is the best way to resolve a criminal situation and reduce the likelihood of an individual reoffending.[4]

Part of this effort is changing how we think about crime and punishment and, in turn, changing how we make decisions. A guiding principle is that of problem solving. Before us is an offender who has broken the law. This situation poses a problem. The question we should ask is, what will it take to significantly reduce the likelihood that this individual will reoffend? Are there solutions to this problem that can significantly reduce the likelihood of reoffending down the road? That, by definition, is a longer-term proposition and requires a reorientation of our thinking from the moment to the future. Closing cases is in the moment. Recidivism reduction is a longer-term proposal.

The American criminal justice system is not currently in the business of asking the right questions and compiling the right information necessary to take actions to effectively reduce recidivism. Many jurisdictions use risk assessments, which are designed to predict the risk of reoffending. Recent research evaluated the predictive accuracy of COMPAS, one of the most widely used risk assessment instruments in the United States today. The analysis shows that COMPAS, which was first used to assess risk in 1998, is no better at predicting recidivism than individuals with little or no criminal justice expertise guessing based on limited information.[5] The individuals were given basic information about defendants' sex, age, and prior criminal history. The COMPAS predictions were based on 137 items in the questionnaire. Not all risk assessment instruments are created equal.

The Texas Department of Criminal Justice has adopted the Texas Risk Assessment System (TRAS), which is a modification of the Ohio Risk Assessment, a commonly used assessment instrument. The TRAS, as is the case with the Ohio Risk Assessment, consists of seven domains: criminal history, education/employment/financial situation, family/social support, neighborhood conditions, substance use, peer associations, and criminal attitudes. This risk assessment and others like it are used to make decisions at the pretrial stage (such as detention or release and pretrial supervision), for plea negotiation, at sentencing, for probation supervision, in prison, and for parole release.

According to the Texas Department of Criminal Justice, the TRAS is

> designed to help community supervision, prison, reentry and aftercare professionals create custom case management programs for individual offenders. The Texas Risk Assessment System or TRAS interprets an offender's criminal history along with their criminogenic needs, allowing criminal justice professionals to devise the most efficient case plans possible, enabling the agency to carefully allocate supervision resources and, in turn, reduce offender recidivism rates and increase public safety.[6]

The intention may be laudable, but the effort falls short. While the TRAS and other similar risk assessment instruments focus on some key predictors of recidivism, there is a great deal of information that is relevant for "custom case management plans" to "reduce offender recidivism rates and increase public safety" that is missing from such risk assessments. For example, there is nothing regarding mental illness, trauma, neurocognitive impairment, or intellectual disability, factors that are commonly implicated in criminality. Risk assessments are designed largely for indicating the level of intensity of supervision and control, not for developing intervention or treatment plans. It makes as much sense as the following. Assume you are having chest pains, so you go to the hospital emergency department. When you arrive, they ask questions that are designed to assess your risk of heart disease, factors such as being overweight/obese, exercise patterns, family history of heart disease, smoking, alcohol consumption, and cholesterol, among others. That's it. They do not perform a physical exam or conduct tests. A diagnosis based on risk factors rather than examination, testing, and identification of actual symptoms is medical malpractice.

Some jurisdictions use separate instruments that may more directly identify criminogenic circumstances. While these instruments are commonly referred to as needs assessments, it is more accurate to call them screeners rather than assessments since they tend to be highly abbreviated, check-box types of instruments. Use of these screeners is highly variable. Whether utilizing a risk assessment alone or a risk and needs assessment, the administration of these assessments usually falls on probation officers or pretrial supervision officers. In some needs assessments we reviewed, such as the Strategies for Case Supervision, the "officer's impression" is a data point for determining the presence of a mental illness.

Expediency is an important consideration in the screening and assessment of criminal offenders. One of the key advantages of instruments like the Ohio Risk Assessment or the TRAS is that administration is quick. But there are obvious trade-offs, one of which is the depth and quality of the information obtained, especially regarding criminogenic or crime-related circumstances.

It is important to emphasize that the evidence we do have regarding criminogenic circumstances and crime indicates that many offenders present with complex histories and situations and complex comorbidities. It is naive to think that generally quick screeners or assessments can discover the presence of all relevant conditions let alone their severity or more complex comorbidities. The point is simple. In order to address and mitigate the relevant crime-related conditions, in turn reducing recidivism, we need to know what they are.

Because of the importance of getting it right and the often complex situations that disordered offenders present with, we recommend an approach that brings necessary expertise into the screening, assessment, and diagnosis of offenders. We propose the use of independent expert panels of behavioral health experts, including psychiatrists, psychiatric nurse practitioners, addiction medicine experts, psychologists, and clinical social workers, who are responsible for utilizing evidence-based assessment and diagnostic tools and protocols in order to identify, on a case-by-case basis, the primary circumstances or disorders related to individuals' criminality. In turn, these expert panels would also be responsible for identifying which of the primary circumstances or disorders should be addressed and how they should be addressed and in what order. In effect, they are responsible for developing treatment plans and overseeing interventions.

These expert panels would also determine risk of reoffending in addition to identifying simple and complex criminogenic needs. The balanced consideration of risks and needs would inform their recommendations regarding whether individual offenders are candidates for diversion from traditional criminal indictment, prosecution, conviction, and punishment or whether they should be incarcerated or otherwise punished with little concern for criminogenic circumstances. Such diversions would not be a "get-out-of-jail-free card" but are situations that include risk management (e.g., supervision, electronic monitoring, and aggressive case management) and clinical intervention and rehabilitation. Incarceration and punishment would be recommended based on the offense (e.g., a violent crime), offense history (such as a habitual offender), and/or the panels' assessment of whether someone is able to be rehabilitated.

This expert assessment and diagnosis should occur as early in the process as possible, even at the point of arrest. The use of crisis intervention teams or mental health units in local law enforcement has expanded in recent years. These specially trained police units respond to mental health situations and crises, often with diversion alternatives to mental health treatment or stabilization facilities rather than jail. In limited jurisdictions, these teams are proactively seeking out the mentally ill in the community and getting them connected to services.

Early assessment and diagnosis is critical so that the information that is generated may be utilized in the early stages of processing. This includes magistration or the initial appearance where the decision to detain in jail or release is made. Such information and the associated recommendations by the expert panel should be important for prosecutors who fairly early on are in the process of making decisions about the parameters of a plea deal and sentencing recommendations. This information should also be essential at sentencing hearings to help the judge make an appropriate decision regarding a sentence in those situations where the judge sets the sentence. If the court is concerned with recidivism, knowing the factors that are associated with offending and, in turn, that should be mitigated is highly relevant information. That, combined with risk and the panel's recommendations, can greatly assist the prosecutor and the judge make informed decisions that provide opportunities for mitigation of criminogenic circumstances while preserving public safety.

We were able to test this concept in the interviews we conducted with prosecutors, defense counsel, and judges. We presented the basics of the concept to interviewees and asked them about their impression of the concept, whether they thought it could be useful and valuable, what concerns they have with it, and how the concept might be best presented to their colleagues. The relevant text from the interview guide is presented below:

> Consider the following idea. Panels of independent experts like psychologists, neuroscientists, addiction specialists, and psychiatrists routinely screen and assess defendants for things like mental illness, substance use disorders, neurocognitive impairments, and intellectual deficits. These experts would determine who is significantly disordered as well as their risk of reoffending, especially for violent crimes. In turn, they would make recommendations to the prosecutor regarding who should be diverted to treatment and supervision/ risk management and who should be traditionally prosecuted and sentenced. Assume for the purposes of this question that there are sufficient diversion resources for diverting and treating these disordered defendants.
>
> Is that something that you view as potentially valuable?
>
> What concerns do you have? What barriers might there be to adoption of this idea?
>
> How might this concept be proposed to defense attorneys/prosecutors? What might serve as an incentive to promote this idea to the defense bar/prosecutors?

Defense Counsel Interview Results

There is essentially universal enthusiasm among public defense for the concept of independent panels of clinical experts who screen and assess, determine risk, make recommendations to prosecutors, develop treatment plans, and oversee interventions. Several noted that the greater need, in terms of numbers, is at the misdemeanor level. Several indicated that it would provide information they currently do not have:

Yes, yes, yes, yes.

Yes, I like the idea of an independent board of experts separated from the state.

Hugely valuable.

I love the idea.

I would love that.

100 percent yes. Not something we currently do.

I think most people would welcome the idea.

Yes, especially in municipal court. There are 12 million arrests for misdemeanors, 2 million for felonies. Misdemeanor court—the vulnerable financially, psychologically, the people who need help are there. It could be a clearinghouse to direct people to services.

We could take that opportunity to identify things other than evil and malice at the root of things people do.

Yeah. For the clients I have that means another layer of investigation for their case and some authority other than me to tell the DA "this person needs mental health treatment, not jail or regular probation." I can think of a ton of clients who should be getting that result.

Absolutely, anything and everything would be better than what we have now because we don't address any of those issues. State courts take the lead because they have mental health courts, veterans' court. Federal court has nothing at all.

This would greatly help reduce recidivism.

More and more psychologists agree that criminal behavior is a direct result of mental disorders and the criminal justice system hasn't changed to reflect that.

Self-medicating is a huge reason for a lot of the crimes I see, and a holistic approach that could speak to that would be beneficial.

Several identified conditions that are required in order for this to be valuable. These include independence from the prosecutor, agreement, or buy-in by prosecutors and availability of adequate capacity for appropriate, competent treatment:

If prosecutors are on board, it would be ridiculously helpful to the community and to clients. It would lead to better outcomes for clients.

I think it could be if it's not under the DA's control. It would be good if it were independent experts.

The actual independence of the committee would be crucial.

If we had all actors committed to moving the mentally ill away more quickly, then we'd have a more efficient and less costly system. . . . They [prosecutors] assume they need to be incarcerated to receive treatment, and that is counterintuitive to the problem.

Yes, if the experts are detached and not working for the government . . . this can be valuable if it leads to better outcomes for my clients.

Only if it comes with attendant services. It's one thing to evaluate them, another thing to treat them.

100 percent. I'm on board. But I don't think prosecutors would welcome it. They are numbers-driven agencies that get their funding from Congress based on prosecutions and not diversions.

Defense counsel had several concerns with the expert panel concept. Most typically, confidentiality and preventing the state from using it against a defendant were key issues raised by defense attorneys:

Possibly an issue where it gets into facts of the offense and the person might not keep their info confidential. We could lose info that was originally protected under attorney/client privilege. If their attorney was present, then that might mitigate that concern.

If it's postadjudication and the chances of him being hurt by that information is limited, then its full sail.

We always want to know more about our clients than anyone else does. If there's a group of people interviewing our clients and gathering information and we don't have control over how that information is used and what it does, we're not going to like that.

Confidentiality is a big concern.

The information could actually hurt my case.

Maybe the information will not help my client.

When, how, and where the information is gathered and disseminated to the state and the court because it is not always beneficial to my client.

My concern is that the DA would have all of this background information to use in the future against my client.

Prosecutors don't want to be seen as not prosecuting someone because of some recommendation by a third party.

If you can get over the hurdle of establishing a clear, independent third party.

There would have to be some policy that the DA actually respects the decision of the panel. Otherwise it will just be more of the same, which is that the DA still has all the power and they only give diversion to a small percentage of people.

Defense counsel indicated that the defense bar would be on board without much effort. Several said that a very important incentive is to emphasize the positive outcomes for clients. A few had suggestions about mitigating potential concerns, including confidentiality and the independence of the panel:

To public defenders, I don't think you would need much convincing . . . you would probably get a lot of support.

I think they'd absolutely agree.

The defense bar would be on board. They would love that.

I would emphasize the positive outcomes for the client.

Better outcomes. Possibility of dismissal.

A better and more through resolution for their client's case. I think that is something everyone would want.

As long as the attorneys understand that they will get more positive outcomes for their clients, it should be an easy sell.

Easy, if it's a way of determining what your client needs.

Assuring confidentiality.

Solving the confidentiality problem.

Don't have it under the auspices of the court or the DA's office.

Having input in how they [expert panelists] are chosen.

If you can get over the hurdle of establishing a clear, independent third party, then I think we wouldn't need much incentive.

Prosecutor Interview Results

Many prosecutors stated it is a good idea because it provides them with information they probably would not have otherwise. They made the point that as lawyers, they do not have the expertise to make determinations about mental illness. They believe that the assistance would be very valuable. Some also indicated that it could produce better, fairer results:

Yes, that is the ideal model I think. We want to be certain that we are doing everything we can for the defendants, and I think this ensures that.

It's an invaluable tool to better assess offenders and make more informed decisions.

I would say in the abstract yes. . . . More info is always better.

I think that is a good idea . . . a lot of lawyers don't have any background in dealing with the mentally ill, so yeah . . . I think that would be a helpful tool.

Absolutely. I think a lot of people fall through the cracks.

I think it could be valuable . . . knowing as much as I can is always of help.

Most definitely. I didn't go to medical school. I'm not a medical professional of any kind. What I know is what I've read. It's my gut feeling. So if there were independent experts, third parties not working for either side, then I think their input would be invaluable to me.

Yeah, it would ease the burden for attorneys to make those evaluations who aren't really trained in mental health.

Most definitely. We are not doctors or counselors. I'm a lawyer. We are not trained in that area, so when you bring this body of people with training, it's invaluable.

It would be because there needs to be something else to help those that are disordered. There is nothing in place at the moment. . . . I also like the fact that it would be coming from a third party outside of what I do.

Any process that gives me more information to make a more informed decision is valuable to me.

Yes, definitely. Especially the evaluation about whether or not incarceration would be an effective punishment. I think we aren't really equipped to make that determination.

If you are a prosecutor and your only goal is convictions, then that wouldn't help you. But if you are hoping for the best resolution possible for the community and for the defendant, we want them to be successful, and we hope we'll never see them again. Expanding these programs to include this idea you're talking about could be even better.

Absolutely. Right now, we're basing a lot of our decisions on what a very small group of people with little training are recommending, and they are connected to the defense bar. I think this is a much more persuasive method.

Definitely. That would make the docket more workable, and it would actually help folks who don't need to be in the criminal justice system.

It seems like a fair thing to do.

Others gave more qualified yes responses. Their concerns included whether there are appropriate resources to actually address mental illness:

Yes and no . . . there is no way to fix some of these mental illnesses.

In a perfect world, yes. However, the resources would never exist. . . . I can agree with the hypothetical, but it will never happen.

You would need money and a place to send these people. You can't have the panel if there is no concrete place to get treatment.

I think that it would be, but I also think that it would eventually become just another bargaining chip.

If it was fair absolutely. As long as it isn't biased in a defense-oriented way.

I think it's a good starting point . . . as long as judges are not involved in that process.

The primary concern the prosecutors had with the expert panel concept was that it could mitigate punishment:

You are going to risk looking lenient by doing these kinds of things when other prosecutors could just put them in prison and be done with it and keep their reputation.

My concern would be that those people wouldn't be held accountable.

I think it's one more way our criminal justice system is tailored to focus on defendants. They have all the rights. Victims of crime are never considered, and this is just one more step in that direction. We are not punishing it, we are just trying to excuse it and fix it with a hug.

Mental illness is something that needs treatment, but you can be a criminal with a mental illness. When it causes it or when it doesn't, if the board says everyone just needs treatment, then that's not helpful.

They are not lawyers. They are looking at it from one standpoint and not taking into consideration what the offender did and the impact on the victim. They don't understand the case from a legal standpoint.

Other concerns involved the potential for error and issues of criminal intent:

But what if they are wrong? What if you go along with the recommendation and they end up killing somebody? You end up being the person responsible for it.

The issue and biggest challenge would be the degree of culpability. . . . You have to show that their mental illness made them unaware that their actions were wrong.

Most of the recommendations for proposing the expert panel concept to prosecutors involved pragmatic considerations, such as reduced caseload and expedited case processing:

It would directly affect [reduce] the caseload.

Tell courts and prosecutors that this would help with their caseloads and move cases quicker.

We are diverting more cases from adjudication and can focus on the cases that matter. This is what we [prosecutors] want.

A pitch would be: We should adopt this idea because those that need to get help and don't belong in the criminal justice system would be out of our way. We would be able to focus on the actual cases plaguing us.

A few emphasized that the expert panel can lead to better decision making:

I think if you tell prosecutors that they can have someone else make the decision, they will be happy. They won't have to think about that anymore and just see what the board recommends.

Just remind everybody that you are here to seek justice, not convictions.

Independence was an issue for a couple:

Emphasizing that it's an independent party would help.

Some prosecutors might be skeptical because in our business we see experts that are not truly independent.

Judicial Interview Results

Across the board, the federal and state judges we interviewed think the expert panel concept is a good idea:

Yes. If we evaluate people on a case-by-case basis and having them evaluated by a group of experts who have knowledge of this, then definitely it would be helpful and welcomed.

I think that would be ideal. This would be a great system if we could get there. I'm all for it.

Sure, yes. I mean, I think the more research we have, the better for us to know how to deal with the population.

It would be hard to argue against that.

That could be really valuable.

I think it'd be great. I see a lot of logistical obstacles, but I think it'd be hard to integrate that and get the resources to accomplish that. But I think it would be very helpful to have a better picture of the person than what we currently get.

I'm not a psychiatrist, so that would be really helpful.

Concerns centered around pushback from the defense bar and funding:

We do get a lot of pushback from the defense bar because they don't believe it's in their best interest for their client to be evaluated.

You have to get the defense bar on board. . . . If the defense objects, it won't happen.

Money is the only concern.

I'd be hard to integrate and get the resources to accomplish that.

I don't know how we would have the resources with the amount of felonies we have.

Judges seem to think their colleagues would embrace the idea:

I think if the concept was proposed to judges I work with, they would welcome it. Everyone wants to see a better result. So if we can divert them and reduce recidivism, then I think that would be a win for everyone.

I think it is a great idea, and I don't think anyone would really be opposed.

It could reduce recidivism. That's an easy sell.

The concept is a long way from design, implementation, and operation, but the initial feedback from a reasonably large number of prosecutors, judges, and public defenders is quite positive. The expert panel concept can substantially change how we go about the business of administering criminal justice in this country but only in conjunction with adequate, appropriate, evidence-based treatment capacity at the community level. We know from a good bit of research[7] and from what the prosecutors and defense lawyers told us that there is a serious lack of adequate diversion options and treatment capacity. Prosecutors, public defenders, and judges stated that while there are some diversion programs, capacity is quite limited, resulting in large gaps between needs and available services. Many believe that not enough is being done to help mentally ill offenders. A good bit of this is due to long-term defunding of public health at the federal, state, and local levels.[8]

Aside from legal and logistical issues regarding the expert panel concept, it is likely that some reorientation of prosecutors' perspectives about their roles and responsibilities will be necessary. Having new, expert information is critical for better decision making, but equally important is who (if anyone) uses it and how it is used. Many prosecutors told us they do not think of themselves as having much of a role with regard to recidivism reduction. That needs to change, especially if expert information regarding disordered defendants is routinely provided along with recommendations regarding diversion, treatment, and case disposition. Perhaps prosecutors believe they do not play much of a role regarding recidivism because historically their playbook has been rather limited. As the options and alternatives expand, prosecutors can play a fundamental role in reducing recidivism, and it is important that they realize that.

We believe that what we have outlined here can provide prosecutors with the information necessary to make better, more informed decisions regarding diversion to treatment versus traditional criminal prosecution, conviction, and punishment. To be clear, we are not saying we should disregard punishment as a consequence for criminal conduct. There are certainly many situations where retribution is an appropriate response, where the moral blameworthiness of an individual offender calls for punishment, pure and simple. Accountability is an important objective as well, as is incapacitation and control in the form of incarceration or community supervision. At the same time, those in charge of making the key decisions in the U.S. criminal justice system—most importantly prosecutors but also judges and defense counsel—must realize the shortcomings of punishment, especially the longer-term limitations in terms of recidivism reduction, as well as longer-term consequences, such as economic productivity, mental health, community and family stability, and educational goals, among others.

We do not see plea bargaining going away, nor do we envision the rate of plea negotiation declining by any significant amount. A variety of structural, procedural, and financial constraints and realities will probably keep plea deals alive and well and as the primary way in which criminal cases are disposed.

What we can change are the significant concerns discussed in chapter 4 and potential remedies we discussed in chapter 5 as well as the role that plea bargaining has played in perpetuating business-as-usual, tough-on-crime, punishment-based justice policies. Plea negotiation has been the pipeline to prison and jail, it seems, because punishment makes sense and is a safe choice for prosecutors and because prosecutors have had limited options in terms of addressing crime. Those limited options and the fact that the criminal justice system is in reality a series of silos with little horizontal integration has probably supported prosecutors' belief that recidivism is someone else's business.

Where this leads us is to providing prosecutors with expertise, information, and effective alternatives to punishment. We need to expand the menu of viable options so that prosecutors can accept that their decisions can and do fundamentally affect recidivism and other outcomes and so that they have the tools to make informed decisions about punishment on the one hand and behavioral change on the other. But it is not just prosecutors that need to be on board. Judges play a fundamental role, especially in terms of sentencing. The defense bar is important as well in advising their clients regarding their options. We often hear anecdotally about situations where a defendant is offered diversion to treatment but opts for jail or prison on advice of counsel because incarceration is quicker and easier than fulfilling the requirements of some diversion program. That may be good advice, but it is potentially shortsighted since there may be very little in the incarceration option that addresses criminogenic circumstances and recidivism.

All of the primary actors in the adjudication of criminal offenders should keep in mind that the end game is public safety, one case at a time. Public safety in many instances may mean incarceration, but wholesale incarceration as we have practiced it is not a model for reducing crime and recidivism. For many cases, public safety means reducing the probability of reoffending by identifying criminogenic circumstances; developing diversion, intervention, and risk management strategies; and having adequate capacity at the community level to carry out the recommendations of the experts. This requires the buy-in and coop-eration of all involved in *advancing the public good of a criminal justice system that effectively and cost efficiently reduces recidivism.*

The good news is that prosecutors and defense counsel are generally interested in the concept of expert assessment and diversion to treat-ment. Those we interviewed seem to welcome more information and expertise. Importantly, the public supports the idea that the justice system should promote rehabilitation and behavioral change (see chap-ter 8).

The concept of expert assessment and diversion sounds rather sim-ple and straightforward. However, we do not pretend that this will be easy. It not only involves fundamental, disruptive change in procedure, process, law, and funding but also requires cultural change in the jus-tice system, adjusting how we think about crime, punishment, human behavior, and behavioral change. It also requires fundamental changes to public health, public health delivery, funding, and capacity. We dis-cuss in some depth how we think the public health system should be reformed in our book *From Retribution to Public Safety: Disruptive Innovation of American Criminal Justice*. Identifying and mediating challenges and barriers are critically important and are the subject of chapter 8.

PLEA MEDIATOR

Expert observers consistently conclude that prosecutors are the most important individuals in the American criminal justice system. Our interviews with defense counsel, prosecutors, and judges confirm that prosecutors have broad discretion in charging, plea agreements, and sentencing.

The power and resource differential between the government and the defendant, between the prosecutor and the public defender, poses significant concerns about fairness. The collateral characteristics of this power and resource divide is the potential for the plea process to be coercive or, in the words of many we interviewed, that defendants often feel pressured to agree to a plea deal. At the same time, the procedural safeguards that are in place in the form of judicial review at the tail end of the process often amount to a perfunctory exchange of questions and rehearsed answers regarding whether the defendant voluntarily and knowingly accepted the plea deal. Moreover, plea negotiation is characterized as a process that occurs in courthouse hallways and jails and over the phone and as a black box to outsiders.

The late Harvard law professor William Stuntz describes plea bargaining as a process that occurs in a legal shadow:

> The defining characteristic of American-style plea bargaining may be that it does exist in the shadows, because it so often fails to internalize the laws that purport to govern it. . . . If plea bargains exist in some legal shadow, the shadow is cast by that law—the law that prosecutors make—and not by the law one reads in code books or case reports.[9]

Several plea negotiation reformers have proposed greater judicial involvement in the process in order to counter the discretion of the prosecutor, guard against coercion or pressure, and enhance the accuracy of the outcomes. Expanding judicial participation would require statutory and procedural changes in many jurisdictions. In most, it would require reallocation of resources and significant changes to court culture. The reason we have plea bargaining is not because it dispenses better justice or is fairer or more accurate than trials. It is not the product of thoughtful consideration of the best way to do the business of the criminal justice system. It is the result of too many offenders and too few resources and excessive and unmanageable dockets and caseloads for judges, prosecutors, and public defenders.

Therein lies one of the major problems with having judges be more involved in the plea process. Plea negotiation exists because it meets the needs of the principals involved in the process. Judges, prosecutors, and public defenders share the common interest in efficient case management, which translates into quickly processing people. Requiring judges to spend more time on plea deals without other adjustments to their dockets seems unworkable. As it currently stands in many metropolitan court systems, the number of cases pending that are carried over year after year is astounding. For example, in Travis County, Texas (Austin), the felony courts typically carry over from year to year up to 25,000 cases. The misdemeanor courts annually carry over around 85,000 cases. With what time are judges supposed to become more involved in the plea process? The Texas Office of Court Administration tracks criminal court activity by county. One of the performance measures used is the backlog index, which is a measure of the pending caseload relative to the courts' capacity to dispose of cases in a specified time period. A backlog index value of 1.0 means the courts disposed of the cases pending in one year. An index value of .5 means the courts dispose of the pending cases in six months. The average backlog index for the eighty counties that reported data in Texas is 10.4. This problem is not unique to Texas or even state courts. Backlog problems in federal courts are causing significant slowdowns in case processing as well.

We propose an option that we believe can address issues associated with plea bargaining, issues including fairness, coercion/pressure to plea, due process concerns, the power and discretion of prosecutors, and others.

Viewed as a dispute to be resolved between parties—the prosecutor on one side and the defendant on the other—a question arises as to whether dispute resolution strategies applied in other legal settings might be useful in the plea negotiation context. A significant proportion of civil legal disputes are resolved through alternative means, such as mediation and arbitration, rather than through formal legal processes. While mediation has occasionally been used in criminal cases, it is most often employed as a part of a restorative justice model to facilitate communication between offenders and victims. While this use of mediation has proven effective in that context, in this section we explore the potential benefits of using mediation not as a part of a restorative justice scheme but rather to facilitate the plea bargaining process in a typical criminal case.

Over the past thirty years, alternative dispute resolution has become an integral and indispensable component of civil litigation. The most common form of alternative dispute resolution mediation employs a neutral third party to facilitate negotiations between the parties in an effort to resolve disputes without the expense and inefficiency of the formal legal process. A skilled mediator assists the parties in recognizing the strengths and weaknesses of their relative positions and helps them explore mutually satisfactory outcomes.

To be sure, many of the features of civil disputes that make them amenable to mediation are not present in the context of criminal plea negotiations. Civil disputes often involve struggles over scarce commodities, failed relationships, broken contracts, hurt feelings, or hostility between parties. The goal of mediation in such circumstances is to divide disputed property equitably, make the aggrieved party whole, or restore strained relationships. While criminal plea negotiations do not have these features in common with civil disputes, we maintain that there are many more applications of mediation that have the potential to apply equally well in civil and criminal cases.

As we imagine the utility of mediation in the context of plea negotiations, we first address the appropriate circumstances for mediation and what it could add to existing practices. We propose that mediation is appropriate when defendants are not contesting their guilt. That is, mediation would be available once a defendant has decided that he or she is willing to accept a plea deal but the terms of the plea have not yet been agreed on. Issues subject to mediation, thus, are those relating to the appropriate disposition of the case, including the potential for diversion, the charge(s) to which the defendant will plead, and the length and circumstances of the sentence to be imposed. For a variety of reasons, mediation would be inappropriate for a defendant who maintains his or her innocence. Given that a guilty plea must be based on a knowing and voluntary admission by the defendant that he or she did indeed commit the offense, there is nothing to be negotiated until he or she is prepared to concede guilt. On the other hand, we believe that mediation offers potential benefits for each side once a defendant is willing and prepared to admit guilt, as discussed below.

While we believe that mediation as outlined below is an appropriate model for the resolution of many criminal cases, we recognize that, for a variety of reasons, such a model would be highly unlikely to be universally employed. It is novel. It adds cost. It might add inefficiency, though we believe that the structure and advantages it would bring to plea negotiations may well increase efficiency and in any event would be justified by the benefits. It raises potential questions about confidentiality and privilege, identified as follows. We do, however, believe that mediation could become an accepted practice in certain (if not all) cases.

An obvious application of mediation would be in those cases where the prosecution and defense have been unable to readily reach an agreement. In cases where plea negotiations have been unsuccessful because of resistance by one or both parties to proposed resolutions, we believe that a formal mediation regime like the one we propose would have great utility. And in the process of increasing efficiency by helping the parties arrive at a negotiated resolution, we have identified a variety of secondary benefits that would likewise result. We suggest that the mediation protocol that we describe be available on request of either party. In the event that this results in mediation being requested in a significant number of cases, we believe that this would only support our hypothesis that the protocol offers benefits unavailable in routine plea negotiations. Likewise, mediation might be appropriate for certain categories of cases and inappropriate for others. Mediation would, for example, be employed most effectively in cases where there is a broad range of possible outcomes, such as where diversion or probation subject to certain conditions are on the table, as opposed to cases with limited possibilities, such as those in which there is a mandatory minimum sentence.

Considering that the vast majority of cases are resolved by plea negotiation, a reasonable question arises as to whether mediation is needed at all. That is, if parties are managing to resolve the vast majority of cases without the benefit of mediation, it is reasonable to question what mediation would add to the process. We offer two plausible responses. First, the fact that most cases are resolved by plea negotiation says nothing about how efficient and fair the negotiations are, notwithstanding their ultimate success rate. Moreover, a good deal of expert analysis, as well as our interviews with public defenders, confirms a variety of due process and procedural concerns associated with plea negotiation. In some (if not most) jurisdictions, there are undeniably significant inequalities in resources between the prosecution and defense. It is not hard to imagine how this disparity of power can affect the fairness and equity of negotiations, much less outcomes. That is, just because most cases are resolved by plea negotiation says nothing about whether the outcomes are just. Although the adversarial system is presumed to ensure that the interests of both sides are sufficiently represented, it is undeniable that a disparity of resources and thus power and discretion might affect the fairness of outcomes. Second, given that current plea negotiations are engaged in informally and without any agreed-on protocols or structure, it is entirely possible that the introduction of a process for communicating information and negotiating offers might well streamline plea negotiations and increase efficiency.

In both civil and criminal cases, parties can benefit from an independent, neutral third party's perspective in a variety of ways. Given the fact that the parties in a criminal case have likely had no prior experience with each other—unlike parties in a civil case who have often had a relationship as competitor, customer, partner, or spouse—there is a case to be made that there is a greater gulf of understanding and communication between a prosecutor and a defendant in a criminal case. As they do in civil cases, mediators in a criminal plea negotiation can offer differing interpretations of events and circumstances. Parties (and even their lawyers) can suffer from tunnel vision, having focused on the situation from only their perspective. A mediator can propose alternate ways to frame the facts and help the parties see the problem from the other side's point of view. They can test assumptions of the strength of the evidence on which the parties have based their positions and expectations. In short, mediators can offer the parties the benefit of an objective, unbiased view of the situation that even the lawyers might miss.

One potential objection to participating in mediation to resolve a criminal case might be the lawyers' reluctance to engage in a process that might necessitate the disclosure of case theories, strategies, evidence, or defenses. As the mediation progresses, a mediator might pressure one side, particularly the prosecutor, to disclose more about their strategy than they might want in order to educate the defendant about the probabilities of conviction or a severe sentence. Given the fact that a failed plea negotiation will then result in a trial before a similarly objective decision maker—whether judge or jury—both parties should welcome the opportunity to test the strength of their positions in a risk-free setting. Mediation in a criminal case, as in a civil case, might serve to minimize the risk of unwanted outcomes. A mediator might point out—to a prosecutor or defense attorney alike—previously unrecognized weaknesses in arguments. Likewise, they may give a "reality check" as to how a judge or jury might respond to particular evidence or arguments. While highlighting potential negative outcomes, a mediator might help parties mitigate risk and identify alternate but mutually acceptable outcomes.

An important function of mediation that could pertain in a criminal setting even more than in a civil case is that of managing power inequalities. In most cases, the prosecution comes to the table with more resources, procedural advantages, and options than a defendant. The state has lawyers, investigators, officers and agents, and the budget to retain expert witnesses. The state generally decides when to seek indictments and warrants. If in custody, the defendant has limited access to counsel, evidence, and legal materials, not to mention the fact that he or she is experiencing the discomforts and disadvantages of incarceration. Finally, while all a prosecutor faces in the event of failure is the disappointment of losing and possible damage to reputation, the stakes for the defendant are serious—his or her personal liberty and property. A neutral mediator can seek to ensure that the prosecutor doesn't take advantage of this imbalance in bargaining power by identifying and confronting inappropriate uses of process or procedure or taking advantage of disparities in resources. A prosecutor inclined to overreach might be discouraged by having the plea negotiations filtered through a neutral third party. Likewise, a mediator might detect ways in which a defense attorney is failing to exploit legal and factual defenses or is simply conceding too readily to the government's position. We also believe that the involvement of an independent, neutral mediator can serve to ensure, through the mediator's inquiry, whether the plea was entered into in a knowing and voluntary manner, reducing the likelihood of involuntary confessions. In important respects, a mediator can serve to level the playing field. Thus, we believe that the mediator can mitigate many of the due process and fairness issues that have been raised about plea negotiation as currently practiced.

Since prosecutors and defense attorneys, especially public or court-appointed defenders, are often overburdened by large caseloads, the need to dispose of cases quickly and efficiently often leads to inadequate communication between the two sides. Plea agreements are often accomplished pursuant to court-imposed deadlines or immediately before trial, potentially depriving the parties of the opportunity to give careful consideration to risks and options. In some jurisdictions, the relationships between prosecutors and defense attorneys do not foster open and effective communication. In some, defense lawyers may find that discovery is difficult to obtain. As a consequence, plea negotiations may be conducted with incomplete information or at the last minute. It is unsurprising, then, that a common basis for claims of ineffective assistance of counsel lodged by defendants following their conviction and sentencing is that the terms and consequences of their plea were not adequately explained to them. They are thus able to claim that their pleas were not made knowingly and intentionally.

The use of an independent, neutral mediator during plea negotiations would serve the dual purpose of ensuring that each side had an adequate opportunity to consider the consequences of a plea as well as possible alternate outcomes. This would serve to give the parties a chance to pause for reflection during a process that is frequently rushed but that may have consequences for the defendant for years to come. And, depending on rules adopted for the use of information from the mediation, it might protect the plea agreement from later claims by the defendant that he or she did not have the opportunity to consider the consequences of and alternatives to his or her plea.

Mediation would also provide a framework to an otherwise unstructured exercise. While is it well understood that the vast majority of cases are resolved via plea negotiation, the lack of any formal process often leads to plea negotiations that are conducted haphazardly. They might be conducted during a brief phone conversation or in a crowded courthouse hallway. They frequently focus on the "end game" and do not entail a detailed analysis of the law, evidence, and needs of a particular case. They are often driven by external factors, such as time constraints, burgeoning caseloads, and scheduling. Mediation would provide some order to this process, giving the parties the opportunity to focus their attention on the appropriate disposition of the case without other distractions. An efficient mediator could assist the parties in concentrating on the core issues, ensuring that all relevant factors are considered before a deal is reached.

Finally, a secondary but important benefit of the mediation of criminal plea negotiations, where such mediations become routine and accepted, would be to provide a window into an otherwise opaque part of the criminal justice system. Because plea negotiations take place in private between the prosecutor and the defense lawyer and usually only the resulting agreement is disclosed, the public has no way to know what happened behind the curtain to get to the end result. Other than a blind faith in the efficacy of the adversarial system, there is virtually no way for the public to be assured that the results of a plea negotiation are fair, just, efficient, or appropriate. But blind faith in the adversarial system must assume the universal good faith of prosecutors and the diligence and competence of lawyers on both sides. While most lawyers in the criminal justice system are undoubtedly competent, diligent, and ethical, the record is replete with examples of overzealous prosecutors, ineffective defense lawyers, and overwhelming caseloads on both sides the docket.

Even if there is no good reason to question the diligence and good faith of the attorneys engaged in plea negotiations, the public should still have the means to test those assumptions and ensure that the players in this important arena are properly reflecting the values and goals of the criminal justice system as well as bigger-picture objectives that the public believe are important (we discuss public opinion about criminal justice policies in chapter 8). A mediator might thus serve as a neutral witness into this otherwise hidden world to identify ways in which either or both parties are behaving that betray their legal, ethical, and public policy obligations. This perspective could be helpful in identifying both systemic and individual problems. Just as one of the stated goals of sentencing guidelines is to ensure that similarly situated offenders receive more or less the same punishment or outcome, a mediator in an individual case might identify how a particular defendant is being treated with reference to how others similarly situated have been treated and try to determine whether the disparate treatment is justified. The mediator might be in a position to judge the outcome in a particular case against the average outcome in a comparable circumstance, identifying outliers, or cases in which one party might have failed to achieve a result that would be appropriate and expected. More broadly, a neutral mediator might, over time, identify ways in which the culture of plea negotiation in a given jurisdiction is systematically favoring one side over another or has evolved in such a way that the interests of justice or the community values are being ignored.

The mediator can also play a critical role with regard to the expert panel concept we discussed earlier in this chapter. A mediator can consider and weigh the recommendations made by the expert panels to ensure that their proposals are being seriously considered in the plea process. Having an independent mediator involved in this can function to increase the likelihood that the recommendations are included in the plea discussions.

As a practical matter, two threshold questions that must be addressed are, who would serve as mediators in a criminal case, and how would they be paid? An appropriate mediator in a criminal case would be an attorney with sufficient experience in criminal practice in the jurisdiction (i.e., local, county, state, or federal) where he or she practices. Regardless of the nature of his or her experience—whether on the prosecution or the defense side—they should be able to act—and be regarded as being able to act—neutrally and without bias. They might be retired or former judges who already appreciate and have experience as a neutral third party. They might also be respected practitioners who have significant experience as litigators on one side or both sides of the docket. They must, however, have the requisite experience and reputation to be regarded by all parties as knowledgeable, evenhanded, independent, neutral, and fair. They should, as is the case with mediators in civil practice, be trained in the best practices of mediation. They should understand and comply with the ethical rules that apply to neutral mediators. They should have a nuanced understanding of their role in facilitating discussion without imposing their own views or opinions. They must understand the importance of respecting the relationship between the defendant and his or her attorney. They must understand the need to respect the limits of the parties in disclosing matters of potential trial strategy should the negotiation be unsuccessful. And they should understand how issues of confidentiality and privilege are implicated during the mediation.

Unlike civil mediation, the cost of which is most often borne by the parties themselves, mediation in the context of criminal plea negotiation would likely have to be funded by a governmental entity, such as the court in which the case is pending or the city, county, or state government having jurisdiction over the proceeding. While courts and governments at every level operate with limited resources, we are confident that the need for and potential important benefits of mediation justify the expense. A well-run mediation program staffed with experienced mediators would add significant value to the system both by streamlining negotiations and by yielding the benefits identified above.

The structure of mediated plea negotiations could take a variety of forms. They could provide a review function whereby all or most plea agreements are subject to examination by the mediator to ensure due process compliance, proper assistance of counsel, and whether the expert panel recommendations were considered in the outcome. Another version would make mediation available as an adjunct to routine negotiations in the event that the parties are unable to reach a settlement readily; mediation could be available at the request of both or either party. In any event, both parties would have to agree to participate. It is also possible that mediation could be suggested by the court should it become apparent that the parties are having difficulty reaching an agreement, as long as it does not appear that the judge is pressuring the parties to settle so as to raise a question as to the voluntariness of the process. Mediation could take place in the context of a formal program in which mediators are full-time employees of the court or of a governmental or quasi-governmental agency. Or the court may refer cases to one of a standing panel of available mediators, much like cases are assigned to defense lawyers in jurisdictions that use assigned counsel for indigent defendants. In such a system, mediators could be paid a flat rate per case or hourly fees out of a fund established for that purpose. In either case, the court would maintain control of the standards of training and qualifications of mediators.

As is the case when any new protocol is proposed for a system, especially a legal system, we have tried to anticipate objections and challenges. To be sure, we allow for the possibility of initial resistance by lawyers on both sides of the docket. Prosecutors may view the process as an intrusion on their discretion to set the terms and parameters of plea negotiations. Defense attorneys may view it as an intrusion on their confidential relationship with their client. But we are confident that skilled and experienced mediators would be sensitive to these issues; thus, these concerns will prove unfounded. There are, however, potential legal and procedural concerns that should be addressed.

We propose a carefully drafted consent form for both parties, making explicit the voluntary nature of the exercise, emphasizing the role of the mediator as facilitator, and reinforcing the ability of the parties to exercise their own judgment as to the acceptability of any proposed resolution. With reference to the defendant, the consent form should make clear that the goals of the exercise are to facilitate communication, examine the risks in light of the facts, and explore possible resolutions. The role of the mediator should be clarified as that of a facilitator whose statements, opinions, and recommendations should be regarded as advisory, rather than binding or coercive. Finally, a plea taken as a result of a successful mediation should include an inquiry into the voluntariness of the mediation, a confirmation of the defendant's understanding that he or she is free to accept or reject the plea deal, and an affirmative confirmation that his or her plea is freely and voluntarily made. The judge should ask directed questions and elicit clear responses to document the voluntariness of the plea as well as other due process criteria, followed by specific findings to support such conclusions.

One issue that needs to be addressed is whether an agreement reached pursuant to mediation would be enforceable should either party fail to comply with its terms. It is hard to imagine that a prosecutor, having agreed to a disposition, would fail to follow through. A more likely scenario is that a defendant, given the opportunity to reflect on the deal, would change his or her mind and refuse to enter the envisioned plea. Given the necessity of voluntariness in entering a guilty plea, a defendant must have the opportunity up to the time his or her plea is taken and the judge confirms that his or her plea is knowing and voluntary to withdraw from any agreement. A question arises, however, as to whether, and the extent to which, a defendant may contest the voluntariness of a plea entered pursuant to a mediated negotiation once the plea is entered. In *State v. Milligan*, the Kansas Court of Appeals was faced with just such a scenario.[10] Milligan was charged with rape and engaged in plea negotiation facilitated by a mediator, a retired judge. Following mediation, during which the mediator expressed his opinion that Milligan would be convicted if he elected to go to trial, Milligan entered a plea of guilty. The terms of the final agreement were considerably better than the terms that the government had offered at the beginning of the negotiation. During the plea hearing, the judge inquired and Milligan confirmed that the plea was being entered into voluntarily and that the mediation had not been coercive. Nonetheless, following the plea but before sentencing, Milligan sought to withdraw his plea, claiming that it had been coerced by the mediator. The trial court denied his request, finding that the record reflected that mediation had not been coercive, and sentenced him consistent with the deal that had been negotiated. Milligan appealed. The Court of Appeals held that, because the trial court made the requisite findings of voluntariness, the denial of Milligan's motion to withdraw was not in error. This case illustrates the importance of a carefully conducted plea hearing during which the judge should make adequate inquiry and affirmative findings establishing that the plea is being freely and voluntarily made.

Another possible objection to mediated plea agreements would be the potential for a mediator to interfere with the relationship between and defendant and his or her attorney. As we have suggested, one role of the mediator would be to challenge assumptions of the parties with regard to the strength of the evidence, the application of the law, and the probabilities relating to conviction and sentencing. What if, during the mediation, the mediator offers an opinion concerning any of those issues that is at odds with the advice of counsel? It's not hard to imagine that such a scenario might cause a defendant to lose confidence in his or her lawyer and counsel to lose confidence in the process. The obvious way to avoid such a circumstance is for the mediator to make clear that his or her observations are offered as possibilities, not as legal advice. As in civil mediations, the mediator must take care to couch his or her perspectives as possibilities to consider rather than as authoritative advice to be followed. Finally, mediators must reiterate frequently the need for defendants to consult with and rely on the advice of counsel on legal and procedural issues.

What if, in the course of mediation, a mediator determines that one of the lawyers is failing to fulfill his or her obligations? What if the mediator believes that the prosecutor is engaging in unethical conduct or that the defense lawyer is offering advice that is contrary to the law or in reckless disregard of the evidence? While the mediator in such a circumstance must tread with care, this may be precisely when a mediator might serve a purpose beyond facilitating a plea. Considering that, in the absence of a third party's awareness of such an irregularity, unethical or unprofessional conduct would go undetected, this shouldn't be a reason to be wary of mediation. To the contrary, it should highlight one benefit of mediation—the presence of a neutral observer—in helping the parties reach a fair result. To be sure, a mediator in such a circumstance will be in the difficult position of addressing the deficiency, but a trained and skilled mediator will be prepared to do so. In most circumstances, a mere suggestion of the mediator's concern might be enough to prompt a corrective response. If not, the mediator can express his or her concerns more directly with the attorney one-on-one.

The final concerns to be identified here, then, are the potential implications of mediation in the context of criminal plea negotiation on privilege and confidentiality. Although it is a fundamental principle of criminal jurisprudence that the communications between a defendant and his or her attorney are privileged and confidential, statements made by a party during a mediation do not always enjoy such protection. In some contexts, statements made during a civil mediation may be made confidential by virtue of a statute, court rule, agreement by parties, or common law. In order for mediation in a criminal case to be viable, however, the defendant must be given every assurance that his or her participation and, in particular, any statements he or she makes will not be used against him or her. The prosecution must not be permitted to use his or her willingness to engage in mediation or any statements he or she makes during mediation as any indication of guilt. Although it is beyond the scope of this book to investigate the ways that privilege and confidentiality might be ensured, we can imagine that they could be protected in one of two ways. First, the parties could enter into a binding agreement stipulating that the fact of the mediation and any statements made by a party during the mediation would not be able to be used against them should the negotiation be unsuccessful. Indeed, it is not an uncommon practice in many jurisdictions to allow a defendant to offer a "proffer" of information to the government prior to or during plea negotiations to give the government a notion of what the defendant intends to say when formally debriefed following an agreement. Such proffer agreements contain representations prohibiting or limiting the use of such statements against the defendant and could serve as models for a mediation confidentiality agreement.

Alternately, the mediator can serve as the communicator of information and offers in a "hypothetical" manner. That is, the parties, rather than making statements to each other that they would otherwise worry about being regarded as admissions, might communicate these statements to the mediator, who could then relay them to the other side in the form of a hypothetical, as in "What if the defendant were willing to show you where the money is buried?" Such a statement would thus not be attributable to the defendant and used against him or her but would nonetheless be useful to explore possible resolutions. The obvious question in such a circumstance is whether, in the event of a failed negotiation, the mediator could be compelled to testify as to statements made in the course of mediation. In order for mediation to be a viable tool, of course, the defendant must be assured that any statements made in the course of negotiations couldn't be used against him or her. As discussed previously, this should be accomplished by means of a clear and binding agreement executed prior to the mediation.

In conclusion, we believe that a well-conceived and professionally administered mediation program could offer significant benefits to plea negation in criminal cases. Not only would the parties realize greater efficiency and improved communication, but mediation would provide another potential check on such concerns as prosecutorial overreach, coercion, and ineffective assistance of counsel, among others. In effect, the mediator can function not only to facilitate fair case disposition but also to level the playing field for the parties involved. While details of funding, organization, and appropriate legal safeguards would have to be worked out, we believe that the potential benefits are compelling.

7

TRANSFORMING PRETRIAL SYSTEMS AND PUBLIC DEFENSE

We now turn to two additional areas of concern that are fundamentally tied to the bigger picture of reforming plea negotiation and reducing recidivism: effectively revising the pretrial process and improving the assistance of counsel for indigent defendants.

The pretrial process defines the context within which plea negotiation takes place. As such, the decisions made during the pretrial stage substantially impact case dispositions and outcomes. We do not see how there can be meaningful renovation of plea negotiation and in turn broader criminal justice reform without addressing primary concerns with the pretrial process.

The Sixth Amendment right to counsel is one of the cornerstones of American jurisprudence. However, for a variety of reasons, it is an empty promise. Effective assistance of counsel is fundamentally tied to reforming plea negotiation. It is also a key component of a fair, just, and effective justice system.

We begin with the pretrial process.

REFORMING PRETRIAL POLICIES AND PROCEDURES

A commonly raised criticism of plea negotiation and the number one concern expressed by the public defenders we interviewed is what is perceived as the excessive use of pretrial detention. That concern is with the unnecessary deprivation of liberty, which has a variety of short-term and longer-term consequences. Critics argue that prosecutors and judges often inappropriately use their own beliefs and attitudes in making detention and release recommendations and decisions. More directly of consequence for plea negotiation is the use of pretrial detention either deliberately or coincidentally for felony and misdemeanor defendants as a way to motivate or leverage a plea deal. This is not an isolated issue as bail reform is one of the more frequently discussed issues that critics of the American criminal justice system raise these days. We will discuss this particular concern and bail reform below. However, there is a bigger picture involving the pretrial system, plea negotiation, and meaningful criminal justice reform. Therefore, we expand this discussion to include broader issues associated with the pretrial justice system.

Pretrial is the status of everyone who is brought into the justice system and follows each individual from arrest through to the point of case disposition. It includes a variety of activities, including arrest, booking into jail, obtaining defense counsel, magistration/initial appearance, detention or release from jail, charging, indictment, prosecution, and plea negotiation. It involves a number of key decisions by several different sets of individuals and organizations, including police, jail personnel, prosecutors, defense counsel, judges and magistrates, grand juries, and pretrial services.

Although the pretrial system affects everyone who comes into the criminal justice system, the decisions that are made and the actions taken have profound consequences. Six decades ago, in 1956, the noted legal expert and law professor Caleb Foote argued that pretrial decisions determine mostly everything. Since then, many have echoed the belief that what occurs in the pretrial stage has substantial downstream consequences.[1]

Pretrial Detention

Approximately 70 percent of the 650,000 jail inmates in the 3,000 local jails across the nation are being detained pretrial, awaiting disposition of their cases.[2] The vast majority of them (90 percent) are there because they have not posted bond.[3] Increased use of pretrial detention is the primary reason that the jail population has grown so dramatically during the past forty years. Over the past several decades, there has been a remarkable decline in the use of pretrial release from jail on personal recognizance or release on recognizance and a commensurate increase in secured release through the use of money bail.[4] Today, the United States largely has a money bail system that governs who is detained pretrial and who is released.

There are two official reasons why individuals are detained awaiting case disposition: flight risk and public safety risk. The logic is to detain those who pose a substantial flight risk or a substantial risk of committing another crime, and the risk of those who are released can be controlled by the financial pledge they have with the court in the form of a money bond often in combination with some kind of pretrial supervision. That bond can be provided by the defendant personally or secured through a third-party bail bond company.

In theory, that is how it is supposed to work. One of the problems is that most jurisdictions to this day do not have reliable ways of determining risk. Only about 10 percent of jurisdictions in 2015 used any kind of validated risk assessment instrument in making pretrial detention decisions.[5] Moreover, a recent survey shows that most judges do not think that risk assessments are any better at assessing risk than are judges' own methods.[6] Thus, it is common to rely on the judgment of prosecutors and judges in making these decisions. That judgment is also a common way of determining the appropriate bond amount for those offered pretrial release, although many jurisdictions use bond guidelines that tie bond amounts to the offense and prior criminal involvement. Regardless of the method of setting bond, the end result is that there is a very clear relationship between pretrial release and financial well-being. The Prison Policy Initiative conducted analyses of Bureau of Justice Statistics reports of characteristics of jail inmates and Census Bureau income data. They found that the median annual income of jail inmates in 2015 was $15,110, which is just one-half of the median income of similar individuals who were not incarcerated. They conclude that the ability to pay the bond or the 10 percent charge to a bail bondsman is the primary driver of who is in jail and who is not. The Pretrial Justice Institute reports that nearly 50 percent of felony defendants with bonds cannot pay that bond and thus remain in jail. While the point of the detention decision is to manage risk, since very few jurisdictions actually use any kind of validated risk assessment instrument, what we end up with is a money-based system that results in excessive numbers of unnecessarily detained individuals. There is an associated annual price tag of $14 billion for detaining mostly low-risk offenders.[7] It is important to remember that these pretrial detainees got to jail because they were arrested, which requires only the standard of proof of probable cause. Many of them will have their charges dropped at some point. Between 2011 and 2015, fully one-third of individuals arrested on felony charges in California who were in pretrial detention were not found guilty of any crime.[8] A recent study of pretrial detention in California found that just six counties spent in just a two-year period nearly $38 million detaining individuals whose cases were dismissed or never filed.[9] A recent study in Maryland found that individuals who were arrested and booked into jail paid $256 million in bail bond fees to get released; $75 million was paid in bail bond fees in cases where the charges were dropped or the individual was acquitted.[10] In Los Angeles between 2012 and 2016, arrestees paid $194 million in fees to bail bond companies.[11] The $75 million in Maryland and the $194 million in Los Angeles, as well as all of the other bail fees charged in the United States, are nonrefundable fees.

There are more than 25,000 bail bond companies in the United States, but the vast majority of the $14 billion market is in the hands of just ten companies. The industry as a whole earns around $2 billion in profits annually.[12] The bail bond lobby is a substantial force in challenging efforts to reform the money bail system.[13]

The Pretrial Justice Institute conducted analyses and issued a report essentially grading the pretrial justice systems across the states. The grading focused on several dimensions of the pretrial systems, including per capita rate of pretrial detention, use of validated risk assessments for determining risk, and the extent to which states have reduced or eliminated money bail. In that sense, it is really a grade focusing on bail and detention rather than an evaluation of the pretrial system in general. The November 2017 State of Pretrial Justice report assigns a grade of D to the United States as a whole. One-third of the states received a grade of F. Together, 60 percent of the states received a grade of D or F.[14]

It seems fair to conclude, as many have, that the pretrial justice system does a rather poor job of managing the risk of offenders through the use of pretrial detention. Moreover, there is substantial financial waste associated with that ineffectiveness. However, it gets worse.

Recent research has focused on identifying the consequences of pretrial detention on case outcomes.[15] At the federal and state levels as well as among misdemeanor and felony offenders, the patterns are similar. Low- and medium-risk defendants who are detained pretrial encounter a variety of negative downstream outcomes that are tied directly and indirectly to pretrial detention. These outcomes include greater probability of criminal conviction, higher likelihood of a sentence of incarceration and for a longer period of time, and heightened risk of longer-term recidivism. All of this of course contributes to mass incarceration and the revolving door of the criminal justice system. Here is what the evidence tells us based on statistically controlled models.

Low-risk defendants who are detained pretrial more than three days (compared to identical individuals who were released pretrial) are more likely to be arrested again during the pretrial phase (74 percent more frequently) and up to two years later (51 percent more frequently). They are also 30 percent more likely to be convicted, meaning that in the vast majority of cases they plead guilty. Low-risk pretrial detainees are also four times more likely to be sentenced to jail and receive a longer sentence than their released counterparts. They are three times more likely to be sentenced to prison and receive a longer sentence.

Length of detention is a contributing factor in these outcomes. A low-risk defendant detained at least three days was 40 percent more likely to commit a new offense during the pretrial phase than a low-risk defendant released within twenty-four hours. Longer-term outcomes are also linked to length of detention. With a comparison to those low-risk offenders released within twenty-four hours, those detained up to three days were 17 percent more likely to reoffend within two years; those low-risk offenders detained up to two weeks were 51 percent more likely to reoffend within two years.[16]

Looking at the released population reveals substantial advantages to not being detained. Compared to those who were identical except for being detained, releasees were more than 300 percent more likely to receive a disposition of deferred adjudication (a form of probation where a finding of guilt is held aside; thus, those who successfully complete the period of supervision will not have a criminal conviction). Those who were released had a greater chance (30 percent) of case dismissal and were 25 percent less likely to be found guilty, and for those who were convicted, they were sentenced to an average of 54 percent fewer days in jail.[17]

A study specifically focusing on misdemeanor defendants found similar patterns.[18] Based on a large sample and carefully controlled statistical analyses, the researchers found that misdemeanor defendants who were detained, compared to similar releasees, are 25 percent more likely to be convicted and nearly 45 percent more likely to be sentenced to jail. Highlighting the probable criminogenic effects of detention, they found that eighteen months out, detained defendants (compared to their released counterparts) were 30 percent more likely to have new felony charges and 30 percent more likely to have new misdemeanor charges.

The authors of the misdemeanor research make clear the point that while the term "misdemeanor" may imply "trivial," that is not the case. In addition to often being a pathway to more serious felony crime,

> [m]isdemeanors matter. Misdemeanor convictions can result in jail time, heavy fines, invasive probation requirements, and collateral consequences that include deportation, loss of child custody, ineligibility for public services and barriers to finding employment and housing. Beyond the consequences of misdemeanor convictions for individuals, the misdemeanor system has a profound impact because it is enormous: while national data on misdemeanors are lacking, a 2010 analysis found that misdemeanors represent more than three-quarters of the criminal caseload in state courts.[19]

We can understand these negative outcomes associated with pretrial detention through a number of consequences. Detention can result in loss of employment and income, loss of housing, family disruption, and loss of public assistance benefits, all of which can contribute to failure to appear and committing new crimes. Detention can also impact one's ability to assist defense counsel, which in turn places a defendant at a significant disadvantage. Moreover, pretrial detention can contribute substantially to debt. We know that the vast majority of individuals entering the criminal justice system are indigent and cannot retain their own counsel. Those financial circumstances then translate to the inability to pay the required bond set by the court. The reality is that most of the 650,000 individuals being detained are in jail because they could not afford the bond amount. The primary way that a defendant can control how long they are detained pretrial is to plead guilty.

Another financial issue associated with pretrial detention is the pay-to-stay system, whereby individuals detained in jail are required to pay a per diem and/or pay for other things like food and medical care. The logic behind requiring jail inmates to pay detention fees is that taxpayers should not have to pay for someone else's mistake. The fact that they are paying for their own detention has some political leverage for sheriffs who typically run local jails and are elected officials. However, the reality of the financial situation of most detainees renders pay-to-stay an excessive burden that undoubtedly plays a role in recidivism.

Decisions in these early stages of processing criminal defendants impact a variety of downstream activities, including prosecution, sentencing, and longer-term outcomes. However, it seems reasonable to us that many of these effects of pretrial decision making find their expression in the plea negotiation process, in particular in the decisions made by prosecutors. This seems especially likely with regard to findings such as the increased likelihood of conviction for detained defendants, the greater probability of a sentence of incarceration compared to probation, and longer sentences in prison or jail compared to released control groups.

There are several reasons for thinking this might be the case. First is the long-standing assertion that pretrial detention serves as leverage to motivate a plea deal (and pay-to-stay requirements likely add significantly to that leverage). It seems reasonable to assume that the increased conviction rate for detained defendants is a product of plea deals. In many cases involving lesser charges, defendants can plead guilty and often get time served. Moreover, prosecutors may engage in more restricted charge bargaining because of the leverage that detention provides them. By that, we mean prosecutors may not negotiate downward as much as they might for released defendants since the lack of the detention incentive may require prosecutors to offer more attractive deals to those who are not detained pretrial. The disadvantages regarding access to defense counsel and the restrictions on assisting with the defense probably also play a role in the greater likelihood of conviction.

More severe sentences for detained defendants may reflect more serious charges to which detained defendants plead because of their relative lack of bargaining power compared to released defendants. Moreover, the problem of access to counsel may contribute to less favorable sentence negotiations. There may also be some subtle perception on the part of prosecutors that defendants in jail are somehow more culpable and thus more deserving of more severe punishment.

Most of the concern with pretrial justice systems revolves around pretrial detention and the money bail system. Bail reform has been in the headlines in recent months involving political opposites such as Kamala Harris (Democratic U.S. senator from California) and Rand Paul (Republican U.S. senator from Kentucky) calling for reductions in the jail population through reforming the bail system (*New York Times* op-ed, July 20, 2017, "To Shrink Jails, Let's Reform Bail"). New Jersey has been gaining attention with the elimination of its money bail system and replacing it with a nonmonetary risk assessment system for determining who is detained and supervision requirements for those who are released. Governor Cuomo of New York is pushing bail reform in New York State. He recently stated,

> The bill will reform our bail system so that anyone facing misdemeanor or nonviolent felony charges should be released without bail. Those who pose a current danger to a person or persons or pose a risk of flight can still be held in detention, with due process, but no longer will people go to jail for the crime of being poor.[20]

New Mexico and Maryland have implemented some versions of bail reform, as have West Virginia, Kentucky, Colorado, Alaska, Arizona, and municipal courts in Alabama, Chicago, and Charlotte, North Carolina, among others. The Harris–Paul effort produced the Pretrial Integrity and Safety Act, which is designed to facilitate state-level innovation in bail reform. As of August 2017, it was reported at the National Conference of State Legislatures that 500 new state laws have been passed addressing various aspects of pretrial reform.[21]

It is also time to abolish pay-to-stay schemes. As other pretrial reforms are implemented, jail populations should decline, which should reduce the financial burdens on jails and counties, reducing the need for offenders to pay their own way. There is some movement in the direction of eliminating pay-to-stay, but that change is very slow. Contra Costa County, California, is reimbursing parents of children who were charged for their children's incarceration. California Governor Jerry

Brown recently banned the California law that permitted charging parents for their children's incarceration.[22]

It seems a bit ironic that a system in which decisions about detention and release are in theory based on the risk of flight and reoffending would be "reformed" by the use of methods that measure the risk of reoffending and failure to appear. Nevertheless, that is where we are. Replacing the money-based system with one that bases detention and release decisions on validated assessments rather than gut feel, intuition, anger, or guesswork is a step in the right direction. The use of validated risk assessment instruments like the Ohio Risk Assessment System or the Texas Risk Assessment System that we discussed in chapter 6 can significantly improve decision making and the accuracy of detention decisions by measuring probabilities of risk.

It is important, however, to clarify that risk assessments do not really predict. They place individuals into broad categories of probabilities, such as low, medium, and high. Moreover, these categories represent probabilities of general recidivism, not necessarily specific types of crime like theft or domestic assault. Finally, they measure the risk of reoffending. The concerns for the court are generally public safety risk and flight risk. These assessments say very little if anything about flight risk.

Risk assessments are not error proof. They can result in false-positive predictions (identifying someone as at high risk of reoffending when in fact they are not) and false negatives (failing to predict a high-risk individual). Examples of errors abound, such as the man in New Jersey who was arrested on a weapons charge, was determined not to be high risk, was released, and then shot a rival twenty-two times, killing him, or the assertion that in New Mexico, the risk assessment results have led to the release of nearly every violent offender in the state.[23] And in San Francisco, the use of risk assessments by judges has caused "many instances of contention" with the district attorney's office.[24]

A more systematic, statistical evaluation of several risk assessment instruments was conducted by the Washington State Institute for Public Policy. They determined the predictive accuracy of five commonly used risk assessment tools based on large samples of offenders in Washington State. The instruments included the Ohio Risk Assessment System that we discussed earlier. The evaluation determined the accuracy of prediction considering both false-positive errors and false-negative errors. The measure of predictive accuracy varies between .5 and 1.0, where .5 is essentially chance and 1.0 is perfect prediction. The average score for the five instruments is .68, which indicates some improvement over chance.[25]

Risk assessment is front and center in the national conversation about bail reform. The Laura and John Arnold Foundation and the Pretrial Justice Initiative, among others, are driving the effort to introduce a more objective, validated approach for making decisions about pretrial detention or release. The use of validated risk assessment instruments is an important step in changing the pretrial justice system by eliminating the reliance on financial means for release and adding scientific validity to the process. Other recommendations for reforming the pretrial system include supervision and monitoring to ensure compliance with supervision conditions, early screening of cases by an experienced prosecutor, and having defense counsel present at initial appearances.[26]

These are reasonable recommendations. There is considerable momentum behind bail reform, and the evidence is clear that reducing unnecessary pretrial detention will help reduce recidivism. Better supervision is a good thing, as is having defense representation in the earliest stages of processing and early screening of cases. The use of a validated risk assessment to inform pretrial supervision, such as assisting in determining the conditions of supervision, is a good idea and increasingly common.

As reliance of pretrial detention is reduced, managing the risk of released offenders increases in importance. A primary tool for managing risk for those who are released is pretrial supervision. Pretrial supervision is shown to be effective at reducing criminal activity and failure to appear for court dates.[27] Several states are moving in the direction of developing pretrial supervision systems designed to manage offender risk. Between 2012 and 2014, Colorado, Hawaii, Nevada, New Jersey, Vermont, and West Virginia passed legislation to establish or bolster risk-based pretrial systems.[28] Risk management tools that well-established pretrial systems typically rely on include court date notification, electronic monitoring, pretrial supervision involving periodic contacts, and drug testing. These tools can be effective in increasing the likelihood that offenders will make court dates and reducing the likelihood of reoffending while on pretrial release.

It seems that pretrial reform is nearly exclusively focused on those who are released and whether they successfully complete supervision. For most, completion of supervision is consummated with a plea deal. It seems like the pretrial phase is sort of a holding pattern until the pieces line up and the parties can get a plea deal worked out. At that point, the typical outcome is some agreed-on period of punishment. The goal of pretrial seems to be to manage the risk of accused offenders until we can convict and punish them. While that is a positive thing, we think there is considerable room for rethinking pretrial justice.

The Bigger Picture of Pretrial Reform

Entering the criminal justice system is triggered by an arrest. That then triggers a series of decisions and actions that ultimately lead to a very limited set of outcomes, most typically criminal conviction and some form of sanction or punishment and often fees to be paid. Unfortunately, in the majority of cases, this fails to do anything to reduce the probability of recidivism and essentially guarantees that the individual will come back into the justice system and the whole process begins again. As we discussed earlier, the decisions that are made at the pretrial stage impact everything downstream. For that reason, significant changes in terms of how we conduct the business of the pretrial system can have substantial benefits down the road. We suggest that the pretrial system is an appropriate and productive opportunity for addressing the overarching goal of transforming the criminal justice system.

It is our contention that the goal of recidivism reduction should begin as soon as someone enters the pretrial justice system. That requires fundamental change in how we currently conduct business and takes the concept of pretrial justice reform well beyond recommendations that have been made by most observers. It is time for us to think more boldly about how meaningful change can be accomplished, especially in the early stages of processing defendants.

Many prosecutors whom we interviewed said that addressing criminogenic problems, those factors that are associated with criminal offending by providing more and higher-quality services, is the appropriate strategy for reducing recidivism:

I think it has a lot to do with the quality of programs we are sending these people to. To reduce recidivism, it's identifying the offender and sending them to quality programs, which we may not be doing.

Personally, my philosophy I think we should be spending more money on education and after-school programs, addiction treatment, smarter policy when it comes to that stuff. Health care, community treatment, we see a lot of crimes due to lacking opportunity.

I think the law should change. I personally believe there needs to be more options and programs for mentally ill and addicted people. . . . But the current legislature doesn't give a crap about that.

To really provide more services.

We need to offer more services. There's just not enough.

The link between mental illness and substance abuse and recidivism makes a lot of intuitive sense. I think we have had plenty of time to learn that treating these things like criminal problems doesn't work.

Judges shared the belief that more needs to be done in dealing with offender circumstances. The primary recommendation centers around better assessment and then funding and professional care for the mentally ill:

Sending them to jail doesn't help at all. They don't have many services there. So, we just have to make sure we evaluate them properly.

We should have more comprehensive assessments. And we would use the assessments to make better recommendations.

A huge increase in funding. More psychologists and psychiatrists. There are not many of those that want to work with these populations.

We need to have more drug and alcohol services. Better mental health services. That's a serious resource issue and one where resources are lacking. Mental health services are the biggest deficit we have in our criminal justice system. But heaven forbid you have a mental health and substance need because we have very limited programs for that.

Not many judges thought that the diversion resources in their jurisdictions were adequate:

> Not much by way of felonies.

> No, I don't think we do enough. I don't think the criminal justice system is adequately prepared to handle mentally ill defendants.

> No, I think we can do more there for sure. We are stretched with what we have currently.

> No, I would say there needs to be more capacity. In my experience, definitely the mental health would need more capacity.

> We don't really have anything like that.

One judge noted the strong association between homelessness and mental illness:

> Housing that is appropriate for needs. There is a lot of substandard housing for mentally ill people, and there are a lot of homeless people with mental illness.

Several prosecutors said that the criminal justice system is not the right set of agencies and people to deal with these kinds of problems, especially mental illness among offenders:

> But something needs to be done for those with mental illness. . . . It is a problem when the only recourse you can provide mentally ill defendants with is prison time.

> We should not ask the CJS to solve all of the problems. I think it is reckless and irresponsible to ask the criminal justice system to fix mental health problems.

> I think the change should come from the legislature if they care about it. We only deal with a small section of the pie as prosecutors.

One of the important consequences of the focus on bail reform and the use of risk assessments is the relative lack of consideration of crime-related factors. Risk assessments do not systematically identify these factors. That is understandable since risk assessments are designed for quick administration with a limited amount of expertise required to administer. For example, the assessment initially used in Kentucky took twenty minutes to administer. That was determined to be too long. The current version takes five minutes.[29] Thus, the growing use of risk assessments poses the problem of crowding out other important information that can be highly relevant to decision making beyond the detention or release question. In addition to often being silent on crime-related factors, risk assessments tell us nothing about things like culpability, moral blameworthiness, or criminal intent. A statistically high risk of recidivism does not mean an individual is guilty of the instant offense, nor does it indicate much about the appropriate sentence. There are many decisions during the pretrial stage that can be greatly assisted by information that is well beyond the scope of risk assessments.

Criminal justice decision making should be based on problem solving. An individual enters the system, and the question that should drive decision making is how we address this situation. The suspect is a "problem." What solutions can we develop to address the short-term needs of processing him or her in the pretrial system as well as longer-term outcomes, such as recidivism, economic productivity, mental health, and family stability? Fundamental to this is the question of what we need to know to accomplish these goals. What do we know about why this person is here? Are there factors that we can identify that help account for his or her criminal behavior? Can we utilize early diversion and intervention to mitigate the effects of these factors and, in turn, reduce the likelihood the individual will reoffend? How do we manage any public safety risk and flight risk posed by the individual? How do we address the matter of accountability? How do we weigh the retributive need to punish against evidence-based policies, practices, and interventions that reduce recidivism, mitigate mental illness and substance abuse, and enhance economic productivity?

Answering these and related questions requires information that is often unavailable, incomplete, or inaccurate. But it is information that prosecutors and judges told us in our interviews is important to have. We also suggest that the earlier they have this information, the better.

What we are proposing is implementing the expert panel screening and assessment process discussed previously up front in the initial stages of processing. If pretrial decisions impact everything downstream, the sooner the better that key individuals have relevant information for optimizing the decision-making process and, in turn, increasing the likelihood of positive outcomes.

Consider, for example, the case of drug offenders. The relation between drug abuse, crime, and the criminal justice system is extraordinarily broad. There are at least four primary ways that substance abuse is related to criminality and criminal justice involvement. First, there are those who get into the criminal justice system for violating drug laws, including possession, manufacture, and distribution. One-third of all prison admissions in state and federal prisons are individuals who have been convicted of drug law violations.[30] Second, approximately 40 percent of state prison and local jail inmates reported using drugs at the time they committed the offense for which they are incarcerated.[31] Third, 21 percent of all state prison and local jail inmates indicated that they committed the offense for which they are incarcerated in order to get money for drugs; 40 percent of property offenders reported that they committed the offense for which they are incarcerated in order to get money for drugs.[32] Fourth, substance abuse impacts criminality through changes to the structure and functioning of the brain. For example, chronic substance abuse, dependence, or addiction can significantly and negatively impact sustained attention, impulse control, valuing future events compared to the present, cognitive flexibility, working memory, planning, emotional regulation, and higher cognitive skills. The evidence is clear that substance abuse has negative consequences for cognitive abilities and, in turn, behavior:

> It is evident . . . that most drugs of abuse may induce adverse effects on brain structures associated with cognitive functions. In most cases, these effects seem to impact brain circuits linked to important aspects of cognition, such as memory and learning, attention, risk taking, motivation, mood and wanting.[33]

There certainly is overlap across these four groups of offenders. For example, someone with a substance use disorder may be caught in possession and also have cognitive dysfunction as a result of drug abuse. Or someone might be using drugs at the time they commit a burglary to secure funds for more drugs.

Regardless, the point is that substance abuse impacts the vast majority of individuals in the criminal justice system. So, how are prosecutors and judges to know what to do with these individuals short of the simple, reflexive imposition of punishment? If the goal is to reduce recidivism, which we suggest requires changing decision making to incorporate evidence-based behavioral change options, those decisions must be informed by accurate, expert opinion regarding the individual being considered. What would the prosecutor or judge get from using the Texas Risk Assessment System or the multitude of similar risk assessment instruments? Five items in the Texas Risk Assessment System are the basis for determining the presence of a substance use problem: age first began regularly using alcohol, ever used illegal drugs, drug use caused problems, drug use caused problems with employment, and drug use caused problems with family and friends. Unfortunately, that will not indicate whether the individual currently has a substance use disorder, let alone its severity or the extent to which the individual wants to engage in treatment. That also does not tell us whether the individual has a comorbid psychiatric disorder. These are clinical, diagnostic questions that require information and expertise that go well beyond a risk assessment. Moreover, we must determine which of these different drug-involved offenders may need treatment and what type and how much and how to deal with a co-occurring psychiatric disorder; such decisions go beyond the expertise of prosecutors, jail intake personnel, judges, defense counsel, and probation officers.

The point is that efforts that target primarily reforming the bail system through implementing more objective, validated risk assessment instruments for making release and detention decisions are important and should be done; however, they miss a bigger and, we think, far more important issue. Better decision making is part of it, but so is assessing and addressing crime-related or criminogenic circumstances, such as disorder, homelessness, and unemployment, in order to reduce recidivism.

The judges we interviewed were clear that the pretrial system in their jurisdictions does not provide adequate services to those who are released after arrest. Several stated that they would like to see more services and more intensive services, such as inpatient treatment for the released population.

> I would have to say that I do have concerns about that. We rely on our counseling center, and we hope they are continuing to use evi-

dence-based practices. I am always nervous about whether they are doing their job well.

I'm not sure we do a very good job with that.

It's stretched pretty thin. I wish we had more services and money for those who are released from jail.

I think we could always use more. I wish there was some kind of pretrial inpatient services. More housing would really help.

The various components and agencies of the American criminal justice system are generally in lockstep in perpetuating tough-on-crime policies and, in turn, high recidivism rates. The pretrial system is no exception. It is designed and functions to keep the flow of offenders moving quickly to plea negotiation, conviction, and punishment. In precisely the same way, the various components of the criminal justice system need to be in lockstep in perpetuating behavioral change, risk management, and recidivism reduction.

Pretrial supervision can be an opportunity for addressing crime-related factors and engaging in meaningful behavioral change. Our recommendations for renovating the pretrial system going forward are to conduct early, comprehensive triage, screening, and assessment that can then inform and direct decision making and problem solving guided by considerations of recidivism reduction and risk management. Recidivism reduction should be based on the volumes of evidence indicating that the way to significantly reduce the probability of reoffending is by identifying and mitigating offenders' primary crime-related circumstances, disorders, impairments, and deficits. Doing this early is important. The evidence is clear that contact with the criminal justice system is criminogenic. Thus, when possible, exposure to the justice system, such as pretrial detention, should be limited when public safety is not seriously compromised.

The National Institute of Corrections (NIC) has identified a number of elements of a "high functioning pretrial services agency."[34] These include universal risk screening utilizing a validated risk assessment instrument, risk-based supervision, supervision conditions specific to the individual rather than "blanket" conditions, and the use of swift and certain sanctions for violations of supervision conditions. The NIC recommendations focus nearly exclusively on assessing risk and utilizing risk-based supervision. Almost as an afterthought, the NIC suggests that agencies also consider using validated needs assessments and provide services to those on pretrial release, services such as substance abuse and mental health treatment. However, they suggest that providing these services be tied to pretrial outcomes. "Pretrial services agencies should offer these services when they help achieve pretrial outcomes and supervision compliance."[35] What is missing here is much consideration of longer-term outcomes, such as recidivism. That is not surprising since recidivism reduction is not something that many individuals in the justice system seem to consider part of their job description.

The 2017 Pretrial Justice Reinvestment Act in Maryland is an illustration of thinking differently about how pretrial services and supervision can not only manage offenders' risk but also engage in evidence-based practices and problem solving to reduce longer-term offending. The Maryland Alliance for Justice Reform outlined what Maryland policymakers have developed for low-risk offenders:

> The most effective pretrial supervision programs evaluate the risk and needs of the arrested person. When community resources are available to reduce a risk and to treat a need, a low risk person may be placed on community supervision with the requirement that instead of pretrial detention, he or she receive and give proof of appropriate services. For example, a former mental health patient may be required to return to treatment, a disturbed veteran may be referred to Veterans Administration programs, a homeless person may be referred to a homeless shelter . . . an unemployed person on community supervision may be directed to job banks or employment services. Taken together, pretrial supervision can help reduce crime and solve social problems, even before an alleged offender gets into a courtroom.[36]

The success of such an approach depends on a number of considerations, such as collecting and using appropriate information about risk and needs, engaging in problem-solving strategies to address crime-related needs, having sufficient evidence-based capacity for referral to treatment, and providing case management when necessary, among others.

It is also important to implement these recommendations at both the felony and the misdemeanor level. As we discussed earlier, misdemeanors can and do have significant consequences in terms of jail time as well as a variety of collateral consequences, such as restrictions on housing and employment. Misdemeanors make up the vast majority of the criminal justice system, amounting to about 80 percent of court dockets.[37] Moreover, failures to effectively address misdemeanor crime can and do lead to misdemeanants becoming more serious offenders, thus ramping up the consequences of ineffective justice policy.

A potentially useful mechanism for what we envision is deferred adjudication (also known as deferred prosecution, probation before judgment, or treatment in lieu of prosecution) but a version of it that occurs much sooner after the point of arrest. This form of diversion shifts offenders away from traditional criminal prosecution and punishment to options that are able to manage the risk that they pose while engaging in meaningful, clinically informed behavioral change. Diversion can reduce the likelihood of reoffending by minimizing contact with the criminal justice system (and thus insulating individuals from its criminogenic effects) and by providing evidence-based behavioral interventions and rehabilitative services. In certain situations, deferred prosecution can be used to leverage participation in programming by rewarding successful completion with a dismissal of charges.

One of the significant challenges is that the diversion programs we are proposing either do not exist in many jurisdictions or, if they do, are of extremely limited capacity. While problem-solving courts have become quite popular over the past thirty years, their capacity is only a fraction of the actual need. The reality going forward is the need to create intervention capacity for the variety of problems and disorders that offenders bring into the justice system. These efforts should be responsive to the needs of felons and especially misdemeanants since greater numbers of them arrive at the justice system requiring intervention and rehabilitation.

What we are proposing is, in principle, fairly straightforward. The concept is that the decision making that occurs in the early stages of the pretrial process should focus on two primary questions: (1) How do we effectively manage the short-term risk of an individual while awaiting case disposition, and (2) how do we reduce the longer-term risk of recidivism? The former question should be guided by relevant, accurate information that reflects short-term risk. That risk can be mitigated in part by supervision. The latter should be based on comprehensive professional assessment of individuals' criminogenic circumstances, including cognitive issues, mental health, substance use, housing, employment, education, and family situation, and providing appropriate, evidence-based interventions, treatment, and rehabilitation services in diversion settings whenever possible.

This directly impacts plea negotiation in several ways. First, it provides new and important information to all parties involved in plea negotiation, including prosecutors, judges and defense counsel, and, often, the plea mediator. That knowledge can be relevant for individual-level, recidivism-focused decision making to facilitate problem solving and alternative case resolution, such as deferred adjudication and referral to diversion programs in lieu of traditional criminal sentencing. Importantly, increased diversion will reduce caseloads for prosecutors and public defenders and reduce court dockets. In the longer run, it will reduce caseloads as recidivism is reduced and fewer offenders repeatedly cycle in and out of the justice system.

This will shift more demand on pretrial services and pretrial supervision, which will require significant reallocation of resources and ramping up of pretrial supervision strategies as more individuals are on pretrial supervision because of bail reform and increased pretrial diversion. In important respects, this involves a reinvention of pretrial services from what has traditionally been more of a holding pattern or stop-off for offenders to a more intensive, intervention-focused landing place or destination for many.

While the ideas we propose are straightforward, we fully appreciate that the actual execution is a monumental task. The experience of designing and implementing similar concepts demonstrate that this kind of initiative is doable but often quite challenging. We have discussed program and policy development elsewhere[38] and discuss such issues in more detail in the next chapter.

PUBLIC DEFENDER/APPOINTED COUNSEL

It is common knowledge even among some casual observers that the indigent defense system in this country is in crisis. As a variety of experts from the American Bar Association, the Brennan Center for Justice, and the Constitution Project note:

> Public defenders' offices are understaffed, underfunded, undertrained and overworked, and they often lack the oversight necessary to ensure constitutionally adequate representation for indigent defendants.[39]

Recent speeches by U.S. Justice Department officials from the Obama administration describe public defense in the United States as "unacceptable," "morally untenable," "unconscionable," and "unworthy of a legal system that stands as an example to the rest of the world."[40]

The problems with indigent defense often aggravate the constitutional and due process concerns we discussed earlier, especially in the context of plea negotiation, where wrongful conviction is a significant issue and there is no jury to serve as a procedural safety net. A substantial cause of the problems with public defense is underfunding, which produces caseload pressures and the need to expedite cases by rapid-fire plea negotiation. To say that indigent defense needs to be appropriately funded is a universal understatement.

Addressing the funding and caseload issues is a critical part of reforming indigent defense. Recommendations generally involve increased resources from Congress and state legislatures to adequately fund local public defender and assigned counsel systems. Fulfilling *Gideon*'s promise requires providing adequate defense counsel to all indigent defendants who want it as well as providing sufficient resources for investigation of the evidence and other collateral activities, maintaining adequate oversight, ensuring that the rights and due process protections of defendants are preserved, and establishing uniform standards for when right to counsel begins, among others.[41] Other strategies include reclassifying some minor crimes to fine only civil matters to reduce criminal defender caseloads and a greater use of prebooking diversion and jail diversion for defendants with mental health problems (the Seattle Law Enforcement Assisted Diversion program is an often-cited jail diversion model). Fixing indigent defense funding, caseload, and related matters is necessary. However, stopping there seems shortsighted. We believe that there is a broader view that many who advocate for indigent defense reform miss.

The current practice of criminal defense has contributed in important ways to the decades-long failures of American criminal justice policy. While an overgeneralization, it is nevertheless true that in many circumstances the primary role of defense counsel is to negotiate less punishment for their clients. In the role of charge and sentence negotiator, defense counsel often engage in and perpetuate the punishment-focused criminal justice system that has failed to effectively reduce crime, recidivism, and victimization and has led to the massive waste of public revenue.

Effective reform of the criminal justice system more broadly and plea negotiation more specifically cannot occur without rethinking the roles and responsibilities of the defense bar. The changes we propose for plea negotiation, the role of the prosecutor, the pretrial system, and the concept of the plea mediator make little sense without substantial changes to how defense attorneys go about the business of representing defendants. Comprehensive criminal justice reform, in particular effectively reducing reoffending and producing more positive longer-term outcomes, requires substantially redefining what the criminal justice system does and how it does it. That includes the defense bar. Since the vast majority of felony and misdemeanor defendants are indigent, much of what we focus on here is redefining indigent defense, although these principles certainly apply to retained counsel.

There are several terms that are used interchangeably to refer to a strikingly different approach to providing criminal defense counsel. Under the umbrella concept of holistic defense are terms such as client-centered defense, problem-solving lawyering, therapeutic defense, and defense with interdisciplinary teams.[42] While these approaches sometimes differ in significant ways, they all share in common the idea of broadening the roles and responsibilities of defense counsel to include not just the legal issues of a case but also the collateral consequences of criminal justice involvement as well as those circumstances and situations that are associated with criminality and recidivism.

The concept seems to have originated in the late 1990s in the South Bronx, when several public defenders decided it was time to provide a new breed of criminal defense counsel. They opened the doors to the Bronx Defenders and launched the concept of holistic defense:

[O]ur experience teaches us that zealous lawyering alone is insufficient to achieve the vision of justice that motivates so many of us to do this work. Thus the question becomes whether it is possible to reimagine the scope of our work in order to become true and lasting agents for change and transformation in the lives of our clients. Holistic defense is a response to this challenge.[43]

The goals are ambitious and include improving case dispositions and legal outcomes as well as reducing the likelihood of longer-term recidivism. This is done generally through collaboration of defense attorneys with social workers and social service professionals who can provide services to address mental health, substance abuse, and other circumstances associated with an offender's criminality as well as investigators, immigration attorneys, and civil attorneys to assist with collateral immigration and civil issues. The end game is to provide the best outcome for the current criminal case while providing the resources and tools necessary to prevent future criminal involvement.

Accomplishing these goals involves implementing four core principles of holistic defense.[44] The point of the four principles is to provide an interdisciplinary, problem-solving, collaborative, community-based approach to the defendant's situation more broadly:

1. Providing seamless access to services for addressing legal and social support needs. The point is to identify and address legal issues as well as those circumstances, situations, disorders, and impairments that are related to clients' criminality and thus risk of reoffending and those collateral consequences of justice involvement that can also contribute to recidivism (such as employment and housing). The "seamless" part of "seamless access" refers to the elimination of as many barriers to services as possible.

2. Dynamic, collaborative communication among members of an interdisciplinary team of advocates, including criminal and civil lawyers, social workers, and other social service experts. "The client sees himself as being represented by a team of dedicated advocates all of whom are in communication with each other, rather than by a single advocate who grasps only part of the big picture."[45]

3. Advocates with an interdisciplinary skill set so that the decisions and actions of each support the efforts of the others. This promotes a real collaborative, problem-solving approach.
4. A robust connection to the community that, among other things, provides important links to essential community-based support services.

Holistic defense initiatives are gaining traction across the country with the primary objective of reducing recidivism. For example, from Montgomery County, Pennsylvania:

> The Montgomery County Public Defender Office is developing programs in an effort to provide a holistic approach to the extra-legal concerns of our clients. Our goal is to improve overall outcomes for our clients in order to ameliorate the conditions that lead to involvement in the justice system and ultimately to reduce recidivism. [46]

Another from Santa Barbara County, California:

> Adult Holistic Defense Case Management is a partnership between Santa Barbara County Public Defender and Family Service Agency. . . . The goal of the program is to stabilize lives, reduce recidivism, and create safer communities through innovative and individualized case management that addresses the dynamic risk factors for the criminal behavior of clients. [47]

There is another brand of innovative public defense called community-oriented defense. Community-oriented defense recognizes the link between poverty and criminal justice involvement. Disinvestment in public assistance and social services places many indigent individuals at risk of financial and other difficulties and without adequate access to mental health and substance abuse treatment. This, in turn, often leads to criminal justice involvement and, for many, to long periods of cycling in and out of the criminal justice system. The Brennan Center for Justice at New York University School of Law developed the Community-Oriented Defender Network to support defense counsel engagement in the three primary advocacy strategies of whole client representation, community engagement, and systemic reform. [48] They have identified ten principles of community-oriented defense that include client-centered defense; identifying and meeting client needs; partnering with the community; collaboration with a variety of agencies, individuals, and institutions; and pursuing a multidisciplinary approach of working with lawyers, social workers, counselors, and the medical community.

A personal communication with James Bethke, former executive director of the Texas Indigent Defense Commission, affirmed the utility and importance of holistic defense. He stated in an e-mail communication that holistic defense "is absolutely the best way to meaningfully represent your client."

The primary concepts of holistic defense and community-oriented defense have been embraced by the American Bar Association. In 2012, it passed Resolution 107C, which urges defense attorneys to adopt this broader approach to criminal defendants' legal, civil, and extralegal circumstances. Resolution 107C states:

> RESOLVED, That the American Bar Association urges defender organizations and criminal defense lawyers to:
>
> 1) Establish and facilitate criminal defense lawyers' linkages and collaborations with civil practitioners, civil legal services organizations, social service program providers and other non-lawyer professionals who can serve, or assist in serving, clients in criminal cases with civil legal and non-legal problems related to their criminal cases, including the hiring of such professionals as experts, or where infrastructure allows, as staff;
>
> 2) Authorize and encourage criminal defense lawyers to provide re-entry and reintegration services to clients in criminal cases including expungement, reestablishment of rights and certificates of reliefs of civil disabilities; and
>
> 3) Create and implement training programs, tools and resources for criminal defense lawyers and their staff regarding how best to serve clients with civil, legal and non-legal problems related to their criminal cases.
>
> FURTHER RESOLVED, That the American Bar Association urges governments, foundations, and other funders of legal services to support, with increased funding, defenders in their efforts to effectively address clients' inter-related criminal, civil and non-legal problems.[49]

While the names differ and there are nuanced differences, these approaches share the basic idea that criminal defense representation can and should be much more than addressing criminal legal issues.

What is remarkable in our minds about this broader conception of criminal defense is the recognition that recidivism reduction is a responsibility of the defense bar. That in and of itself is a major step forward in reforming criminal adjudication, in particular plea bargaining.

Evaluation research of these public defense innovations is limited. However, what is available indicates that both short-term and longer-term outcomes are positive for defendants who had holistic defense from the Bronx Defenders.[50] Preliminary results from a large-scale study reveal that holistic defense reduces the probability of a sentence of incarceration and reduces sentence length.[51] Clearly, more research is needed to determine what impacts holistic defense and community-oriented defense have on a variety of outcomes.

Moreover, there are a variety of national-level organizations advocating for the reinvention of indigent defense. These include the Smart on Crime Coalition, the Obama administration's and former Attorney General Eric Holder's Smart on Crime initiative, and Right on Crime. These groups believe indigent defense reform fits squarely within the broader agenda of criminal justice reform. The Smart on Crime Coalition consists of dozens of organizations, including the American Bar Association, the Counsel on State Governments, the Drug Policy Alliance, the Constitution Project, Human Rights Watch, the National Association of Criminal Defense Lawyers, and the Open Society Institute. Right on Crime has a long list of conservative signatories, including Jeb Bush, Asa Hutchinson, Jim DeMint, Newt Gingrich, Edwin Meese, Grover Norquist, and William Bennett.

The logic of reforming indigent defense and how it fits into broader criminal justice reform is nicely summarized by law professor Roger Fairfax:

> As we celebrate the golden anniversary of *Gideon*, it is important to contextualize our commitment to improving indigent criminal defense within the broader criminal justice policy agenda. Whether it is the focus on reducing our reliance on incarceration, tackling over-criminalization, or working with other criminal justice actors to find cost-effective ways to reduce crime and recidivism, much of the new smart-on-crime agenda is compatible with the aims of the indigent defense reform effort. In turn, the stronger our indigent defense

system is, the more cost-effective and efficient our criminal justice system will be.[52]

8

CONCLUSIONS, CHALLENGES, AND INCENTIVES

THE GOALS OF CRIMINAL JUSTICE REFORM

Most of the criticism of the American criminal justice system in recent years has been directed toward incarceration, including state and federal prisons and local jails. Attacking incarceration makes sense since it is a highly visible, stark metric of our tough-on-crime policy. The most common concern is the scale of incarceration. The media have labeled it "mass incarceration" and "warehousing offenders" and have noted how much prison populations have grown in recent decades and how much higher our incarceration rates are than those of most other countries. There has also been a good bit of attention paid to the cost to government to maintain such large prison and jail populations. A fair amount of criticism in recent years has also revolved around racial disparities in incarceration. Several high-profile books on this topic have caught the attention of experts and the public alike, including *Jim Crow: Mass Incarceration in the Age of Colorblindness* and *Locking Up Our Own: Crime and Punishment in Black America* by James Forman Jr., among many others.

Incarceration is also an important focus of criticism because of the toll it takes on individual offenders, their families, and communities as well as the extraordinary financial cost incurred by local, state, and federal governments in operating jails and prisons. Moreover, there are rather staggering broader social and economic costs associated with such heavy reliance on prison and jail, estimated to be $1 trillion per year.[1] This includes things like lost wages and productivity, marital instability, the criminogenic effect of incarceration and future recidivism, health implications, homelessness, and twenty other indicators that are not typically captured in government criminal justice budgets.

A common focal point of many reform discussions is cutting the prison population. Reducing incarceration was a significant target of many state legislatures and governors during the recession that began in 2007. Between 2007 and 2015, incarceration rates declined by about 13 percent in the thirty states that enacted policies to reduce incarceration.[2] Observers note that these prison reductions did not have any measurable impact on crime rates, which continued their longer-term decline that began in the early 1990s.[3] Reducing prison populations while crime rates continue to decline is a good outcome. However, many things impact crime rates and crime trends. Correctional policy is only one of those and one that historically has had a relatively small impact.

While reducing incarceration rates and prison populations is important, it is not, in our opinion, the ultimate goal of justice reform. The clear majority of offenders in U.S. jails and prisons have been through the criminal justice system before, either in prison or jail or on probation. Roughly two-thirds of the individuals on prosecutors' and public defenders' caseloads and judges' court dockets have been cycling in and out of the justice system. The point is simple. Many of the problems with American criminal justice are self-imposed failures to significantly reduce recidivism.

Thus, a more meaningful outcome—and one that gets to the core of fundamental, meaningful change—is recidivism. Recidivism is a much more direct and realistic measure of the impact of criminal justice policy and should drive and inform decisions and policies regarding criminality and criminal offenders. This broader question of how to effectively reduce recidivism shifts the focus upstream from corrections, away from simply smaller incarceration numbers or shorter periods on probation or parole, to what transpires well before someone ends up in the correctional system. We are reminded once again of the words of Caleb Foote: What happens in the pretrial stage determines mostly everything else.

We think of this in terms of reducing correctional numbers and budgets, achieving smaller prison and jail populations and probation and parole caseloads not simply by shortening or otherwise modifying sentences. Rather, our intent is reducing the size of the criminal justice system by reducing recidivism. While there are many impediments to significantly reducing recidivism, we believe that plea negotiation is a prime obstacle. We also believe that the pretrial system is a key barrier.

Imagine delivering health care the way we administer criminal justice. There would be little attention paid to examining patients and arriving at a symptom-based diagnosis. It would be largely one-or-two-sizes-fit-all, with a limited number of treatment options available to patients, treatment options that do not have much evidence-based validation. Patients would get the same medication regardless of the aliment and regardless of the medication's effectiveness and side effects. It sounds ludicrous, the outcomes would be devastating, and we would not tolerate it. But this is largely how the criminal justice system operates.

Part of the problem we face today is that most criminal justice reform initiatives tend to be quite specific, focusing on a relatively narrow issue or concern. Issue-driven reform targets things like mandatory minimums; marijuana policy; jail crowding; mental health; the death penalty; overcriminalization; law enforcement practices such as use-of-force, stop-and-frisk, and zero-tolerance policing; truth-in-sentencing laws that extend time served in prison; civil asset forfeiture; innocence; and "banning the box" to reduce restrictions on employment for those with a criminal record, to name a few. Issue-driven reform is important. The organizations that promote particular issues do a substantial service by identifying the problems and developing strategies for change. Many also provide technical assistance to state and local government in implementing reforms. The problem, however, is that issue-specific reform is not big-picture, comprehensive reform. It is by definition a particular slice, sometimes a very narrow slice of the criminal justice system. As such, issue-driven reform necessarily keeps policymakers and elected officials focused on separate issues or slices of the justice system, leading to fragmented or piecemeal change.

One way to guide broader, comprehensive reform is to identify a common denominator that can capture a number of issues and provide guidance for broader reform. We believe that recidivism reduction is a reasonable candidate for that common denominator. Recidivism reduction should include changes to many of the particular concerns identified by issue-driven initiatives. For example, recidivism reduction should include changes to sentencing laws, drug laws and policies, mental health of offenders, truth-in-sentencing laws, prosecutorial discretion, and overcriminalization, among others. As such, recidivism reduction can serve as an umbrella for much criminal justice reform. It undoubtedly misses many important things. Nevertheless, we think it is a useful starting point for thinking about and implementing comprehensive justice reform.

PUBLIC OPINION ABOUT CRIME POLICY

The public is quite supportive of criminal justice reform and has been for some time. A 2002 national survey found that by a two-to-one margin (65 to 32 percent), the public favors addressing the causes of crime over just strict punishment. The same poll reported that 56 percent of respondents prefer changes to sentencing policy by eliminating mandatory sentences, such as three-strikes laws. Public support for sentencing reform has grown since then. A 2016 survey shows that three-quarters now support sentencing reform.[4]

A trend analysis conducted by Gallup shows that Americans are less likely to believe today that the criminal justice system is "not tough enough." In 2003, two-thirds of Americans said that the system was not tough enough. Today, it is 45 percent. The percentage that believe that we are not tough enough on drug crimes is lower still at 34 percent.[5]

An RTI International and Zogby Analytics national poll conducted in March 2017 found that the public believes that the purpose of the criminal justice system is to rehabilitate. Two-thirds of Americans believe that rehabilitating or treating nonviolent offenders is preferred to punishing them (deterrence) or keeping them off the street (incapacitation). Three-quarters believe that alternatives such as diversion to rehabilitation rather than jail or prison is the most appropriate response for nonviolent offenders who are mentally ill. A 2016 poll commissioned by the Legal Action Center shows that the vast majority of respondents (78 percent) believe that drug and alcohol addiction should be treated as a health problem, not a criminal justice problem.[6]

A national poll taken in October 2017 reveals even stronger support for criminal justice reform across the political divide, even among individuals who voted for Trump.[7] The survey by the American Civil Liberties Union Campaign for Smart Justice shows that 91 percent of Americans support criminal justice reform. The vast majority support reducing the size of the prison population and reinvesting that money in drug and mental health treatment, including 65 percent of Trump supporters. Eighty-four percent believe that individuals with a mental health disability should be in treatment, not prison. Nearly three-quarters support abolishing mandatory minimum sentences and believe that incarceration is often counterproductive since inmates receive little rehabilitation while in prison. This includes 65 percent of Trump voters.

Oklahoma and Louisiana are two of the toughest-on-crime states as evidenced by the fact that they have the highest incarceration rates in the nation. A 2017 survey found that residents of these states strongly support alternatives to lengthy prison sentences:

> These results echo those of previous national and state-level public opinion research dating to 2010 that found overwhelming support for policy changes that shift nonviolent offenders from prison to more effective, less expensive alternatives. . . . In both states, majorities of Republicans, Democrats and independents backed general reform concepts, such as diverting less serious, nonviolent offenders from prison to alternative programs, reducing the length of incarceration, and reinvesting cost savings in treatment interventions and community-based supervision.[8]

An interesting take on attitudes about crime and punishment is a survey of victims of crime. A 2017 survey[9] asked crime victims what they thought contributed to crime and where governments should invest going forward. Drug and alcohol addiction (54 percent) and poor parenting (31 percent) are the top two reasons for criminal offending identified by crime victims. Only 4 percent believe that it is because there are too few people in prison. The majority (54 percent) of crime victims believe that more investment in rehabilitation and drug and mental health treatment is what is necessary. Only 6 percent said that the solution is more prisons and jails.

Another important survey of crime victims confirms the preference for changing behavior.[10] The results show that by a margin of two to one, crime victims believe that the criminal justice system should focus more on rehabilitation than punishment. One in three crime victims believe that it is better to hold offenders accountable through rehabilitation, mental health and drug treatment, and community supervision rather than incarceration. Seventy percent of crime victims believe that local prosecutors should focus more on reducing recidivism through rehabilitation, even if it results in fewer criminal convictions and sentences of incarceration.

The bottom line is that the public is ready for significant changes to the criminal justice system. The public clearly believes that tough punishment is not productive. Large majorities across the political divide believe that reducing crime and recidivism through rehabilitation and treatment is a more effective way to enhance public safety.

While among the public, criminal justice reform is not a partisan issue, it is still being treated that way by many elected officials. It is puzzling that in this environment of strong bipartisan support for criminal justice reform, Trump ran for and won the presidency in part as the "law-and-order" candidate. Moreover, U.S. Attorney General Jeff Sessions has implemented new policies for federal prosecutors requiring them to charge the maximum offense possible in drug cases, and Sessions has recently expressed his preference for mandatory sentences and successfully kept repeal of mandatory sentencing off the White House's criminal justice reform agenda. On January 3, 2018, Sessions repealed the Cole memo, the Obama administration's policy of not enforcing federal marijuana laws in states that have legalized recreational use. As of January 2018, eight states and the District of Columbia have legalized recreational use of marijuana. On January 23, 2018, Sessions wrote an op-ed in *USA Today* claiming that tough-on-crime policies are responsible for the great crime decline that began in the 1990s and that Trump's initiatives have, since he took office, resulted in further declines in violent crime.[11] Maybe this is what they mean by alternative facts. Despite the scientific evidence and strong public opinion, the Trump administration appears to be working from the old, tired, discredited tough-on-crime playbook from the 1980s.

GOING FORWARD

In our minds, the four sets of recommendations we make here—transforming plea negotiation, reforming the pretrial system, plea negotiation mediators, and addressing the problems with public defense—are fundamentally intertwined. The problems with plea negotiation are in part due to deficiencies in the pretrial system and the public defense system. It is obvious to us that comprehensive criminal justice reform requires not only fundamental changes to the plea negotiation process but transformative changes to the pretrial system and public defense as well. For example, prosecutorial discretion cannot be addressed without a well-functioning public defense system and oversight of the plea process by a neutral third party. Recidivism-focused problem solving cannot occur without expert clinical advice regarding assessment and diagnosis, risk management, and recommendations about diversion and treatment. The pretrial system is an appropriate setting for implementing sophisticated screening and assessment and diversion to needs-based services. Reinventing the pretrial system by incorporating competent screening and assessment early in the pretrial process and diversion to appropriate services takes a pretrial system that in many jurisdictions has largely been a lost opportunity and transforms it into a significant player in recidivism reduction. These changes will affect the plea process in productive ways.

Challenges

We are quite aware that what we recommend is not easy, to say the least. It is extraordinarily ambitious and involves a sea change in public policy regarding the administration of criminal justice. It will require substantial changes to law, procedure, policy, funding, and, importantly, how we think about crime and punishment.

We are trying to shift the philosophy of justice from retribution, anger-based decision making resulting in the reflexive imposition of punishment toward problem solving and more frequent considerations of disorder, deficit, impairment, intervention, mitigation, behavioral change, and, ultimately, recidivism reduction. Among other things, we are proposing that the key individuals in the justice system, primarily prosecutors, judges, and defense counsel, collectively accept responsibility for the outcomes of the system they administer.

An indispensable component of that is the adoption of a problem-solving approach to how they deal with individual offenders. But we appreciate that these principal individuals are lawyers, and when recidivism reduction becomes the goal, we are introducing complexities that require expertise that goes beyond their training and experience. Several of the prosecutors, judges, and public defenders we interviewed said just that:

> I didn't go to medical school. I'm not a medical professional of any kind. What I know is what I've read. It's my gut feeling. So if there were independent experts, third parties not working for either side, then I think their input would be invaluable to me.

> Yeah, it would ease the burden for attorneys to make those evaluations who aren't really trained in mental health.

> Most definitely. We are not doctors or counselors. I'm a lawyer. We are not trained in that area, so when you bring this body of people with training, it's invaluable.

> I'm not a psychiatrist, so that would be really helpful.

> I'm a lawyer not a doctor. That's [dealing with mental health problems] not what I do, and we can use all the help we can get.

> Making decisions about who is mentally ill is usually up to me. I'm not trained to do that.

To make things even more formidable, the initiatives and reforms that we propose are largely local. Prosecutors and judges are local. Pretrial systems are local. Public defenders and appointed counsel are local. Jails are local. Moreover, decisions about these matters will be made by a variety of county and city government officials, prosecutors, judges, the defense bar and various other administrators, stakeholders, and interested and affected agencies and organizations.

One of the reasons this is challenging is that there are 3,142 counties and county equivalents in the United States, most of which are, to a significant extent, self-contained criminal justice systems. This is not to say that state legislatures are irrelevant. Their cooperation will be required to the extent that statutory changes are necessary. Funding will also be a substantial consideration, as diversion will require significant increases in capacity for treatment of mental health problems, substance abuse, and neurodevelopmental and neurocognitive impairments, among others.

There are many roadblocks that will make effective transformation of the justice system difficult. One is the scale of the changes that we propose and have recommended elsewhere, which is best described as comprehensive and transformative.[12] We are certainly capable of such change. After all, where we are today bears little resemblance to the justice system of 1980.

The adversarial process necessarily pits prosecution and defense against each other and places judges in their own unique role, so it should be obvious that they would approach things with their own goals, perceptions, beliefs, values, constraints, and cultures. Prosecutors, judges, and public defenders work in three often disparate cultures (silos). Although the interviews did not directly focus on judges', prosecutors', and public defenders' roles relative to the justice system more broadly, we suggest that they probably see themselves as separate from the rest of the system. There is considerable agreement among critical observers that the silo metaphor is quite fitting for the American criminal justice system.[13] Breaking those silos down will be a major effort.

There are many moving parts in what we propose: local government, state legislatures, agencies and commissions (especially local prosecutors, judges, and defense attorneys), pretrial services, probation, law enforcement, nonprofits and foundations, public health agencies, employment and education resources, and many other stakeholders. Cooperation, trust, turf, money, power, and control will all come into play. Agencies and organizations that may not be used to working together and collaborating, such as prosecutors and public health agencies, will need to dismantle silos and forge new relationships.

Perhaps the toughest challenge is cultural, and that will manifest in many ways. First is changing how we think about crime and punishment. Prosecutors were asked to describe their job—how they think about what they do. While they did not express consensus regarding how they view their job, most of what they said reflected a way of thinking that limits their options. Prosecutors think in terms of justice, law enforcement, accountability, and punishment:

> I enforce the criminal laws . . . if someone is accused of a crime, we convict if there's enough evidence. If we believe they're innocent, then we dismiss the case.

> I enforce the law.

> My job is to impose consequences on people for their criminal choices.

> My job is to prosecute the cases that are presented by a police department and get indicted by a grand jury.

> We look at what they [defendants] do and figure if they should go to jail or not.

> I determine who is guilty and then impose the right punishment.

A few prosecutors tend to think in terms of justice:

> We are there to seek justice. I seek to do what is right by the facts given.

> To seek justice regarding the criminal law.

> Justice for victims. We want them to feel like they've had their day in court.

> To make sure the victims are satisfied. Doing justice for them.

> Fairness.

A couple were more pragmatic:

> A lot of my work is negotiation.

> I'm just working a docket.

What is striking is that none of the prosecutors we interviewed said anything about public safety. This underscores the challenge associated with changing how key individuals in the justice system think about crime and punishment.

We also asked prosecutors how they define success. The prosecutors we interviewed have a variety of definitions or measures of success. Many prosecutors were quick to say that success is not measured in terms of convictions:

> I definitely don't track my convictions.

> I'll tell you it's not convictions.

Several think of success in terms of victims:

> I measure success by making sure victims are satisfied or receive closure.

> I think it's in the places where I can help a victim in a case. . . . I do like to see my cases move.

Others believe that holding offenders accountable is important:

> If the victim is happy and the defendant is held accountable.

> I would say for me it's holding people accountable and responsible for their actions.

For some prosecutors, success is justice:

> If the outcome has achieved some justice in the case.

> Do I feel like I actually accomplish something that is good and just, it is the right result.

A couple mentioned the proportionality of punishment:

> Does the punishment fit the crime.

> Did they receive the right punishment.

One respondent sees success in more practical terms:

> Caseload management.

Once again, what is particularly noteworthy is that none of the prosecutors we interviewed said anything about success being measured in terms of public safety or recidivism reduction.

Defense attorneys were asked whether they consider the prosecutors they work with to be tough on crime. Nearly all said that in their experience, the prosecutors they work with are tough on crime and do not seem to care much about recidivism:

> I don't think they care about recidivism.

> I'd say they are tough on offenders.

> Yes, that's all they care about, numbers [convictions].

> In our jurisdiction they just prosecute everyone. That's being stupid on crime.

> Hard 5 on the 1-to-5 scale.

> Very tough. Not known for coddling.

> They just keep giving tougher sentences rather than listening to why it's [crime] happening.

> Yes. They don't let the little things go.

> They are [tough]. For the most part, they are very unreasonable.

Federal public defenders have already seen changes due to the new charging guidance coming out of the Sessions Justice Department:

> With the new administration [Trump and Sessions] we already see tipping in the other direction, mitigation is being ignored, lock 'em up and let it get sorted later is a growing attitude.

The public seems to understand the bigger picture of the relationship between public safety and rehabilitation. What has yet to occur is that recognition by key individuals such as prosecutors, judges, and defense counsel. That needs to be accompanied by recognizing the critical importance of implementing evidence-based behavioral change interventions. What stands in the way is a well-entrenched culture of retribution, tough on crime, one-size-fits-all punishment, and failure to accept responsibility for reducing recidivism.

Part of the cultural shift involves redefining relationships and roles. Prosecutors and defense attorneys have traditionally had an adversarial relationship. That is understandable based on the ideal image of criminal prosecution as a criminal trial. However, the problem-solving focus going forward will require prosecutors and defense attorneys to collaborate more than they have historically. That will require renegotiating these relationships.

Then there is the matter of having outsiders, such as the plea mediator and the expert panels, involved in the business of the criminal justice system. While the prosecutors and defense counsel we interviewed for the most part welcome the idea of the expert panels, it will require some adjustment for outsiders to be involved in decision making that has traditionally been essentially unilateral. The participation of the expert panels and the plea mediator will certainly change the dynamics of the interactions among the key players as well as alter the distribution of power. It will also require changing the culture to focus on collaboratively working on reducing reoffending.

Creating capacity for diversion is another challenge. Thirty-nine states have statutory diversion programs for offenders with substance abuse problems (e.g., drug courts). Twenty-four states have diversion programs for offenders with mental illness (mental health courts and similar programs), and twenty-four states also provide diversion for veterans and active military personnel (e.g., veterans courts).[14] Thirty-six states and the District of Columbia have pretrial diversion for a variety of circumstances.[15] Although this is a step in the right direction, it is inadequate by a large margin.

Availability of effective treatment is a significant challenge. The two operative words in the last sentence are "availability" and "effective." Specialty courts like drug, mental health, and veterans courts and a variety of others have become a popular alternative to traditional criminal prosecution and punishment. While common, they are not ubiquitous, and in those jurisdictions that have them, the evidence indicates that capacity is not close to the need.[16] Most of the prosecutors, judges, and defense attorneys we interviewed stated that they do not think that the diversion programs in their jurisdictions had sufficient capacity to meet the need.

For example, many substance abuse treatment facilities have adopted the twelve-step model of Alcoholics Anonymous as the primary protocol, which is not evidence based. Moreover, treatment for the current opioid crisis is inadequate. Only about one-third of the addiction treatment programs in the United States use evidence-based protocols, which include maintenance doses of methadone or buprenorphine. Many treatment facilities reject medication as appropriate care for opioid abuse; thus, many individuals who are in treatment are not receiving evidence-based care.[17]

The good news is that there are probably a dozen or so progressive, reform-oriented district attorneys who have recently been elected and taken office. Examples include Kim Ogg in Houston, Larry Krasner in Philadelphia, and Mark Gonzalez in Corpus Christi, Texas. At the same time, there is certainly considerable pushback to reform from prosecutors, starting with U.S. Attorney General Sessions. Another example includes district attorneys in Louisiana who are hindering an effort in that state to overhaul felony sentencing laws.[18] The Florida Prosecuting Attorneys Association and those like it in every other state advocate for prosecutors, and a general theme they support is tough on crime. This association opposed DNA testing to prove wrongful conviction, changes to the death penalty, and efforts to divert first-time drug offenders to treatment rather than jail. The California District Attorneys Association sued to prevent Proposition 57, which included a variety of justice reforms, such as reduced prison sentences and early release for some inmates. Udi Ofer, the director of the Campaign for Smart Justice at the American Civil Liberties Union, stated,

> They [prosecutors and district attorney associations] all too often act
> as a roadblock to significant reforms. In state after state, we've seen
> DA associations hold back reforms that are supported by Democrats
> and Republicans alike.[19]

Despite some progress like modest reductions in the prison population, the existence of diversion programs like drug courts, and significant change in public attitudes about crime and punishment, there still appears to be significant political comfort in being tough on crime. While it may not have the salience it had in the 1980s, 1990s, and early 2000s, taking a tough stance on crime apparently still sells. One way to counter that is labeling reform "smart on crime" and highlighting the two primary positives: effectiveness and cost savings.

Then there is the fear of uncertainty and fear of change. While the evidence indicates that these reform initiatives can work, whether they do is dependent on a large number of factors. Getting it right requires a good bit of hard work. Investing resources as well as one's reputation in criminal justice reform may be too politically risky for some.

One of the most important elements in implementing such change is the presence of high-profile leadership in a jurisdiction that champions reform. Judges and district attorneys are obvious choices for this role. Their leadership will have more credibility than someone outside of the justice system.

Figuring out how to fund this is particularly difficult. Part of the problem is that what we propose will require reallocation of funds within the criminal justice system. The justice system involves different levels of government and thus different budgets. States pay for prison and parole, and local jurisdictions typically have primary responsibility for paying for law enforcement, the courts, indigent defense, jails, pretrial services, diversion programs, and probation. The funding models differ by state, so in many instances, state government also funds some of these local activities. But the point is the same: Different agencies, different sets of interests, and different budgets within the broader criminal justice system come into play in the reallocation of resources.

One relatively new funding model is already well established. The Justice Reinvestment Initiative is defined by the Bureau of Justice Assistance as follows:

> Justice reinvestment is a data-driven approach to improve public safety, reduce corrections and related criminal justice spending, and reinvest savings in strategies that can decrease crime and strengthen neighborhoods. The purpose of justice reinvestment is to manage and allocate criminal justice resources more cost-effectively, generating savings that can be reinvested in evidence-based strategies that increase public safety.[20]

Justice reinvestment provides technical assistance and funding to states to assess their justice policies, identify poorly performing policies, revamp those policies (e.g., reducing the prison population), and then reinvesting the savings in community-based programs that have been shown to effectively reduce recidivism. The primary drivers of justice reinvestment are the Justice Center at the Counsel of State Governments, the Pew Charitable Trusts, and the Vera Institute of Justice.

The logic of justice reinvestment is quite sound: defund poor performance and increase funding to policies that have been shown to be effective and cost efficient. Thirty-three states have participated in justice reinvestment to various degrees since 2007. The evidence to date indicates that justice reinvestment is an effective, viable strategy for redirecting funding to high-performing (i.e., recidivism reduction) programs and policies.[21] It is important to repeat that public opinion data we discussed earlier in this chapter show that the public is clearly behind such reinvestment strategies.

The other funding issue involves the fact that what we propose requires the participation of other sectors of government. Addressing the mental health, substance abuse, and neurocognitive disorders and deficits will require expertise from agencies and organizations outside of the justice system. That invariably requires expenditures from those agencies' budgets in creating sufficient treatment capacity. This will be particularly challenging until there is widespread recognition of and appreciation for the fact that the crime and recidivism problem is not just a criminal justice problem.

There will undoubtedly be other issues that arise in the process of implementing change. As is the normal course for such reform efforts, local jurisdictions develop pilot programs that can then be adapted, modified, and adopted in other jurisdictions. The early adopters will do a good bit of the heavy lifting, and lessons learned from their efforts will facilitate the path for others. For example, the Lone Star Justice Alliance in Austin, Texas, is in the process of developing and implementing the expert panel concept in several local jurisdictions around the country. Their efforts will provide proof of concept and lessons learned in the process and will facilitate adoption in other jurisdictions.

Incentives

There are many incentives that should motivate consideration of these recommendations. First and foremost is the potential to significantly and substantially reduce recidivism. As the justice system transitions from primarily retribution and punishment focused to a more balanced behavioral change, risk management, and punishment model, recidivism rates will decline. That is, after all, what the criminal justice system is supposed to do. As recidivism declines, so will criminal victimization. That certainly is a public good.

Some of the key concepts we propose, such as the expert panel concept and the diversion of offenders to treatment, were generally embraced by the prosecutors, defense attorneys, and judges we interviewed. Many stated that this would greatly assist them from day to day in their jobs. Defense counsel noted the potential for better outcomes for their clients. They also indicated that with the exception of some public defenders being concerned with confidentiality, their colleagues would likely welcome the concept as well. The confidentiality issue will need to be addressed. Judges noted that there could be pushback from the defense bar, so addressing their concerns is important.

Our interviews were in a limited number of jurisdictions, so the beliefs and opinions that prosecutors, defense attorneys, and judges have could be different in different venues. Thus, it is important that implementation efforts include understanding the opinions and concerns of local practitioners and making modifications accordingly.

Reducing crime, recidivism, and victimization is a public good. So is saving money. The logic regarding financial benefit is straightforward. Every time someone reoffends, all of the criminal justice costs are incurred again—costs associated with law enforcement, jail, pretrial services, a public defender or assigned counsel, the court, the prosecutor, a grand jury, and corrections, among others. In turn, every time someone does not reenter the justice system, all of those costs are avoided, not to mention the broader costs of crime and victimization. If we are able to interrupt the offending behavior of a typical repeat offender and thus avoid multiple criminal events over a period of years, those cost savings increase dramatically.

What we propose involves substantial investment in addressing criminogenic disorders, impairment, and deficits. Cost-benefit analyses consistently show that evidence-based screening and assessment, intervention/treatment, rehabilitation, and, in turn, behavioral change all amount to a very wise investment.[22] Not only do the cost-benefit analyses show favorable ratios in the short term, but those relative benefits also become greater over time as future crime is avoided.

However, there are additional economic and social costs that do not normally enter into the cost-benefit analyses. These involve the collateral costs of crime and criminal justice involvement, things that affect the offender, his or her family, victims, neighborhoods, and communities. They include issues such as lost productivity, lost wages, barriers to economic mobility for justice-involved individuals as well as their families and children, marital and household disruption, increased criminality of children of justice-involved parents, impacts of crime on property values, and victim costs, such as lost property, physical harm, and quality of life, among many others.

There needs to be a greater appreciation on the part of policymakers and elected officials of the fundamental interrelationships among criminal justice and other institutions, such as public health and public education, to name just two. One of the very common concerns raised by the individuals we interviewed is the lack of resources to effectively support expert assessment, diversion, and treatment.

What is apparent is that the neglect and underfunding of public institutions, such as public health and public education, have profound consequences for crime and criminal justice. Two current examples illustrate the point. Repealing and replacing the Affordable Care Act and states' decisions not to extend Medicaid have significant implications for criminal justice. Both negatively affect insurance coverage for things like mental health, neurocognitive disorders, and substance abuse and may indirectly impact capacity for treatment of these disorders. Either by design or by default, the criminal justice system is the repository for the consequences of underfunding these other institutions. One would be hard-pressed to make a valid case that dealing with those consequences this way is fiscally prudent. Does it make economic sense to repeatedly lock up rather than effectively treat mentally ill and/ or substance-abusing individuals?

There are clear benefits from what we propose to those directly involved in the administration of criminal justice. One chronic problem in the U.S. criminal justice system is crowding—excessive caseloads for judges, prosecutors, public defenders, probation and parole officers, and pretrial supervision officers. This is not a consequence of high crime rates. We have been at or near historically low crime for twenty years or so. Rather, this is fueled primarily by high recidivism rates. In time, as these proposals are implemented, assuming that crime rates remain stable and recidivism rates fall, the number of people entering the justice system should decline, reducing caseloads and court dockets. Moreover, as the number of individuals who are diverted to pretrial diversion programs and deferred adjudication increases, there will be corresponding reductions in prosecutors' and public defenders' caseloads and court dockets. In fact, several prosecutors noted that is an important selling point to their colleagues.

The approach that U.S. criminal justice policy has taken over the past forty-five or fifty years is in some respects analogous to a payday loan. A payday loan may seem like a good idea in the moment as a way to address an immediate problem. But the longer-term consequences are often catastrophic, resulting in individuals being in an endless cycle of debt. Being tough on crime and sentencing someone to prison may seem like a good idea in the moment as a way to address an immediate problem, but there are longer-term consequences that can be catastrophic as well. Ninety-eight percent of all prison and jail inmates will get out, and the vast majority will reoffend.

The bottom line is that today we have the evidence base required to reinvent the criminal justice system. It is possible to administer an effective, fair, and cost-efficient justice system, and we believe that what we propose is a path to those goals. The public is behind reform, there are some vocal elected officials and policymakers backing it, and there are numerous prominent and many less well known nonprofits and foundations at the national level and locally that are advocating and supporting criminal justice reform. What appears to be missing is the political will to make meaningful, comprehensive reform a priority.

APPENDIX

Interview Discussion Guides

DEFENSE COUNSEL

Plea Negotiation and Criminal Justice Reform

Public Defender Interview Guide

Date _____

Interviewer _____

Public Defender or Assigned Counsel

PLEASE ANSWER THESE QUESTIONS BASED ON YOUR IN-
DIVIDUAL BELIEFS, ATTITUDES, AND EXPERIENCES.

A. BACKGROUND

A1. How long have you been a public defender/assigned counsel?

A2. Have you spent all of that time here?

Y

N

A3. Do you handle both felonies and misdemeanors?

BOTH

FELONIES ONLY

MISDEMEANORS ONLY

IF BOTH

A4. What is the mix of the two for you (percentage)?

FELONY PERCENTAGE

MISDEMEANOR PERCENTAGE

A5. How many cases do you typically have per year (separate felony and misdemeanor)?

FELONY

MISDEMEANOR

B. PLEA PROCESS

B1. The statistics vary, but in general about 95 percent of all criminal convictions are plea negotiations. Why do you think the percentage is so high? (PROBE: CASELOADS PRESSURE, NOT ENOUGH RESOURCES TO HOLD MORE TRIALS, PLEA DEALS ARE BETTER FOR MY CLIENTS?)

B2. When does plea negotiation typically commence? At what stage of processing?

B3. Is plea negotiation usually a matter of the prosecutor offering a deal and the defendant then takes that offer? Or does it usually involve more negotiation, more back and forth?

B4. How do you determine what is appropriate for a plea offer? How do you gauge the "going rate" for a particular case or what is fair?

B5. What kinds of leverage do prosecutors typically use to motivate defendants to accept a plea deal?

B6. Do you ever feel that a client of yours has been coerced by the prosecutor to accept a plea deal? Is "coercion" the right word? If not, what is? How often does this happen?

B7. How often are sentences embedded in or agreed on in the plea deal? (PROBE: IS IT ROUTINE/COMMON OR PRETTY RARE?)

B8. What resources do you consider important for providing an effective defense? (PROBE: TIME, INVESTIGATORS, FORENSIC EXPERTS, OTHER EXPERTS, PSYCHOLOGISTS, PSYCHIATRISTS?)

B8a. Are these resources routinely available to you when you need them?

B9. All else equal, if the policy in the prosecutor's office changed such that the percentage of cases that are plea negotiated dropped by say 20 percentage points (assume it's 90 percent and it dropped to 70 percent, so that the percent that went to trial increased from 10 to 30 percent), what do you think would be the impact on the public defender's office? On you? How would your job change?

C. PROBLEMS WITH PLEA NEGOTIATION

Much has been written about plea negotiation in recent years. A good bit of it focuses on a variety of problems or concerns. Based on your experience as a defense attorney, which of the following do you consider significant problems or concerns with plea negotiation in your jurisdiction? Using a scale from 1 to 5, where 1 is Not a Problem at All and 5 is a Substantial Problem, please indicate the extent to which you think each is a problem. WE ARE LOOKING FOR A SCORE AND SOME DISCUSSION.

C1. Lack of due process protections? (THE ARGUMENT THAT DUE PROCESS PROTECTIONS PERTAIN MAINLY TO A CRIMINAL TRIAL, NOT PLEA NEGOTIATION)

C2. Lack of mens rea requirements in the law? (TOO MANY STRICT LIABILITY CRIMES, MEANING CRIMES FOR WHICH MENS REA IS NOT REQUIRED)

C3. Mens rea is often just ignored by the prosecutor? (NOT PART OF THE EVIDENCE OR THE PLEA NEGOTIATION)

REMIND INTERVIEWEE: Again, using a scale from 1 to 5, where 1 is Not a Problem at All and 5 is Substantial Problem.

C4. Excessive use of pretrial detention?

C5. Limited investigation of the case? (THE ARGUMENT THAT PLEA DEALS OFTEN OCCUR BEFORE A THROUGH INVESTIGATION OF THE CASE)

C6. Limited discovery? (DEFENSE IS NOT PROVIDED WITH MUCH OF THE GOVERNMENT'S EVIDENCE IN THE CASE)

SKIP IF B6 IS NO

C7. Coerced confessions? (IF RAISED AS A CONCERN, FOLLOW UP WITH)

SKIP IF C7 IS NO

C7a. How are confessions coerced? What tactics are used?

C8. Fact that the evidence is not litigated?

C9. Probable cause is the standard for conviction, not reasonable doubt?

C10. What else that we have not covered do you consider a problem or concern with plea negotiation?

D. RECIDIVISM, DIVERSION, THE DISORDERED DEFENDANT

D1. Criminal offenders often have one or more disorders and impairments, such as mental illness, substance use disorders, intellectual deficits, and neurocognitive impairments. By neurocognitive impairments, I mean things like impaired memory, attention, impulse control, goal directed behavior, and planning. These can be caused by traumatic brain injury and other trauma in the environment.

Today, the recidivism rates for mentally ill offenders or offenders with substance use disorders is over 80 percent. Similarly, those with neurocognitive disorders have extraordinarily high recidivism. The evidence indicates that what we have been doing with these types of offenders is not working.

D2. Are defendants routinely screened or assessed for such disorders and impairments in your jurisdiction? (NOT AT ALL, VERY RARELY, OFTEN, ROUTINELY)

IF OFTEN OR ROUTINELY

D2a. Who initiates the screening and assessment? (PROSECUTOR, COURT, DEFENSE, PRETRIAL SERVICES)

IF OFTEN OR ROUTINELY

D2b. Who does the screening and assessment? (PSYCHOLO-GISTS, PSYCHIATRISTS, SOCIAL WORKERS, PROBATION OFFICERS)

D3. Is it pretty routine, or is it the exception that significant psychological, intellectual, or cognitive disorders are considered in the plea negotiation?

D3a. IF IT IS A CONSIDERATION, how is information about a disorder or impairment used in the plea process? (IS IT USED TO MITIGATE CULPABILITY, SENTENCE REDUCTION, ETC.?)

D3b. IF IT IS USED, what are some common disorders or impairments that in your experience are considered in the plea process?

D4. What types of diversion options are there for disordered defendants in this county?

D5. Is the diversion decision pretty much up to the prosecutor? What is your role?

Consider the following idea. Panels of independent experts, like psychologists, neuroscientists, addiction specialists, and psychiatrists, routinely screen and assess defendants for things like mental illness, substance use disorders, neurocognitive impairments, and intellectual deficits. These experts would determine who is significantly disordered as well as their risk of reoffending, especially for violent crimes. In turn, they would make recommendations to the prosecutor regarding who should be diverted to treatment and supervision/risk management and who should be traditionally prosecuted and sentenced. Assume for the purposes of this question that there are sufficient diversion resources for diverting and treating these disordered defendants.

D6. Is that something that you view as potentially valuable to you and your clients?

D7. What concerns do you have? What barriers might there be to adoption of this idea?

D8. How might this concept be proposed to defense attorneys? What might serve as an incentive to promote this idea to the defense bar?

D9. Is it your experience that prosecutors in your jurisdiction tend to be tough on crime?

VARIES

USUALLY TEND TO BE TOUGH

DON'T USUALLY TEND TO BE TOUGH

THANK AND TERMINATE

PROSECUTORS

Plea Negotiation and Criminal Justice Reform

Prosecutor Interview Guide

Date _____

Interviewer _____

PLEASE ANSWER THESE QUESTIONS BASED ON YOUR IN-DIVIDUAL BELIEFS, ATTITUDES, AND EXPERIENCES.

A. BACKGROUND

A1. How long have you been a prosecutor?

A2. Have you spent all of that time here?

Y

N

A3. Do you prosecute both felonies and misdemeanors?

BOTH

FELONIES ONLY

MISDEMEANORS ONLY

IF BOTH

A3a. What is the mix of the two (percentage)?

FELONY PERCENTAGE

MISDEMEANOR PERCENTAGE

A4. How many cases do you typically have per year? (separate felony and misdemeanor if they do both)

FELONY

MISDEMEANOR

A5. How do you describe your role as a prosecutor? If someone asked you what does a prosecutor do, what would you say?

B. PLEA PROCESS

B1. The statistics vary, but in general about 95 percent of all criminal convictions are plea negotiations. Why do you think the percentage is so high? (PROBE: CASELOADS PRESSURE, NOT ENOUGH RE-SOURCES TO HOLD MORE TRIALS, MORE EXPEDIENT?)

B2. When does negotiation typically commence?

B3. Is it usually a matter of you offering a deal and the defendant then takes that offer, or does it usually involve more negotiation? More back and forth?

B4. How do you determine what is appropriate in a plea offer? How do you determine the "going rate" in a particular case?

B5. Do you have pretty broad discretion in determining the parameters of the plea? How much does the district attorney set the standards?

B6. What kinds of incentives do you use to motivate defendants to plea?

B7. Does your office use any kind of plea bargaining guidelines? If so, please describe. Are they advisory or required? IF THEY USE THEM, FIND OUT MORE DETAIL ABOUT THEM; ARE THEY GENERAL OR SPECIFIC?

B8. How often are sentences embedded in or agreed on in the plea deal? (PROBE: IS IT ROUTINE/COMMON OR PRETTY RARE?)

B8a. Is it typically a recommendation, or is it binding on the court?

B9. If the percentage of cases that are plea negotiated dropped by say 20 percentage points (assume it's 90 percent now and it dropped to 70 percent, so that the percent that went to trial increased from 10 to 30 percent), what do you think would be the impact on the prosecutor's office? On you as a prosecutor? How would your job change?

B10. Does your office keep systematic records of plea agreements? Does your office keep systematic records of the outcomes of the agreements, such as successful completion of diversion, rearrest, etc.?

C. PROBLEMS WITH PLEA NEGOTIATION

C1. Based on your experience as a prosecutor, what concerns do you have about plea negotiation and the plea negotiation process? (PROBE: FOR EXAMPLE, DUE PROCESS ISSUES)

C2. How do you measure success in what you do? (PROBE: CONVICTIONS, CASELOAD MANAGEMENT, RECIDIVISM)

D. RECIDIVISM, DIVERSION, THE DISORDERED DEFENDANT

D1. Recidivism is a common outcome measure for the criminal justice system. What role do you think you and your colleagues play with regard to recidivism? (WE WANT TO GET A SENSE OF WHETHER THEY FEEL THEY CAN IMPACT RECIDIVISM AND, IF SO, HOW)

D2. Why do you think offenders reoffend at such a high rate?

Criminal offenders often have one or more disorders and impairments, such as mental illness, substance use disorders, neurocognitive impairments, and intellectual deficits.

D3. Are defendants routinely screened or assessed for such disorders and impairments in your jurisdiction? IF YES, when does that happen? IF YES, who typically does the screening? (PSYCHOLOGISTS, PSYCHIATRISTS, SOCIAL WORKERS, PROBATION OFFICERS?; I WANT A SENSE OF HOW QUALIFIED THE PERSON IS WITHOUT ASKING THE QUESTION)

D3a. Who typically gets screened? Obvious cases, or is it more broadly done?

D3b. Are such disorders or impairments that a defendant has a consideration in the plea negotiation process? (PROBE: ROUTINELY, OFTEN, RARELY, NOT AT ALL) IF SO, how is that information used?

D4. What types of diversion options are there for defendants in this county? What types of circumstances are defendants diverted for? (PROBE: SUBSTANCE ABUSE? MENTAL ILLNESS? INTELLECTUAL DEFICITS? NEUROCOGNITIVE DYSFUNCTION?)

D4a. Is the capacity for such diversion adequate for meeting the need?

D5. Is the diversion decision pretty much up to you? Who else is involved in the decision?

D6. Today, the recidivism rates for mentally ill offenders or offenders with substance use disorders is over 80 percent. Similarly, those with neurocognitive disorders have extraordinarily high recidivism. The evidence indicates that what we have been doing with these types of offenders is not working.

D6a. What should we be doing to address such high recidivism rates? What should change?

Consider the following idea. Having panels of independent experts like psychologists, neuroscientists, addiction specialists, and psychiatrists who routinely screen and assess defendants for things like mental illness, substance use disorders, neurocognitive impairments, and intellectual deficits. These experts would determine who is significantly disordered as well as their risk of reoffending, especially for violent crimes. In turn, they would make recommendations to you regarding who should be diverted to treatment and risk management and who should be traditionally prosecuted and sentenced. Assume for the purposes of this question that there are sufficient diversion resources for diverting and treating these disordered defendants.

D6b. Is that something that is potentially valuable to you? (HOW? WHY?)

D6c. What concerns do you have about this idea? What barriers might there be to adoption of this idea?

D6d. How might this concept be proposed to prosecutors? What might serve as an incentive to promote adoption of this idea? Are there legislative changes that would have to occur? What are they?

THANK AND TERMINATE

JUDGES

Plea Negotiation and Criminal Justice Reform

Judge Interview Guide

Date _____

Interviewer _____

PLEASE ANSWER THESE QUESTIONS BASED ON YOUR IN-
DIVIDUAL BELIEFS, ATTITUDES, AND EXPERIENCES.

A. BACKGROUND

A1. How long have you been a judge?

A2. Have you spent all of that time here?

Y

N

A3. Do you preside over felonies and misdemeanors?

FELONIES ONLY

MISDEMEANORS ONLY

A4. How many cases do you typically have per year?

FELONY

MISDEMEANOR

A5. How do you describe your role as a judge? If someone asked you
what does a judge do, what would you say?

A6. Many observers have concluded that prosecutors have an extraordinary amount of power and discretion in the American criminal
justice system. In your experience, do you find that to be the case?
Please explain.

IF YES TO A6

A7. What would you say are the positives and negatives of prosecutorial discretion?

B. PLEA PROCESS

B1. The statistics vary, but in general about 95 percent of all criminal
convictions are plea negotiations. Why do you think the percentage is so
high? (PROBE: CASELOADS PRESSURE, NOT ENOUGH RE-
SOURCES TO HOLD MORE TRIALS, MORE EXPEDIENT?)

B2. What is your role in plea negotiation?

B3. What do you think your role should be? How would you change the process of plea negotiation with regard to your role?

B4. What do you think are the benefits of plea negotiation?

B5. What do you think are the problems with plea negotiation? (PROBE IF NECESSARY—What about innocent individuals pleading guilty, due process problems, coercion or excessive pressure, pretrial detention, limited discovery, prosecutorial discretion? Other?)

B6. How often do you impose the sentence versus accepting what the prosecutor recommended or stipulated in the plea deal?

B7. How do you determine what is appropriate in a plea offer? How do you determine the "going rate" in a particular case?

B8. If the percentage of cases that are plea negotiated dropped by say 20 percentage points (assume it's 90 percent now and it dropped to 70 percent, so that the percent that went to trial increased from 10 to 30 percent), what do you think would be the impact on the courts? On you as a judge? How would your job change?

C. THE PRETRIAL SYSTEM

It has been said by many experts that pretrial decisions determine everything. The evidence indicates the pretrial detention affects the probability of conviction, the type and severity of the sentence, and longer-term recidivism.

C1. How well do you think the pretrial system in your jurisdiction is working?

C1a. Are the right people being detained and released?

C1b. Is supervision adequate?

C1c. Are those who need pretrial services getting appropriate services?

C1d. What do you think needs to change with the pretrial system? PROBE IF NECESSARY—DETENTION DECISION, SUPERVISION, SERVICES?

D. RECIDIVISM, DIVERSION, THE DISORDERED DEFENDANT

D1. Recidivism is a common outcome measure for the criminal justice system. What role do you think you and your colleagues play with regard to recidivism? (WE WANT TO GET A SENSE OF WHETHER THEY FEEL THEY CAN IMPACT RECIDIVISM AND, IF SO, HOW)

D2. Why do you think offenders reoffend at such a high rate?

Criminal offenders often have one or more disorders and impairments, such as mental illness, substance use disorders, neurocognitive impairments, and intellectual deficits.

D3. Are defendants routinely screened or assessed for such disorders and impairments in your jurisdiction? IF YES, when does that happen? IF YES, who typically does the screening? (PSYCHOLOGISTS, PSYCHIATRISTS, SOCIAL WORKERS, PROBATION OFFICERS?; I WANT A SENSE OF HOW QUALIFIED THE PERSON IS WITHOUT ASKING THE QUESTION)

D3a. Who typically gets screened? Obvious cases, or is it more broadly done?

D4. What types of diversion options are there for defendants in this jurisdiction? What types of circumstances are defendants diverted for? (PROBE: SUBSTANCE ABUSE? MENTAL ILLNESS? INTELLECTUAL DEFICITS? NEUROCOGNITIVE DYSFUNCTION?)

D4a. Is the capacity for such diversion adequate for meeting the need?

D5. Is the diversion decision pretty much up to you? Who else is involved in the decision?

D6. Today, the recidivism rates for mentally ill offenders or offenders with substance use disorders is over 80 percent. Similarly, those with neurocognitive disorders have extraordinarily high recidivism. The evidence indicates that what we have been doing with these types of offenders is not working.

D6a. What should we be doing to address such high recidivism rates? What should change?

Consider the following idea. Having panels of independent experts like psychologists, neuroscientists, addiction specialists, and psychiatrists who routinely screen and assess defendants for things like mental illness, substance use disorders, neurocognitive impairments, and intellectual deficits. These experts would determine who is significantly disordered as well as their risk of reoffending, especially for violent crimes. In turn, they would make recommendations to you regarding who should be diverted to treatment and risk management and who should be traditionally prosecuted and sentenced. Assume for the purposes of this question that there are sufficient diversion resources for diverting and treating these disordered defendants.

D6b. Is this something that is potentially valuable to you? (HOW? WHY?)

D6c. What concerns do you have about this idea? What barriers might there be to adoption of this idea?

D6d. How might this concept be proposed to your colleagues? What might serve as an incentive to promote adoption of this idea? Are there legislative changes that would have to occur? What are they?

NOTES

1. THE RELENTLESS PURSUIT OF PUNISHMENT

1. This and the next profile were obtained from the website of Families Against Mandatory Minimums at http://famm.org.

2. Kelly, *The Future of Crime and Punishment: Smart Policies for Reducing Crime and Saving Money*; Kelly et al., *From Retribution to Public Safety: Disruptive Innovation of American Criminal Justice.*

3. Kelly, *Criminal Justice at the Crossroads: Transforming Crime and Punishment*; Kelly, *The Future of Crime and Punishment*; Kelly et al., *From Retribution to Public Safety*; Travis et al., *The Growth of Incarceration in the United States: Exploring Causes and Consequences.*

4. Kelly, *Criminal Justice at the Crossroads*; Kelly, *The Future of Crime and Punishment.*

5. Travis et al., *The Growth of Incarceration in the United States.*

6. Kelly, *Criminal Justice at the Crossroads.*

7. Pfaff, *Locked In: The True Causes of Mass Incarceration and How to Achieve Real Reform.*

8. The last two examples were obtained from Levin, "At the State Level, So-Called Crimes Are Here, There, Everywhere."

9. Copland et al., "Overcriminalizing the Wolverine State: A Primer and Possible Reforms for Michigan."

10. Copland et al., "Overcriminalizing the Wolverine State."

11. Copland et al., "Overcriminalizing the Wolverine State."

12. Copland and Gorodetski, "Overcriminalizing the Old North State: A Primer and Possible Reforms for North Carolina."

13. Dutton, "She Went to the Hospital for Mental Illness. She Ended Up Charged with 2 Felonies."

14. Kelly et al., *From Retribution to Public Safety*.

15. Kelly et al., *From Retribution to Public Safety*.

16. Kelly, *The Future of Crime and Punishment*.

17. Kelly et al., *From Retribution to Public Safety*.

18. National Center on Addiction and Substance Abuse, "Addiction Medicine: Closing the Gap between Science and Practice."

19. National Center on Addiction and Substance Abuse, "Addiction Medicine," 2.

20. Glaser, "The Irrationality of Alcoholics Anonymous."

21. National Center on Addiction and Substance Abuse, "Addiction Medicine: Closing the Gap between Science and Practice."

22. Fletcher, *Inside Rehab: The Surprising Truth about Addiction Treatment and How to Get Help That Works*.

23. American Society of Addiction Medicine, "Public Policy Statement on the Relationship between Treatment and Self Help: A Joint Statement of the American Society of Addiction Medicine, the American Academy of Addiction Psychiatry, and the American Psychiatric Association."

24. National Institute on Drug Abuse, "Principles of Drug Addiction Treatment: A Research-Based Guide (Third Edition)."

25. Glaser, "The Irrationality of Alcoholics Anonymous."

26. Chandler et al., "Treating Drug Abuse and Addiction in the Criminal Justice System: Improving Public Health and Safety."

27. Chandler et al., "Treating Drug Abuse and Addiction in the Criminal Justice System."

28. Kelly, *Criminal Justice at the Crossroads*; Kelly, *The Future of Crime and Punishment*.

29. Cooke and Respaut, "How a Respected Drug-Rehab Program Spun Out of Control."

30. Harris and Walter, "They Thought They Were Going to Rehab. They Ended Up in Chicken Plants," 4.

31. Elizabeth Brown, "The Real 'Modern Slavery'? Inside America's Court-Ordered Corporate Labor Camps."

32. National Center on Addiction and Substance Abuse, "Addiction Medicine," 1.

33. Mental Health America, "2017 State of Mental Health in America—Access to Care Data."

34. HRSA (Health Resources and Services Administration) Data Warehouse, "Designated Health Professional Shortage Areas Statistics."

35. Mental Health America, "2017 State of Mental Health in America."

36.   Bishop et al., "Acceptance of Insurance by Psychiatrists and the Implications for Access to Mental Health Care."

37.   National Conference of State Legislatures, "Affordable Care Act Medicaid Expansion."

38.   Wen et al., "The Effect of Medicaid Expansion on Crime Reduction."

39.   Bondurant et al., "Substance Abuse Treatment Centers and Local Crime."

40.   Vogler, "Access to Health Care and Criminal Behavior: Short-Run Evidence from the ACA Medicaid Expansions."

41.   Kelly et al., *From Retribution to Public Safety*.

42.   James and Glaze, "Mental Health Problems of Prison and Jail Inmates."

43.   Richard Williams, "Addressing Mental Health in the Justice System."

44.   Kelly et al., *From Retribution to Public Safety*.

45.   Kelly, *The Future of Crime and Punishment*.

46.   Federal Bureau of Investigation, U.S. Department of Justice, "Crime in the United States, 2013, Clearances."

47.   Baillargeon et al., "Psychiatric Disorders and Repeat Incarcerations: The Revolving Prison Door."

48.   Byron, "Criminals Need Mental Health Care."

49.   Kelly, *Criminal Justice at the Crossroads*; Kelly, *The Future of Crime and Punishment*.

50.   Kelly et al., *From Retribution to Public Safety*.

51.   Lopez, "The New War on Drugs."

2. PLEA BARGAINING IN PRACTICE

1.   Langbein, "On the Myth of Written Constitutions."

2.   Scott and Stuntz, "Plea Bargaining as Contract."

3.   Palmer, "Abolishing Plea Bargaining: An End to the Same Old Song and Dance."

4.   See discussion by Alkon, "The U.S. Supreme Courts Failure to Fix Plea Bargaining: The Impact of *Lafler* and *Frye*."

5.   Burger, "The State of the Judiciary—1970."

6.   Caldwell, "Coercive Plea Bargaining: The Unrecognized Scourge of the Justice System."

7.   Kelly, *The Future of Crime and Punishment : Smart Policies for Reducing Crime and Saving Money*; Kelly et al., *From Retribution to Public Safety : Disruptive Innovation of American Criminal Justice*.

8.   Stuntz, "The Pathological Politics of Criminal Law," 512.

9. Dervan, "Overcriminalization 2.0: The Symbiotic Relationship between Plea Bargaining and Overcriminalization," 646.

10. Fisher, *Plea Bargaining's Triumph*, 2.

11. Fisher, *Plea Bargaining's Triumph*, 178.

12. *Brady v. United States*, 397 U.S. 742, 753 (1970).

13. *Santobello v. New York*, 404 U.S. 257 (1971).

14. American Bar Association, "Pleas of Guilty."

15. Wan, "The Unnecessary Evil of Plea Bargaining: An Unconstitutional Conditions Problem and a Not-so-Least Restrictive Alternative."

16. *Brodenkircher v. Hayes*, 364.

17. *U.S. Supreme Court v. Hayes*, 434.

18. Taslitz, "Prosecutorial Preconditions to Plea Negotiations: 'Voluntary' Waivers of Constitutional Rights."

19. *Missouri v. Frye* at 1399, 1408.

4. PLEA BARGAINING'S CRITICS

1. Bibas, "Designing Plea Bargaining from the Ground Up: Accuracy and Fairness without Trials as Backstops," 1058.

2. Guidorizzi, "Should We Really 'Ban' Plea Bargaining? The Core Concerns of Plea Bargaining Critics," 768, 769.

3. Taslitz, "Prosecutorial Preconditions to Plea Negotiations: 'Voluntary' Waivers of Constitutional Rights."

4. Guidorizzi, "Should We Really 'Ban' Plea Bargaining?," 770.

5. Ross, "The Entrenched Position of Plea Bargaining in United States Legal Practice," 724.

6. Hessick and Saujani, "Plea Bargaining and Convicting the Innocent: The Role of the Prosecutor, the Defense Counsel, and the Judge."

7. Taslitz, "Prosecutorial Preconditions to Plea Negotiations"; Ma, "Prosecutorial Discretion and Plea Bargaining in the United States, France, Germany, and Italy: A Comparative Perspective"; Schulhofer, "A Wake-Up Call from the Plea Bargaining Trenches."

8. Schwartzapfel, "Defendants Kept in the Dark about Evidence, until It's Too Late."

9. Bibas, "Regulating the Plea-Bargaining Market: From Caveat Emptor to Consumer Protection."

10. Petegorsky, "Plea Bargaining in the Dark: The Duty to Disclose Exculpatory Brady Evidence during Plea Bargaining"; Yaroshefsky, "Ethics and Plea Bargaining: What's Discovery Got to Do with It?"; Ma, "Prosecutorial Discre-

tion and Plea Bargaining in the United States, France, Germany, and Italy"; Bibas, "Designing Plea Bargaining from the Ground Up."

11. Petegorsky, "Plea Bargaining in the Dark," 3599.

12. Bibas, "Regulating the Plea-Bargaining Market."

13. Bibas, "Regulating the Plea-Bargaining Market."

14. Bibas, "Regulating the Plea-Bargaining Market," 1153.

15. In re Winship, 397 U.S. 358, 90 S. Ct. 1068, 25 L. Ed. 2d 368 (1970).

16. United States Courts for the Ninth Circuit, "Model Jury Instructions."

17. New York Courts, "Criminal Jury Instructions."

18. Bacigal, "Making the Right Gamble: The Odds on Probable Cause"; International Bridges to Justice, "Standards of Proof"; Congressional Research Service, "Probable Cause, Reasonable Suspicion, and Reasonableness Standards in the Context of the Fourth Amendment and Foreign Intelligence Surveillance Act."

19. Lynch, "Our Administrative System of Criminal Justice," 2124.

20. Darryl Brown, *Free Market Criminal Justice: How Democracy and Laissez Faire Undermine the Rule of Law*.

21. Rakoff, "Why Prosecutors Rule the Criminal Justice System—and What Can Be Done about It," 1430, 1432.

22. Devers, "Plea and Charge Bargaining."

23. Andiloro et al., "Cumulative Disadvantage: Examining Racial and Ethnic Disparity in Prosecution and Sentencing"; Andiloro et al., "Does Evidence Really Matter?"; Andiloro et al., "Opening Pandora's Box: How Does Defendant Race Influence Plea Bargaining?"

24. Davis, *Arbitrary Justice: The Power of the American Prosecutor*, 5.

25. Lynch, "Our Administrative System of Criminal Justice," 2123, 2124.

26. D. Brown, *Free Market Criminal Justice*.

27. U.S. Supreme Court, *Wayte v. United States*, 470 U.S. 598 (1985) at 607.

28. Ross, "The Entrenched Position of Plea Bargaining in United States Legal Practice."

29. Guidorizzi, "Should We Really 'Ban' Plea Bargaining?"

30. *Newman v. United States* 382, F. 2d 479 (D.C. Cir. 1967) at 480.

31. Ma, "Prosecutorial Discretion and Plea Bargaining in the United States, France, Germany, and Italy."

32. The Innocence Project. "Prosecutorial Oversight: A National Dialogue in the Wake of Connick v. Thompson," https://www.innocenceproject.org/wp-content/uploads/2016/04/IP-Prosecutorial-Oversight-Report_09.pdf.

33. *Berger v. United States*, 295 U.S. 78, 88 (1935).

34. *Gideon v. Wainwright*, 372 U.S. (1963) at 344.

35. Cummings, "KC Public Defenders Say High Caseloads Mean Losing Their Licenses, Going to Jail, or Quitting."

36. Walsh, "On the Defensive."

37. Hager, "When Real Estate and Tax Lawyers Are Forced to Do a Public Defender's Job."

38. Timothy Williams, "Courts Sidestep the Law, and South Carolina's Poor Go to Jail."

39. Sixth Amendment Center, "Utah's Right to Counsel Deficiencies."

40. Walsh, "On the Defensive."

41. Sixth Amendment Center, "Actual Denial of Counsel in Misdemeanor Courts."

42. *The Guardian*, "The Human Toll of America's Public Defender Crisis."

43. CBS News, "Innocents Have Gone to Jail, Say NOLA Public Defenders."

44. Coburn, "Maryland Public Defenders Juggle Heavy Caseloads; Critics Say Indigent Clients Suffer."

45. *The Guardian*, "The Human Toll of America's Public Defender Crisis."

46. Brownwell et al., "Charts: Why You're in Deep Trouble If You Can't Afford a Lawyer."

47. Farole and Langton, "County-Based and Local Public Defender Offices, 2007."

48. American Constitution Society, "Toward a More Perfect Union"; American Bar Association, "Gideon's Broken Promise: America's Continuing Quest for Equal Justice"; Brink et al., "Minor Crimes, Massive Waste: The Terrible Toll of America's Broken Misdemeanor Courts"; Sixth Amendment Center, "The Right to Counsel in America Today."

49. Van Brunt, "Poor People Rely on Public Defenders Who Are Too Overworked to Defend Them."

50. Ewing, "When Does the Right to an Attorney Kick In?"

51. Ewing, "When Does the Right to an Attorney Kick In?"

52. Hessick and Saujani, "Plea Bargaining and Convicting the Innocent."

53. Bibas, "Regulating the Plea-Bargaining Market."

54. Klein, "The Emperor Gideon Has No Clothes: The Empty Promise of the Sixth Amendment Right to Effective Assistance of Counsel," 627.

55. Constitution Project, "Indigent Defense: Ensuring the Constitutional Right to Counsel."

56. Zeidman, "Gideon: Looking Backward, Looking Forward, Looking in the Mirror."

57. Zeidman, "Gideon."

58. Rakoff, "Why Innocent People Plead Guilty," 5.

59. Dervan, "Bargained Justice: Plea Bargaining's Innocence Problem and the Brady Safety-Valve."

60. *Brady v. United States*, 397 U.S. 742 (1970), 750.

61. *Brady v. United States*, 397 U.S. 742 (1970), 758.

62. Ma, "Prosecutorial Discretion and Plea Bargaining in the United States, France, Germany, and Italy," 26.

63. Devers, "Plea and Charge Bargaining"; McCoy, "Plea Bargaining as Coercion: The Trial Penalty and Plea Bargaining Reform"; Ulmer and Bradley, "Variation in Trial Penalties among Serious Violent Offenses."

64. Human Rights Watch, "An Offer You Can't Refuse: How US Federal Prosecutors Force Drug Defendants to Plead Guilty."

65. *United States v. Kupa*, 976 F. Supp. 2nd 417, 432 (Eastern District of New York 2013).

66. D. Brown, *Free Market Criminal Justice*.

67. Dibber, "American Plea Bargains, German Lay Judges, and the Crisis of Criminal Procedure," 547, 598.

68. For example, Levenson, "Peeking behind the Plea Bargaining Process: *Missouri v. Frye* & *Lafler v. Cooper*"; Caldwell, "Coercive Plea Bargaining: The Unrecognized Scourge of the Justice System"; Alkon, "The U.S. Supreme Court's Failure to Fix Plea Bargaining: The Impact of *Lafler* and *Frye*"; Taslitz, "Prosecutorial Preconditions to Plea Negotiations"; Work, "Creating Constitutional Procedure: Frye, Lafler, and Plea Bargaining Reform."

69. Kang-Brown and Subramanian, "Out of Sight: The Growth of Jails in Rural America."

70. Pretrial Justice Institute, "Pretrial Justice: How Much Does It Cost?"

71. Subramanian et al., "Incarceration's Front Door: The Misuse of Jails in America."

72. Kang-Brown and Subramanian, "Out of Sight."

73. Prison Policy Initiative, "Detaining the Poor."

74. McCullough, "Poor Inmates Sue Dallas County over Bail System Following Harris County Ruling."

75. Subramanian et al., "Incarceration's Front Door."

76. Heaton et al., "The Downstream Consequences of Misdemeanor Pretrial Detention"; Dobbie et al., "The Effects of Pre-Trial Detention on Conviction, Future Crime, and Employment: Evidence from Randomly Assigned Judges"; Leslie and Pope, "The Unintended Impact of Pretrial Detention on Case Outcomes: Evidence from NYC Arraignments"; Stevenson, "Distortion of Justice: How the Inability to Pay Bail Affects Case Outcomes."

77. Lynch, "Our Administrative System of Criminal Justice," 2146.

78. Connor Brown, "Man Cleared of Molestation Sues over Withheld Evidence," 8.

79. National Registry of Exonerations, "Innocents Who Plead Guilty."

80. *McMann v. Richardson*, 397 U.S. 759 (1970).

81. Blume and Helm, "The Unexonerated: Factually Innocent Defendants Who Plead Guilty," 19.

82. Blume and Helm, "The Unexonerated."

83. Ross, "The Entrenched Position of Plea Bargaining in United States Legal Practice."

84. Natapoff, "Why Misdemeanors Aren't So Minor"; Brink et al., "Minor Crimes, Massive Waste."

85. Natapoff, "Misdemeanors."

86. Natapoff, "Misdemeanors," 1313, 1315.

87. Natapoff, "Misdemeanors"; Brink et al., "Minor Crime, Massive Waste"; Heaton et al., "The Downstream Consequences of Misdemeanor Pretrial Detention"; Roberts, "Why Misdemeanors Matter: Defining Effective Advocacy in the Lower Criminal Courts"; Natapoff, "Gideon Skepticism"; Natapoff, "Aggregation and Urban Misdemeanors."

88. Heaton et al., "The Downstream Consequences of Misdemeanor Pretrial Detention."

89. Jackson, "Mass Justice in Southern Court Replete with Rights Violations, ABA Observers Say."

90. Hanlon et al., "Denial of the Right to Counsel in Misdemeanor Cases: Court Watching in Nashville, Tennessee"; Brink et al., Minor Crimes, Massive Waste."

91. Natapoff, "Aggregation and Urban Misdemeanors," 1046.

5. PLEA BARGAINING'S REMEDIES

1. Jan, "America's Affordable-Housing Stock Dropped by 60 Percent from 2010 to 2016."

2. Batra, "Judicial Participation in Plea Bargaining: A Proposal for Plea Reform."

3. Jaffe, *Insane Consequences: How the Mental Health Industry Fails the Mentally Ill.*

4. Jaffe, *Insane Consequences*, 44.

5. James and Glaze, "Mental Health Problems of Prison and Jail Inmates."

6. Statistics are cited in Jaffe, *Insane Consequences*.

7. National Association for Public Defense, "Alternatives to Traditional Prosecution Can Reduce Defender Workload, Save Money, and Reduce Recidivism."

8. Lopez, "The New War on Drugs."

9. Gelb, "The Lack of a Relationship between Drug Imprisonment and Drug Problems," 1.

10. Blume and Helm, "The Unexonerated: Factually Innocent Defendants Who Plead Guilty"; Work, "Creating Constitutional Procedure: Frye, Lafler, and Plea Bargaining Reform"; Schulhofer, "Plea Bargaining as Disaster"; Alschuler, "Implementing the Criminal Defendant's Right to Trial: Alternatives to the Plea Bargaining System."

11. Alschuler, "Implementing the Criminal Defendant's Right to Trial"; Schulhofer, "Is Plea Bargaining Inevitable?"

12. Hessick and Saujani, "Plea Bargaining and Convicting the Innocent: The Role of the Prosecutor, the Defense Counsel, and the Judge"; Turner, "Plea Bargaining."

13. Work, "Creating Constitutional Procedure"; Flynn, "Plea-Negotiations, Prosecutors, and Discretion: An Argument for Legal Reform"; Turner, "Plea Bargaining."

14. Benner, "Eliminating Excessive Public Defender Workloads"; Santo, "How Conservatives Learned to Love Free Lawyers for the Poor"; Lefstein, "The Failure to Implement the Right to Counsel Due to Excessive Caseloads: Securing Reasonable Caseloads Ethics and Law in Public Defense."

15. Balko, "In Texas, a Novel Idea to Address the Public Defender Crisis."

16. Turner, "Plea Bargaining"; Hessick and Saujani, "Plea Bargaining and Convicting the Innocent"; Work, "Creating Constitutional Procedure"; Schulhofer, "Plea Bargaining as Disaster"; Bibas, "Regulating the Plea Bargaining Market: From Caveat Emptor to Consumer Protection."

17. Schwartzapfel, "How New York Could Change the Game for Its Criminal Defendants."

18. Turner, "Plea Bargaining."

19. King and Wright, "The Invisible Revolution in Plea Bargaining: Managerial Judging and Judicial Participation in Negotiations."

20. Hessick and Saujani, "Plea Bargaining and Convicting the Innocent"; Blume and Helm, "The Unexonerated."

21. Turner, "Plea Bargaining."

22. Burke, "Will Alaska's Plea Bargain Plan Serve Justice, or Cause It to Grind to a Halt?"

23. Batra, "Judicial Participation in Plea Bargaining"; Rakoff, "Why Innocent People Plead Guilty"; Beekman, "Judge Says Plea-Deal Process Must Be Fixed."

24. Caldwell, "Coercive Plea Bargaining: The Unrecognized Scourge of the Justice System."

25. Blume and Helm, "The Unexonerated."

26. Applebaum, "The Plea Jury."

27. Bibas, "Regulating the Plea-Bargaining Market."
28. Fair Trials International, "The Disappearing Trial: Towards a Rights-Based Approach to Trial Waiver Systems."
29. Fair Trials International, "The Disappearing Trial."
30. Ma, "Prosecutorial Discretion and Plea Bargaining in the United States, France, Germany, and Italy"; Brook et al., "A Comparative Look at Plea Bargaining in Australia, Canada, England, New Zealand and the United States"; Turner, *Plea Bargaining across Borders.*
31. Ma, "Prosecutorial Discretion and Plea Bargaining in the United States, France, Germany, and Italy."
32. King and Wright, "The Invisible Revolution in Plea Bargaining."

6. PLEA NEGOTIATION AND MEANINGFUL CRIMINAL JUSTICE REFORM

1. Yoffe, "Innocence Is Irrelevant," 19.
2. Natapoff, "Aggregation and Urban Misdemeanors," 1046.
3. Kelly, *Criminal Justice at the Crossroads*; Kelly et al., *From Retribution to Public Safety.*
4. Kelly et al., *From Retribution to Public Safety*, 132.
5. Dressel and Farid, "The Accuracy, Fairness, and Limits of Predicting Recidivism."
6. Criminal Justice Connections, https://www.tdcj.state.tx.us/connections/JanFeb2015/agency_vol22no3.html.
7. Kelly, *Criminal Justice at the Crossroads*, Kelly et al., *From Retribution to Public Safety.*
8. Kelly et al., *From Retribution to Public Safety.*
9. Stuntz, "Plea Bargaining and Criminal Law's Disappearing Shadow," 2569.
10. No. 108,094, 2013 WL 2919942 (Kan. Ct. App. June 27, 2013) (unpublished opinion).

7. TRANSFORMING PRETRIAL SYSTEMS AND PUBLIC DEFENSE

1. McCoy, "Caleb Was Right: Pretrial Decisions Determine Mostly Everything"; Bechtel et al., "A Meta-Analytic Review of Pretrial Research: Risk Assessment, Bond Type, and Interventions"; VanNostrand, "Measuring and

Managing Pretrial Risk: Improving Public Safety, Fairness, and Cost Effectiveness"; Rowings, "Pretrial Decisions Have Major Effects on Post-Trial Life."

2. Prison Policy Initiative, "Detaining the Poor."

3. Pretrial Justice Institute, "Bail in America: Unsafe, Unfair, Ineffective."

4. Prisoner Reentry Institute, "Pretrial Practice: Building a National Research Agenda for the Front End of the Criminal Justice System."

5. Laura and John Arnold Foundation, "More Than 20 Cities and States Adopt Risk Assessment Tool to Help Judges Decide Which Defendants to Detain prior to Trial."

6. Stevenson, "Risk Assessment: The Devil's in the Details."

7. Pretrial Justice Institute, "Pretrial Justice: How Much Does It Cost?"

8. Human Rights Watch, "Not in It for Justice."

9. Human Rights Watch, "Not in It for Justice."

10. Pretrial Justice Institute, "Pretrial Justice."

11. TCR [The Crime Report] Staff, "Los Angeles Study Finds $19 Billion Levied in Money Bail between 2012–2016."

12. White, "Who Really Makes Money off of Bail Bonds?"

13. Vitale, "Bail Bond Industry Fights Back against Reform."

14. Pretrial Justice Institute, "The State of Pretrial Justice in America."

15. These include Lowenkamp and VanNostrand, "Exploring the Impact of Supervision on Pretrial Outcomes"; Heaton et al., "The Downstream Consequences of Misdemeanor Pretrial Detention"; Lowenkamp et al., "The Hidden Costs of Pretrial Detention"; Dobbie et al., "The Effects of Pre-Trial Detention on Conviction, Future Crime, and Employment: Evidence from Randomly Assigned Judges"; Gupta et al., "The Heavy Costs of High Bail: Evidence from Judge Randomization"; Leslie and Pope, "The Unintended Impact of Pretrial Detention on Case Outcomes: Evidence from NYC Arraignments"; Stevenson, "Distortion of Justice: How the Inability to Pay Bail Affects Case Outcomes"; and Didwania, "The Immediate Consequences of Pretrial Detention: Evidence from Federal Criminal Cases."

16. Texas Appleseed, "Bail and Pretrial Release: Summary of Recent Research on What Works."

17. Texas Appleseed, "Bail and Pretrial Release."

18. Heaton et al., "The Downstream Consequences of Misdemeanor Pretrial Detention."

19. Heaton et al., "The Downstream Consequences of Misdemeanor Pretrial Detention," 715.

20. Cuomo, "Governor Cuomo: The Way to a More Just New York State."

21. Lannan, "A Broad Push for Pretrial Justice Reforms from the States."

22. Hager, "The Check Is in the Mail (for Real)."

23. Siddall, "Bail Reform: Why Judges Should Reject 'Risk Assessment.'"

24. Siddall, "Bail Reform."

25. Drake, "Predicting Criminal Recidivism: A Systematic Review of Offender Risk Assessments in Washington State."

26. Pretrial Justice Institute, "The Solution."

27. Laura and John Arnold Foundation, "Pretrial Criminal Justice Research"; Lowenkamp and VanNostrand, "Exploring the Impact of Supervision on Pretrial Outcomes."

28. Harvard Law School Criminal Justice Policy Program, "Moving beyond Money: A Primer on Bail Reform."

29. Lyons, "Predicting Pretrial Success."

30. Rothwell, "Drug Offenders in American Prisons: The Critical Distinction between Stock and Flow."

31. Berzofsky et al., "Drug Use, Dependence, and Abuse among State Prisoners and Jail Inmates, 2007–2009."

32. Berzofsky et al., "Drug Use, Dependence, and Abuse among State Prisoners and Jail Inmates, 2007–2009."

33. Nyberg, "Cognitive Impairments in Drug Addicts," 235.

34. Pilnik, "A Framework for Pretrial Justice: Essential Elements of an Effective Pretrial System and Agency."

35. Pilnik, "A Framework for Pretrial Justice," 49.

36. Maryland Alliance for Justice Reform, "Maryland's Pretrial/Bail Troubles—How and Why to Fix Them," 8.

37. Natapoff, "Misdemeanors."

38. Kelly, *Criminal Justice at the Crossroads: Transforming Crime and Punishment*; Kelly, *The Future of Crime and Punishment: Smart Policies for Reducing Crime and Saving Money*; Kelly et al., *From Retribution to Public Safety: Disruptive Innovation of American Criminal Justice*.

39. Constitution Project, "Indigent Defense: Ensuring the Constitutional Right to Counsel," 71.

40. Carroll, "Gideon's Despair: Four Things the Next Attorney General Needs to Know about America's Indigent Defense Crisis."

41. National Association for Public Defense, "Alternatives to Traditional Prosecution Can Reduce Defender Workload, Save Money, and Reduce Recidivism."

42. Lee et al., "The Measure of Good Lawyering: Evaluating Holistic Defense in Practice."

43. Center for Holistic Defense, "The Holistic Defense Toolkit," 3.

44. These are quoted and paraphrased from Center for Holistic Defense, "The Holistic Defense Toolkit," 4–5.

45. Center for Holistic Defense, "The Holistic Defense Toolkit," 4.

46. Anderson and Heaton, "Does Holistic Defense Improve Criminal Justice Outcomes?," 3.

47. Anderson and Heaton, "Does Holistic Defense Improve Criminal Justice Outcomes?," 3.

48. Clark and Savner, "Community Oriented Defense: Stronger Public Defenders."

49. American Bar Association, "Resolution 107C."

50. Steinberg, "Heeding Gideon's Call in the Twenty-First Century: Holistic Defense and the New Public Defense Paradigm."

51. Anderson and Heaton, "Does Holistic Defense Improve Criminal Justice Outcomes?," 3.

52. Fairfax, "Searching for Solutions to the Indigent Defense Crisis in the Broader Criminal Justice Reform Agenda," 2335.

8. CONCLUSIONS, CHALLENGES, AND INCENTIVES

1. McLaughlin et al., "The Economic Burden of Incarceration in the U.S."

2. Pew Center on the States, "State Reforms Reverse Decades of Incarceration Growth."

3. Pew Center on the States, "State Reforms Reverse Decades of Incarceration Growth."

4. Legal Action Center, "Public Opinion Favors Criminal Justice and Drug Policy Reform, Making Now the Time to Act."

5. Hart, "Changing Public Attitudes toward the Criminal Justice System."

6. Legal Action Center, "Public Opinion Favors Criminal Justice and Drug Policy Reform, Making Now the Time to Act."

7. American Civil Liberties Union, "91 Percent of Americans Support Criminal Justice Reform, ACLU Polling Finds."

8. Gelb and Page, "Voters in Louisiana and Oklahoma Strongly Favor Alternatives to Incarceration," 2.

9. Alliance for Safety and Justice, "Crime Survivors' Views on Trump Administration's Criminal Justice Agenda."

10. Alliance for Safety and Justice, "Crime Survivors Speak: The First-Ever National Survey of Victims' Views on Safety and Justice."

11. Sessions, "Jeff Sessions: Trump Promised to End 'American Carnage.' Promise Delivered."

12. Kelly, *Criminal Justice at the Crossroads: Transforming Crime and Punishment*; Kelly, *The Future of Crime and Punishment: Smart Policies for Reducing Crime and Saving Money*; Kelly et al., *From Retribution to Public Safety: Disruptive Innovation of American Criminal Justice*.

13. Kelly, *The Future of Crime and Punishment*; TCR [The Crime Report] Staff, "Justice Reform Means 'Thinking outside Silos,' Says New John Jay President"; Borakove et al., "From Silo to System: What Makes a Criminal Justice System Operate Like a System?"

14. National Conference of State Legislatures, "Pretrial Diversion."

15. National Conference of State Legislatures, "Pretrial Diversion."

16. National Conference of State Legislatures, "Pretrial Diversion."

17. Szalavitz, "The Wrong Way to Treat Opioid Addiction."

18. O'Donoghue, "Louisiana District Attorneys Continue to Push Back on Criminal Sentencing Changes."

19. Pishko, "Prosecutors Are Banding Together to Prevent Criminal Justice Reform."

20. Justice Reinvestment Initiative, "What Is JRI?"

21. Justice Reinvestment Initiative, "What Is JRI?"; LeVigne et al., "Justice Reinvestment Initiative State Assessment Report"; Public Safety Performance Project, "33 States Reform Criminal Justice Policies through Justice Reinvestment."

22. Aos et al., "Evidence-Based Treatment of Alcohol, Drug, and Mental Health Disorders: Potential Benefits, Costs, and Fiscal Impacts for Washington State"; Kelly, *Criminal Justice at the Crossroads*; Kelly et al., *From Retribution to Public Safety*.

REFERENCES

Alkon, Cynthia. "The U.S. Supreme Court's Failure to Fix Plea Bargaining: The Impact of *Lafler* and *Frye*." *Hastings Constitutional Law Quarterly* 41, no. 3 (2014): 561–621.

Alliance for Safety and Justice. "Crime Survivors Speak: The First-Ever National Survey of Victims' Views on Safety and Justice." July 2016. http://www.allianceforsafetyandjustice. org/wp-content/uploads/documents/Crime%20Survivors%20Speak%20Report.pdf.

Alliance for Safety and Justice. "Crime Survivors' Views on Trump Administration's Criminal Justice Agenda." David Binder Research. August 1, 2017. https://www.alliancefor safetyandjustice.org/wp-content/uploads/2017/08/DBR-US-Crime-Victim-Survey-Sum-mary-v20.pdf.

Alschuler, Albert W. "Implementing the Criminal Defendant's Right to Trial: Alternatives to the Plea Bargaining System." *University of Chicago Law Review* 50, no. 3 (1983): 931–41.

American Bar Association. "Gideon's Broken Promise: America's Continuing Quest for Equal Justice." December 2004. https://www.americanbar.org/content/dam/aba/adminis-trative/legal_aid_indigent_defendants/ ls_sclaid_def_bp_right_to_counsel_in_criminal_proceedings.authcheckdam.pdf.

American Bar Association. "Pleas of Guilty." 2018. https://www.americanbar.org/publica-tions/criminal_justice_section_archive/crimjust_standards_guiltypleas_toc.html.

American Bar Association. "Resolution 107C." 2012. https://www.americanbar.org/content/ dam/aba/administrative/criminal_justice/ABAResolution107c.authcheckdam.pdf.

American Civil Liberties Union. "91 Percent of Americans Support Criminal Justice Reform, ACLU Polling Finds." November 16, 2017. https://www.aclu.org/news/91-percent-americans-support-criminal-justice-reform-aclu-polling-finds.

American Constitution Society, "Toward a More Perfect Union: A Progressive Blueprint for the Second Term." https://www.acslaw.org/publications/progressive-blueprint-for-a-sec-ond-term

American Society of Addiction Medicine. "Public Policy Statement on the Relationship be-tween Treatment and Self Help: A Joint Statement of the American Society of Addiction Medicine, the American Academy of Addiction Psychiatry, and the American Psychiatric Association." https://www.asam.org/docs/default-source/public-policy-statements/1treat-ment-and-self-help---joint-12-971.pdf?sfvrsn=d32ab2d5_0.

Anderson, James, and Paul Heaton. "Does Holistic Defense Improve Criminal Justice Out-comes?" Quattrone Center for the Fair Administration of Justice. RAND. December 2017.

Andiloro, Nancy R., Besiki Luka Kutateladze, and Brian D. Johnson. "Opening Pandora's Box: How Does Defendant Race Influence Plea Bargaining?" *Justice Quarterly* 33, no. 3 (2016): 398–426. http://www.tandfonline.com/doi/abs/10.1080/07418825.2014.915340.

Andiloro, Nancy R., Besiki L. Kutateladze, Brian D. Johnson, and Cassia C. Spohn. "Cumulative Disadvantage: Examining Racial and Ethnic Disparity in Prosecution and Sentencing." *Criminology* 52, no. 3 (2014): 514–51. doi:10.1111/1745-9125.12047.

Andiloro, Nancy R., Besiki L. Kutateladze, and Victoria Z. Lawson. "Does Evidence Really Matter?" *Law and Human Behavior* 39, no. 5 (2015): 431–42.

Aos, Steve, Jim Mayfield, Marna Miller, and Wei Yen. "Evidence-Based Treatment of Alcohol, Drug, and Mental Health Disorders: Potential Benefits, Costs, and Fiscal Impacts for Washington State." Washington State Institute for Public Policy. June 2006.

Appleman, Laura I. "The Plea Jury." *Indiana Law Journal* 85, no. 3 (2010): 731–76.

Bacigal, Ronald J. "Making the Right Gamble: The Odds on Probable Cause." *Mississippi Law Journal* 74 (2004): 279–335.

Baillargeon, Jacques, Ingrid A. Binswanger, Joseph V. Penn, Brie A. Williams, and Owen J. Murray. "Psychiatric Disorders and Repeat Incarcerations: The Revolving Prison Door." *American Journal of Psychiatry* 166, no. 1 (2009): 103–9.

Balko, Radley. "In Texas, a Novel Idea to Address the Public Defender Crisis." *Washington Post*. January 28, 2014. https://www.washingtonpost.com/news/opinions/wp/2014/01/28/in-texas-a-novel-idea-to-address-the-public-defender-crisis/?utm_term=.59b13a3ce83e.

Batra, Rishi. "Judicial Participation in Plea Bargaining: A Proposal for Plea Reform." September 2, 2015. https://casetext.com/posts/judicial-participation-in-plea-bargaining-a-proposal-for-plea-reform.

Bechtel, Kristin, Alexander Holsinger, Christopher T. Lowenkamp, and Madeline Warren. "A Meta-Analytic Review of Pretrial Research: Risk Assessment, Bond Type, and Interventions." 2016. http://doi.org/10.2139/ssrn.2741635. *American Journal of Criminal Justice* 42, no. 2 (2017): 443–67.

Beekman, Daniel. "Judge Says Plea-Deal Process Must Be Fixed." *New York Daily News*. May 27, 2014. http://www.nydailynews.com/news/crime/judge-plea-deal-process-fixed-article-1.1806358.

Benner, Laurence A. "Eliminating Excessive Public Defender Workloads." *Criminal Justice* 26, no. 2 (2011): 134–54.

Berzofsky, Marcus, Jennifer Bronson, Jessica Stroop, and Stephanie Zimmer. "Drug Use, Dependence, and Abuse among State Prisoners and Jail Inmates, 2007–2009." Bureau of Justice Statistics. *Special Report*. June 2017.

Bibas, Stephanos. "Designing Plea Bargaining from the Ground Up: Accuracy and Fairness without Trials as Backstops." *William and Mary Law Review* 57, no. 4 (2016): 1055–81.

Bibas, Stephanos. "Regulating the Plea-Bargaining Market: From Caveat Emptor to Consumer Protection." *California Law Review* 99, no. 4 (2011): 1117–61.

Bishop, Tara F., Matthew J. Press, Salomeh Keyhani, and Harold Alan Pincus. "Acceptance of Insurance by Psychiatrists and the Implications for Access to Mental Health Care." *JAMA Psychiatry* 71, no. 2 (2014): 176–81. doi:10.1001/jamapsychiatry.2013.2862.

Blume, John H., and Rebecca K. Helm. "The Unexonerated: Factually Innocent Defendants Who Plead Guilty." *Cornell Law Review* 100, no. 1 (2014): 157–91.

Bondurant, Samuel R., Jason M. Lindo, and Issac D. Swensen. "Substance Abuse Treatment Centers and Local Crime." National Bureau of Economic Research. NBER Working Paper no. 22610, https://www.nber.org/papers/w22610. September 2016.

Borakove, M. Elaine, Robin Wosje, Franklin Cruz, Aimee Wickman, Tim Dibble, and Carolyn Harbus. "From Silo to System: What Makes a Criminal Justice System Operate Like a System?" Justice Management Institute, prepared for MacArthur Foundation. April 30, 2015.

Brink, Malia N., Robert C. Boruchowitz, and Maureen Dimino. "Minor Crimes, Massive Waste: The Terrible Toll of America's Broken Misdemeanor Courts." National Association of Criminal Defense Lawyers. April 2009. https://www.nacdl.org/reports/misdemeanor.

Brook, Carol A., Bruno Fiannaca, David Harvey, Paul Marcus, and Jenny McEwan. "A Comparative Look at Plea Bargaining in Australia, Canada, England, New Zealand, and the United States." *William and Mary Law Review* 57, no. 4 (2016): 1167–79.

Brown, Connor. "Man Cleared of Molestation Sues over Withheld Evidence." *Austin American Statesman.* January 24, 2018. https://pressreader.com/usa/austin-american-statesman/20180124/textview.

Brown, Darryl K. *Free Market Criminal Justice: How Democracy and Laissez Faire Undermine the Rule of Law.* New York: Oxford University Press, 2016.

Brown, Elizabeth Nolan. "The Real 'Modern Slavery'? Inside America's Court-Ordered Corporate Labor Camps." *Reason.* October 5, 2017. http://reason.com/blog/2017/10/05/human-trafficked-by-uncle-sam.

Brownwell, Brett, Hannah Levintova, and Jaeah Lee. "Charts: Why You're in Deep Trouble If You Can't Afford a Lawyer." *Mother Jones.* May 6, 2013. http://www.motherjones.com/politics/2013/05/public-defenders-gideon-supreme-court-charts.

Burger, Warren. "The State of the Judiciary—1970." *American Bar Association Journal* 56, no. 10 (October 1970): 929–34.

Burke, Jill. "Will Alaska's Plea Bargain Plan Serve Justice, or Cause It to Grind to a Halt?" *Alaska Dispatch News.* August 13, 2013. https://www.adn.com/alaska-news/article/will-alaskas-plea-bargain-plan-serve-justice-or-cause-it-grind-halt/2013/08/14.

Byron, Robert. "Criminals Need Mental Health Care." *Scientific American.* March 1, 2004. https://www.scientificamerican.com/article/criminals-need-mental-health-care.

Caldwell, H. Mitchell. "Coercive Plea Bargaining: The Unrecognized Scourge of the Justice System." *Catholic University Law Review* 61, no. 1 (2011): 63–96.

Carroll, David. "Gideon's Despair: Four Things the Next Attorney General Needs to Know about America's Indigent Defense Crisis." January 2, 2015. https://www.themarshallproject.org/2015/01/02/four-things-the-next-attorney-general-needs-to-know-about-america-s-indigent-defense-crisis.

CBS News. "Innocents Have Gone to Jail, Say NOLA Public Defenders." CBS. April 13, 2017. https://www.cbsnews.com/news/innocents-have-gone-to-jail-say-nola-public-defenders.

Center for Holistic Defense. "The Holistic Defense Toolkit." http://www.apainc.org/wp-content/uploads/Holistic-Defense-Toolkit.pdf.

Chandler, Redonna K., Bennett W. Fletcher, and Nora D. Volkow. "Treating Drug Abuse and Addiction in the Criminal Justice System: Improving Public Health and Safety." *Journal of the American Medical Association* 301, no. 2 (2009): 183–90.

Clark, Melanca, and Emily Savner. "Community Oriented Defense: Stronger Public Defenders." Brennan Center for Justice at New York University School of Law. July 2010. https://www.brennancenter.org/publication/community-oriented-defense-stronger-public-defenders.

Coburn, Jesse. "Maryland Public Defenders Juggle Heavy Caseloads; Critics Say Indigent Clients Suffer." *Baltimore Sun.* August 20, 2016. http://www.baltimoresun.com/news/maryland/investigations/bs-md-public-defender-caseloads-20160819-story.html.

Congressional Research Service. "Probable Cause, Reasonable Suspicion, and Reasonableness Standards in the Context of the Fourth Amendment and Foreign Intelligence Surveillance Act." January 30, 2006. https://fas.org/sgp/crs/intel/m013006.pdf.

Constitution Project. "Indigent Defense: Ensuring the Constitutional Right to Counsel." 2014. https://constitutionproject.org/wp-content/uploads/2014/10/Chapter_07.pdf.

Cooke, Kristina, and Robin Respaut. "How a Respected Drug-Rehab Program Spun Out of Control." Reuters. September 2, 2015. https://www.reuters.com/investigates/special-report/usa-rehab-phoenixhouse.

Copland, James R., and Isaac Gorodetski. "Overcriminalizing in the Old North State: A Primer and Possible Reforms for North Carolina." Manhattan Institute. Issue Brief no. 28 (2014). https://www.manhattan-institute.org/html/overcriminalizing-old-north-state-primer-and-possible-reforms-north-carolina-5721.html.

Copland, James R., Isaac Gorodetski, and Michael J. Reitz. "Overcriminalizing the Wolverine State: A Primer and Possible Reforms for Michigan." Manhattan Institute and Mackinac Center. Issue Brief no. 31 (2014). https://www.manhattan-institute.org/pdf/ib_31.pdf.

Cummings, Ian. "KC Public Defenders Say High Caseloads Mean Losing Their Licenses, Going to Jail, or Quitting." *Kansas City Star*. October 19, 2017. http://www.kansascity.com/news/politics-government/article179852406.html.

Cuomo, Andrew M. "Governor Cuomo: The Way to a More Just New York State." *New York Times*. January 15, 2018. https://www.nytimes.com/2018/01/15/opinion/cuomo-prison-reform-new-york.html.

Davis, Angela. *Arbitrary Justice: The Power of the American Prosecutor*. New York: Oxford University Press, 2007.

Davis, Angela J. "The Prosecutor's Ethical Duty to End Mass Incarceration." *Hofstra Law Review* 44, no. 4 (2016): 1063–85.

Dervan, Lucian E. "Bargained Justice: Plea Bargaining's Innocence Problem and the Brady Safety-Valve." *Utah Law Review* 51, no. 1 (2012): 51–97.

Dervan, Lucian E. "Overcriminalization 2.0: The Symbiotic Relationship between Plea Bargaining and Overcriminalization." *Journal of Law, Economics and Policy* 7, no. 4 (2011): 645–55.

Devers, Lindsey. "Plea and Charge Bargaining." U.S. Department of Justice, Bureau of Justice Assistance. 2011. https://www.bja.gov/Publications/PleaBargainingResearchSummary.pdf.

Dibber, Markus. "American Plea Bargains, German Lay Judges, and the Crisis of Criminal Procedure." *Stanford Law Review* 49, no. 3 (1997): 547–606.

Didwania, Stephanie. "The Immediate Consequences of Pretrial Detention: Evidence from Federal Criminal Cases." February 17, 2018. https://papers.ssrn.com/abstract=2809818.

Dobbie, Will, Jacob Goldin, and Crystal Yang. "The Effects of Pre-Trial Detention on Conviction, Future Crime, and Employment: Evidence from Randomly Assigned Judges." *American Economic Review* 108, no. 2 (2018): 201–40.

Drake, E. "Predicting Criminal Recidivism: A Systematic Review of Offender Risk Assessments in Washington State." Washington State Institute for Public Policy. February 2014. http://www.wsipp.wa.gov/ReportFile/1554/Wsipp_Predicting-Criminal-Recidivism-A-Systematic-Review-of-Offender-Risk-Assessments-in-Washington-State_Final-Report.pdf.

Dressel, Julia, and Hany Farid. "The Accuracy, Fairness, and Limits of Predicting Recidivism." *Science Advances* 4, no. 1 (January 17, 2018). http://advances.sciencemag.org/content/4/1/eaao5580.full.

Dutton, Audrey. "She Went to the Hospital for Mental Illness. She Ended Up Charged with 2 Felonies." *Idaho Statesman*. January 20, 2018. http://www.idahostatesman.com/news/politics-government/state-politics/article195828984.html.

Ewing, Maura. "When Does the Right to an Attorney Kick In?" *The Atlantic*. September 15, 2017. https://www.theatlantic.com/politics/archive/2017/09/when-does-the-right-to-an-attorney-kick-in/539898.

Fair Trials International. "The Disappearing Trial: Towards a Rights-Based Approach to Trial Waiver Systems." https://www.fairtrials.org/campaigns/the-disappearing-trial.

Fairfax, Roger A., Jr. "Searching for Solutions to the Indigent Defense Crisis in the Broader Criminal Justice Reform Agenda." *Yale Law Journal* 122, no. 8 (2013): 2316–35.

Farole, Donald J., Jr., and Lynn Langton. "County-Based and Local Public Defender Offices, 2007." Bureau of Justice Statistics. *Special Report*. September 2010.

Federal Bureau of Investigation, U.S. Department of Justice. "Crime in the United States, 2013, Clearances." https://ucr.fbi.gov/crime-in-the-u.s/2013/crime-in-the-u.s.-2013/offenses-known-to-law-enforcement/clearances/clearancetopic_final.

Fisher, George. *Plea Bargaining's Triumph: A History of Plea Bargaining in America*. Stanford, CA: Stanford University Press, 2003.

Fletcher, Anne M. *Inside Rehab: The Surprising Truth about Addiction Treatment and How to Get Help That Works*. New York: Penguin Books, 2013.

Flynn, Asher. "Plea-Negotiations, Prosecutors, and Discretion: An Argument for Legal Reform." *Australian and New Zealand Journal of Criminology* 49, no. 4 (2015): 564–82.

Gelb, Adam. "The Lack of a Relationship between Drug Imprisonment and Drug Problems." Public Safety Performance Project, Pew Charitable Trusts. June 18, 2017.

Gelb, Adam, and Andrew Page. "Voters in Louisiana and Oklahoma Strongly Favor Alternatives to Incarceration." Public Safety Performance Project, Pew Charitable Trusts. June
   28, 2017.

Glaser, Gabrielle. "The Irrationality of Alcoholics Anonymous." *The Atlantic*. April 2015.
   https://www.theatlantic.com/magazine/archive/2015/04/the-irrationality-of-alcoholics-
   anonymous/386255.

Guidorizzi, Douglas D. "Should We Really 'Ban' Plea Bargaining? The Core Concerns of
   Plea Bargaining Critics." *Emory Law Journal* 47 no. 2 (1998): 753–83.

Gupta, Arpit, Christopher Hansman, and Ethan Frenchman. "The Heavy Costs of High Bail:
   Evidence from Judge Randomization." *Journal of Legal Studies* 45, no. 2 (June 2016):
   471–505.

Hager, Eli. "The Check Is in the Mail (for Real)." The Marshall Project. January 7, 2018.
   https://www.themarshallproject.org/2018/01/07/the-check-is-in-the-mail-for-real.

Hager, Eli. "When Real Estate and Tax Lawyers Are Forced to Do a Public Defender's Job."
   The Marshall Project. September 8, 2016. https://www.themarshallproject.org/2016/09/
   08/when-real-estate-and-tax-lawyers-are-forced-to-do-a-public-defender-s-job.

Hanlon, Stephen F., Thomas B. Harvey, and Norman Lefstein. "Denial of the Right to
   Counsel in Misdemeanor Cases: Court Watching in Nashville, Tennessee." American Bar
   Association, Section on Civil Rights and Social Justice. 2017.

Harris, Amy, and Shoshana Walter. *All Work. No Pay*. "They Thought They Were Going to
   Rehab. They Ended Up in Chicken Plants." October 7, 2017. *Reveal* from the Center for
   Investigative Reporting. https://www.revealnews.org/article/they-thought-they-were-go-
   ing-to-rehab-they-ended-up-in-chicken-plants.

Hart, Peter D. "Changing Public Attitudes toward the Criminal Justice System." Open Society Foundations. February 2012. https://www.opensocietyfoundations.org/reports/chang-
   ing-public-attitudes-toward-criminal-justice-system.

Harvard Law School Criminal Justice Policy Program. "Moving beyond Money: A Primer on
   Bail Reform." October 2016. http://cjpp.law.harvard.edu/assets/FINAL-Primer-on-Bail-
   Reform.pdf.

Heaton, Paul, Sandra Mayson, and Megan Stevenson. "The Downstream Consequences of
   Misdemeanor Pretrial Detention." *Stanford Law Review* 69, no. 3 (2017): 711–94.

Hessick, Andrew, III, and Reshma M. Saujani. "Plea Bargaining and Convicting the Innocent: The Role of the Prosecutor, the Defense Counsel, and the Judge." *Brigham Young
   University Journal of Public Law* 16, no. 2 (2002): 189–242.

HRSA (Health Resources and Services Administration) Data Warehouse. "Designated
   Health Professional Shortage Areas Statistics." Bureau of Health Workforce, Health Re-
   sources and Services Administration, U.S. Department of Health and Human Services.
   January 1, 2018. https://ersrs.hrsa.gov/ReportServer?/HGDW_Reports/BCD_HPSA/
   BCD_HPSA_SCR50_Smry_HTML&rc:Toolbar=false.

Humans Rights Watch. "An Offer You Can't Refuse: How US Federal Prosecutors Force
   Drug Defendants to Plead Guilty." 2013. https://www.hrw.org/report/2013/12/05/offer-
   you-cant-refuse/how-us-federal-prosecutors-force-drug-defendants-plead.

Human Rights Watch. "Not in It for Justice." 2017. https://www.hrw.org/report/2017/04/11/
   not-it-justice/how-californias-pretrial-detention-and-bail-system-unfairly.

International Bridges to Justice. "Standards of Proof." Criminal Defense Wiki. 2011. http://
   defensewiki.ibj.org/index.php/Standards_of_Proof#Various_Standards_of_Proof.

Jackson, Daniel. "Mass Justice in Southern Court Replete with Rights Violations, ABA Observers Say." *Courthouse News*. August 21, 2017. https://www.courthousenews.com/ob-
   servers-find-violations-nashville-misdemeanor-court.

Jaffe, D. J. *Insane Consequences: How the Mental Health Industry Fails the Mentally Ill*.
   Amherst, NY: Prometheus Books, 2017.

James, Doris J., and Lauren E. Glaze. "Mental Health Problems of Prison and Jail Inmates."
   Bureau of Justice Statistics, U.S. Department of Justice. *Special Report*, September 2006.
   http://bjs.gov/content/pub/pdf/mhppji.pdf.

Jan, Tracy. "America's Affordable-Housing Stock Dropped by 60 Percent from 2010 to
   2016." *Washington Post*. October 23, 2017. https://www.washingtonpost.com/news/wonk/

wp/2017/10/23/americas-affordable-housing-stock-dropped-by-60-percent-from-2010-to-2016/?utm_term=.a83a818a0b97.

Justice Reinvestment Initiative. "What Is JRI?" U.S. Department of Justice, Bureau of Justice Assistance. 2007. https://www.bja.gov/programs/justicereinvestment/what_is_jri.html.

Kang-Brown, Jacob, and Ram Subramanian. "Out of Sight: The Growth of Jails in Rural America." New York: Vera Institute of Justice, June 2017.

Kelly, William R. *Criminal Justice at the Crossroads: Transforming Crime and Punishment.* New York: Columbia University Press, 2015.

Kelly, William R. *The Future of Crime and Punishment: Smart Policies for Reducing Crime and Saving Money.* Lanham, MD: Rowman & Littlefield, 2016.

Kelly, William R., Robert Pitman, and William Streusand. *From Retribution to Public Safety: Disruptive Innovation of American Criminal Justice.* Lanham, MD: Rowman & Littlefield, 2017.

King, Nancy J., and Ronald F. Wright. "The Invisible Revolution in Plea Bargaining: Managerial Judging and Judicial Participation in Negotiations." *Texas Law Review* 95, no. 2 (2016): 325–97.

Klein, Richard. "The Emperor Gideon Has No Clothes: The Empty Promise of the Sixth Amendment Right to Effective Assistance of Counsel." *Hastings Constitutional Law Quarterly* 13 (Summer 1986): 625–93.

Langbein, John. "On the Myth of Written Constitutions." Yale Law School Faculty Scholarship Series, Paper 548. 1992. http://digitalcommons.law.yale.edu/cgi/viewcontent.cgi?article=1541&context=fss_papers.

Lannan, Katie. "A Broad Push for Pretrial Justice Reforms from the States." *Boston Globe.* August 8, 2017. https://www.bostonglobe.com/metro/2017/08/08/broad-push-for-pretrial-justice-reforms-from-states/STJtFCEULXsajIXbxk8GDM/story.html.

Oliver Laughland, "The Human Toll of America's Public Defender Crisis," *The Guardian,* September 7, 2016.

Laura and John Arnold Foundation. "More Than 20 Cities and States Adopt Risk Assessment Tool to Help Judges Decide Which Defendants to Detain prior to Trial." June 26, 2015. http://www.arnoldfoundation.org/more-than-20-cities-and-states-adopt-risk-assessment-tool-to-help-judges-decide-which-defendants-to-detain-prior-to-trial.

Laura and John Arnold Foundation. "Pretrial Criminal Justice Research." November 2013. http://www.arnoldfoundation.org/wp-content/uploads/2014/02/LJAF-Pretrial-CJ-Research-brief_FNL.pdf.

LaVigne, Nancy, Samuel Bieler, Lindsey Cramer, Helen Ho, Cybele Kotonias, Deborah Mayer, David McClure, et al. "Justice Reinvestment Initiative State Assessment Report." Urban Institute, Bureau of Justice Assistance, U.S. Department of Justice. January 2014. https://www.urban.org/sites/default/files/publication/22211/412994-Justice-Reinvestment-Initiative-State-Assessment-Report.PDF.

Lee, Cynthia G., Brian J. Ostrom, and Matthew Kleiman. "The Measure of Good Lawyering: Evaluating Holistic Defense in Practice." *Albany Law Review* 78, no. 3 (2015): 1215–38.

Lefstein, Norman. "The Failure to Implement the Right to Counsel Due to Excessive Caseloads: Securing Reasonable Caseloads Ethics and Law in Public Defense." https://www.americanbar.org/content/dam/aba/publications/books/ls_sclaid_def_securing_reasonable_caseloads.authcheckdam.pdf.

Legal Action Center. "Public Opinion Favors Criminal Justice and Drug Policy Reform, Making Now the Time to Act." 2018. https://lac.org/public-opinion-favors-criminal-justice-and-drug-policy-reform-making-now-the-time-to-act.

Leslie, Emily, and Nolan G. Pope. "The Unintended Impact of Pretrial Detention on Case Outcomes: Evidence from New York City Arraignments." *Journal of Law and Economics* 60, no. 3 (August 2017): 529–57.

Levenson, Laurie L. "Peeking behind the Plea Bargaining Process: Missouri v. Frye & Lafler v. Cooper." *Loyola of Los Angeles Law Review* 46, no. 2 (2013): 457–90.

Levin, Mark A. "At the State Level, So-Called Crimes Are Here, There, Everywhere." *Criminal Justice* 28, no. 1 (2013): 4–10.

Lopez, German. "The New War on Drugs." *Vox*. September 13, 2017. https://www.vox.com/policy-and-politics/2017/9/5/16135848/drug-war-opioid-epidemic.

Lowenkamp, Christopher T., and Marie VanNostrand. "Exploring the Impact of Supervision on Pretrial Outcomes." Laura and John Arnold Foundation. November 2013. http://www.arnoldfoundation.org/wp-content/uploads/2014/02/LJAF_Report_Supervision_FNL.pdf.

Lowenkamp, Christopher T., Marie VanNostrand, and Alexandra Holsinger. "The Hidden Costs of Pretrial Detention." Laura and John Arnold Foundation. November 2013. http://arnoldfoundation.org/wp-content/uploads/2014/02/LJAF_Report_hidden-costs_FNL.pdf.

Lynch, Gerald E. "Our Administrative System of Criminal Justice." *Fordham Law Review* 66, no. 6 (1998): 2117–51.

Lyons, Donna. "Predicting Pretrial Success." National Conference of State Legislatures. February 1, 2014.

Ma, Yue. "Prosecutorial Discretion and Plea Bargaining in the United States, France, Germany, and Italy: A Comparative Perspective." *International Criminal Justice Review* 12, no. 1 (2002): 22–52.

Maryland Alliance for Justice Reform. "Maryland's Pretrial/Bail Troubles—How and Why to Fix Them." http://www.ma4jr.org/wp-content/uploads/2014/10/pretrial-IssueBrief.pdf.

McCoy, Candace. "Caleb Was Right: Pretrial Decisions Determine Mostly Everything." *Berkeley Journal of Criminal Law* 12, no. 2 (2007): 135–50.

McCoy, Candace. "Plea Bargaining as Coercion: The Trial Penalty and Plea Bargaining Reform." *Criminal Law Quarterly* 50 (2005): 1–41.

McCullough, Jolie. "Poor Inmates Sue Dallas County over Bail System Following Harris County Ruling." *Texas Tribune*. January 22, 2018. https://www.texastribune.org/2018/01/22/following-harris-county-ruling-poor-inmates-sue-dallas-county-over-bail.

McLaughlin, Michael, Carrie Pettus-Davis, Derek Brown, Chris Veeh, and Tanya Renn. "The Economic Burden of Incarceration in the U.S." Concordance Institute for Advancing Justice, George Warren Brown School of Social Work, Washington University, St. Louis. 2017. https://joinnia.com/wp-content/uploads/2017/02/The-Economic-Burden-of-Incarceration-in-the-US-2016.pdf.

Mental Health America. "2017 State of Mental Health in America—Access to Care Data." October 17, 2016. http://www.mentalhealthamerica.net/issues/2017-state-mental-health-america-access-care-data.

Natapoff, Alexandra. "Aggregation and Urban Misdemeanors." *Fordham Urban Law Journal* 40, no. 3 (2013): 1043–89.

Natapoff, Alexandra. "Gideon Skepticism." *Washington and Lee Law Review* 70, no. 2 (2013): 1049–87.

Natapoff, Alexandra. "Misdemeanors." 85 *Southern California Law Review* 101 (2012): 1313–76.

Natapoff, Alexandra. "Why Misdemeanors Aren't So Minor." *Slate*. April 27, 2012. http://www.slate.com/articles/news_and_politics/jurisprudence/2012/04/misdemeanors_can_have_major_consequences_for_the_people_charged.html.

National Association for Public Defense. "Alternatives to Traditional Prosecution Can Reduce Defender Workload, Save Money, and Reduce Recidivism." March 2017. http://www.publicdefenders.us/files/NAPD%20Demand%20Side%20paper_FINAL.pdf.

National Center on Addiction and Substance Abuse at Columbia University. "Addiction Medicine: Closing the Gap between Science and Practice." CASA Columbia National Advisory Commission. June 2012.

National Conference of State Legislatures. "Affordable Care Act Medicaid Expansion." November 2017. http://www.ncsl.org/research/health/affordable-care-act-expansion.aspx.

National Conference of State Legislatures. "Pretrial Diversion." September 28, 2017. http://www.ncsl.org/research/civil-and-criminal-justice/pretrial-diversion.aspx.

National Institute on Drug Abuse. "Principles of Drug Addiction Treatment: A Research-Based Guide (Third Edition)." *Advancing Addiction Science*. https://www.drugabuse.gov/publications/principles-drug-addiction-treatment-research-based-guide-third-edition/principles-effective-treatment.

National Registry of Exonerations. "Innocents Who Plead Guilty." November 24, 2015. http:/
/www.law.umich.edu/special/exoneration/Documents/NRE.Guilty.Plea.Article1.pdf.

New York Courts. "Criminal Jury Instructions." http://www.nycourts.gov/judges/cji/index.
shtml.

Nyberg, Fred. "Cognitive Impairments in Drug Addicts" in *Brain Damage: Bridging between Basic Research and Clinics*, ed. Alina Gonzalez-Quevedo. INTECH Open Access Publisher. 2012. doi: 10.577237661.

O'Donoghue, Julia. "Louisiana District Attorneys Continue to Push Back on Criminal Sentencing Changes." October 18, 2017. http://www.nola.com/politics/index.ssf/2017/10/district_attorneys_sentences.html.

Palmer, Jeff. "Abolishing Plea Bargaining: An End to the Same Old Song and Dance." *American Journal of Criminal Law* 26, no. 3 (1999): 505–37.

Petegorsky, Michael Nasser. "Plea Bargaining in the Dark: The Duty to Disclose Exculpatory Brady Evidence during Plea Bargaining." *Fordham Law Review* 81, no. 6 (2013): 3599–650.

Pew Center on the States. "State Reforms Reverse Decades of Incarceration Growth." Public Safety Performance Project. March 21, 2007.

Pfaff, John F. *Locked In: The True Causes of Mass Incarceration and How to Achieve Real Reform.* New York: Basic Books, 2017.

Pfaff, John F. "The Causes of Growth in Prison Admissions and Populations." Fordham University School of Law. 2011. http://dx.doi.org/10.2139/ssrn.1884674.

Pilnik, Lisa. "A Framework for Pretrial Justice: Essential Elements of an Effective Pretrial System and Agency." National Institute of Corrections. February 2017. https://university.pretrial.org/HigherLogic/System/DownloadDocument-
File.ashx?DocumentFileKey=c8bd044e-0215-9ab6-c22e-b1a4de912044.

Pishko, Jessica. "Prosecutors Are Banding Together to Prevent Criminal Justice Reform." *The Nation*. October 18, 2017. https://www.thenation.com/article/prosecutors-are-banding-together-to-prevent-criminal-justice-reform.

Pretrial Justice Institute. "Bail in America: Unsafe, Unfair, Ineffective." 2018. http://
www.pretrial.org/the-problem.

Pretrial Justice Institute. "Pretrial Justice: How Much Does It Cost?" 2017. https://university.pretrial.org/HigherLogic/System/DownloadDocument-
File.ashx?DocumentFileKey=4c666992-0b1b-632a-13cb-b4ddc66fadcd.

Pretrial Justice Institute. "The Solution." http://www.pretrial.org/solutions.

Pretrial Justice Institute. "The State of Pretrial Justice in America." November 2017. https://
www.pretrial.org/state-pretrial-justice-america.

Prison Policy Initiative. "Detaining the Poor." May 10, 2016. https://www.prisonpolicy.org/
reports/incomejails.html.

Prisoner Reentry Institute. "Pretrial Practice: Building a National Research Agenda for the Front End of the Criminal Justice System." John Jay College of Criminal Justice. October 26–27, 2015. http://johnjaypri.org/wp-content/uploads/2016/05/ArnoldReport2_webversion.pdf.

Public Safety Performance Project. "33 States Reform Criminal Justice Policies through Justice Reinvestment." Pew Center on the States. November 2016.

Rakoff, Jed S. "Why Innocent People Plead Guilty." *New York Review of Books*. November 20, 2014. http://www.nybooks.com/articles/2014/11/20/why-innocent-people-plead-guilty.

Rakoff, Jed S. "Why Prosecutors Rule the Criminal Justice System—and What Can Be Done about It." *Northwestern University Law Review* 111, no. 6 (2017): 1429–36.

Roberts, Jenny M. "Why Misdemeanors Matter: Defining Effective Advocacy in the Lower Criminal Courts." American University Washington College of Law. *Articles in Law Reviews and Other Academic Journals*. Paper 289. 2011. http://digitalcommons.wcl.
american.edu/facsch_lawrev/289.

Ross, Jacqueline E. "The Entrenched Position of Plea Bargaining in United States Legal Practice." *American Journal of Comparative Law* 54, supp. 1 (Fall 2006): 717–32.

Rothwell, Jonathan. "Drug Offenders in American Prisons: The Critical Distinction between Stock and Flow." Brookings, The Brookings Institution. November 25, 2015. https://

www.brookings.edu/blog/social-mobility-memos/2015/11/25/drug-offenders-in-american-prisons-the-critical-distinction-between-stock-and-flow.

Rowings, Kathy. "Pretrial Decisions Have Major Effects on Post-Trial Life." National Association of Counties. October 29, 2013. http://www.naco.org/blog/pretrial-decisions-have-major-effects-post-trial-life.

Santo, Alysia. "How Conservatives Learned to Love Free Lawyers for the Poor." *Politico.* September 24, 2017. https://www.politico.com/magazine/story/2017/09/24/how-conservatives-learned-to-love-free-lawyers-for-the-poor-215635.

Schulhofer, Stephen J. "Is Plea Bargaining Inevitable?" *Harvard Law Review* 97, no. 5 (1984): 1037–107.

Schulhofer, Stephen J. "Plea Bargaining as Disaster." *Yale Law Journal* 101, no. 8 (1992): 1979–2009.

Schulhofer, Stephen J. "A Wake-Up Call from the Plea-Bargaining Trenches." *Law and Social Inquiry* 19, no. 1 (1994): 135–44.

Schwartzapfel, Beth. "Defendants Kept in the Dark about Evidence, until It's Too Late." *New York Times.* August 7, 2017. https://www.nytimes.com/2017/08/07/nyregion/defendants-kept-in-the-dark-about-evidence-until-its-too-late.html.

Schwartzapfel, Beth. "How New York Could Change the Game for Its Criminal Defendants." The Marshall Project. January 3, 2018. https://www.themarshallproject.org/2018/01/03/how-new-york-could-change-the-game-for-its-criminal-defendants.

Scott, R., and William Stuntz. "Plea Bargaining as Contract." *Yale Law Journal* 101, no. 8 (1992): 1909–68.

Sessions, Jeff. "Jeff Sessions: Trump Promised to End 'American Carnage.' Promise Delivered." *USA Today.* January 23, 2018. https://www.usatoday.com/story/opinion/2018/01/23/trump-promised-end-american-carnage-has-come-true-jeff-sessions-column/1057630001.

Siddall, Eric W. "Bail Reform: Why Judges Should Reject 'Risk Assessment.'" *The Crime Report.* August 25, 2017. https://thecrimereport.org/2017/08/25/bail-reform-why-judges-should-think-twice-about-risk-assessment.

Sixth Amendment Center. "Actual Denial of Counsel in Misdemeanor Courts." May 2015. http://sixthamendment.org/wp-content/uploads/2015/05/Actual-Denial-of-Counsel-in-Misdemeanor-Courts.pdf.

Sixth Amendment Center. "The Right to Counsel in America Today." 2018. http://sixthamendment.org/the-right-to-counsel-in-america-today.

Sixth Amendment Center. "Utah's Right to Counsel Deficiencies." 2015. http://sixthamendment.org/utahs-right-to-counsel-deficiencies.

Steinberg, Robin. "Heeding Gideon's Call in the Twenty-First Century: Holistic Defense and the New Public Defense Paradigm." *Washington and Lee Law Review* 70, no. 2 (2013): 962–1017.

Stevenson, Megan T. "Distortion of Justice: How the Inability to Pay Bail Affects Case Outcomes." 2017. https://ssrn.com/abstract=2777615; http://dx.doi.org/10.2139/ssrn.2777615.

Stevenson, Megan T. "Risk Assessment: The Devil's in the Details." *The Crime Report.* August 31, 2017. https://thecrimereport.org/2017/08/31/does-risk-assessment-work-theres-no-single-answer.

Stuntz, William J. "Plea Bargaining and Criminal Law's Disappearing Shadow." *Harvard Law Review* 117, no. 8 (2004): 2548–69. doi:10.2307/409340.

Subramanian, Ram, Ruth Delaney, Stephen Roberts, Nancy Fishman, and Peggy McGarry. "Incarceration's Front Door: The Misuse of Jails in America." New York: Vera Institute of Justice, Center on Sentencing and Corrections, February 2015.

Szalavitz, Maia. "The Wrong Way to Treat Opioid Addiction." *New York Times.* January 17, 2018. https://www.nytimes.com/2018/01/17/opinion/treating-opioid-addiction.

Taslitz, Andrew E. "Prosecutorial Preconditions to Plea Negotiations: 'Voluntary' Waivers of Constitutional Rights." *Criminal Justice* 23, no. 3 (Fall 2008): 14–27.

TCR Staff. "Justice Reform Means 'Thinking outside Silos,' Says New John Jay President." *The Crime Report,* Center on Media and Crime at John Jay College. November 9, 2017.

https://thecrimereport.org/2017/11/09/justice-reform-means-thinking-outside-silos-says-new-john-jay-president.

TCR Staff. "Los Angeles Study Finds $19 Billion Levied in Money Bail between 2012–2016." *The Crime Report*, Center on Media and Crime at John Jay College. December 7, 2017. https://thecrimereport.org/2017/12/07/los-angeles-study-finds-19-billion-levied-in-money-bail-between-2012-2016.

Texas Appleseed. "Bail and Pretrial Release: Summary of Recent Research on What Works." https://www.texasappleseed.org/sites/default/files/Bail%20Reform%20Summary.pdf.

Travis, Jeremy, Bruce Western, and Steve Redburn. *The Growth of Incarceration in the United States: Exploring Causes and Consequences.* Washington, DC: National Academies Press, 2014.

Turner, Jenia I. "Plea Bargaining." Southern Methodist University Dedman School Law of Legal Studies. Research Paper no. 348 (2017).

Turner, Jenia I. *Plea Bargaining across Borders.* New York: Aspen, 2009.

Ulmer, Jeffrey T., and Mindy S. Bradley. "Variation in Trial Penalties among Serious Violent Offenses." *Criminology* 44, no. 3 (2006): 631–70.

United States Courts for the Ninth Circuit. "Model Jury Instructions." December 2016. http://www3.ce9.uscourts.gov/jury-instructions/node/338.

Van Brunt, Alexa. "Poor People Rely on Public Defenders Who Are Too Overworked to Defend Them." *The Guardian*, U.S. edition. June 17, 2015. https://www.theguardian.com/commentisfree/2015/jun/17/poor-rely-public-defenders-too-overworked.

VanNostrand, Marie. "Measuring and Managing Pretrial Risk: Improving Public Safety, Fairness, and Cost Effectiveness." California Pretrial Summit. 2015. http://www.courts.ca.gov/documents/PretrialSummit2015-10MeasuringManagingRisk.pdf.

Vitale, Alex S. "Bail Bond Industry Fights Back against Reform." *Injustice Today.* July 27, 2017. https://injusticetoday.com/bail-bond-industry-fights-back-against-reform-b4bacb510140.

Vogler, Jacob. "Access to Health Care and Criminal Behavior: Short-Run Evidence from the ACA Medicaid Expansions." 2017. https://ssrn.com/abstract=3042267; http://dx.doi.org/10.2139/ssrn.3042267.

Walsh, Dylan. "On the Defensive." *The Atlantic.* June 2, 2016. https://www.theatlantic.com/politics/archive/2016/06/on-the-defensive/485165.

Wan, Tina. "The Unnecessary Evil of Plea Bargaining: An Unconstitutional Conditions Problem and a Not-So-Least Restrictive Alternative." *Review of Law and Social Justice* 17, no. 1 (2007): 33–61.

Wen, Hefei, Jason Hockenberry, and Janet Cummings. "The Effect of Medicaid Expansion on Crime Reduction." *Journal of Public Economics* 154 (October 2017): 67–94.

White, Gillian B. "Who Really Makes Money off of Bail Bonds?" *The Atlantic.* May 12, 2017. https://www.theatlantic.com/business/archive/2017/05/bail-bonds/526542.

Williams, Richard. "Addressing Mental Health in the Justice System." *National Conference of State Legislatures* 23, no. 31 (2015): 1–2.

Williams, Timothy. "Courts Sidestep the Law, and South Carolina's Poor Go to Jail. *New York Times.* October 12, 2017. https://www.nytimes.com/2017/10/12/us/south-carolina-jail-no-lawyer.html.

Work, Mike. "Creating Constitutional Procedure: Frye, Lafler, and Plea Bargaining Reform." *Journal of Criminal Law and Criminology* 104, no. 2 (2014): 457–86.

Yaroshefsky, Ellen. "Ethics and Plea Bargaining: What's Discovery Got to Do with It?" *Criminal Justice* 23, no. 3 (2008): 28–33.

Yoffe, Emily. "Innocence Is Irrelevant." *The Atlantic.* September 2017. https://www.theatlantic.com/magazine/archive/2017/09/innocence-is-irrelevant/534171.

Zeidman, Steven. "Gideon: Looking Backward, Looking Forward, Looking in the Mirror." *Seattle Journal for Social Justice* 11, no. 3 (2013): 933–62.

INDEX

ABOUT THE AUTHORS

William R. Kelly, PhD, is a professor of sociology at the University of Texas at Austin. He has taught, researched, and written about criminology, criminal justice, and criminal justice reform for thirty-five years. He has also spent years evaluating a variety of justice programs and policies for numerous local, state, and federal criminal justice agencies. His recent books include *Criminal Justice at the Crossroads: Transforming Crime and Punishment* (2015), *The Future of Crime and Punishment: Smart Policies for Reducing Crime and Saving Money* (Rowman & Littlefield, 2016), and *From Retribution to Public Safety: Disruptive Innovation of American Criminal Justice* (Rowman & Littlefield, 2017).

Robert Pitman, JD, MSt (Oxon), was appointed in 2014 by President Obama and confirmed by the U.S. Senate to serve as a U.S. district judge for the Western District of Texas. In 2011, Pitman was appointed by President Obama and confirmed by the Senate to be the U.S. attorney for the Western District of Texas, during which time he was appointed to the U.S. Attorney General's Advisory Committee. Prior to that, he served as the interim U.S. attorney for the Western District of Texas, as the deputy U.S. attorney, and as a U.S. magistrate judge in the Western District of Texas.